Your All-in-One Resource

On the CD that accompanies this book, you'll find additional resources to extend your learning.

The reference library includes the following fully searchable titles:

- *Microsoft Computer Dictionary*, 5th ed.
- Windows Vista Product Guide

The CD interface has a new look. You can use the tabs for an assortment of tasks:

- Check for book updates (if you have Internet access)
- Install the book's practice files
- Go online for product support or CD support
- Send us feedback

The following screen shot gives you a glimpse of the new interface.

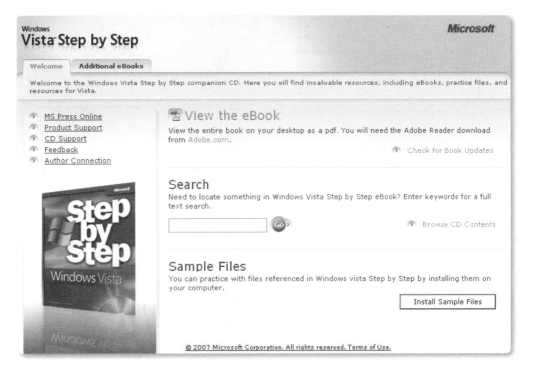

Microsoft® Office SharePoint® Designer 2007 Step by Step

Penelope Coventry

PUBLISHED BY
Microsoft Press
A Division of Microsoft Corporation
One Microsoft Way
Redmond, Washington 98052-6399

Library of Congress Control Number: 2007941086

Printed and bound in the United States of America.

2 3 4 5 6 7 8 9 QWT 3 2 1 0 9 8

Distributed in Canada by H.B. Fenn and Company Ltd.

A CIP catalogue record for this book is available from the British Library.

Microsoft Press books are available through booksellers and distributors worldwide. For further information about international editions, contact your local Microsoft Corporation office or contact Microsoft Press International directly at fax (425) 936-7329. Visit our Web site at www.microsoft.com/mspress. Send comments to mspinput@microsoft.com.

Acquisitions Editor: Juliana Aldous Atkinson
Developmental Editor: Sandra Haynes
Project Editor: Rosemary Caperton
Editorial Production: Online Training Solutions, Inc.
Technical Reviewer: Mitch Tulloch, Technical Review services provided by Content Master, a member of CM Group, Ltd.

Body Part No. X14-38540

Contents

What do you think of this book? We want to hear from you!

Microsoft is interested in hearing your feedback so we can continually improve our books and learning resources for you. To participate in a brief online survey, please visit:

www.microsoft.com/learning/booksurvey/

What do you think of this book? We want to hear from you!

Microsoft is interested in hearing your feedback so we can continually improve our books and learning resources for you. To participate in a brief online survey, please visit:

www.microsoft.com/learning/booksurvey/

Acknowledgments

I want to thank my husband for his support while writing this book, for providing me with food and drink, and for generally keeping me going through those long nights and days—too often I was going to bed as he got up. I would also like to mention my dog, Poppy, whose tail never stopped wagging and who was always pleased to see me, in those odd moments when I did leave my computers. I ignored them both while writing this book, and they still love me. I'd like to include a special thanks to Rosemary Caperton (Microsoft Press Project Editor), Susie Bayers (OTSI Project Manager), Mitch Tulloch (Technical Reviewer), and all the people at Microsoft Press and Online Training Solutions, Inc. who kept me on track and provided such excellent suggestions. This is the fifth book project I've done with the Microsoft Press team, and without their attention to detail, humor, and dedication, this book could not have been produced. I would like to thank Nikander and Margriet Bruggeman, and Errin O'Connor, who stepped in at the last moment as contributing authors so we could meet the publishing time-scales. Lastly, I would like to thank the SharePoint and Microsoft Expression Web MVPs. I am truly honored to be part of this unique community. I have learned much from their e-mail messages, blog posts, newsletters, presentations, and books.

Thank you all!

–Penny Coventry

Information for Readers Running Windows XP

The graphics and operating system–related instructions in this book reflect the Windows Vista user interface, but you can also use a computer running Windows XP with Service Pack 2 (SP2) installed. If you want to complete the workflow exercises, you will also need Microsoft .NET Framework 3.0 installed, which you can download from the Microsoft Download Center.

Most of the differences you will encounter when working through the exercises in this book on a computer running Windows XP relate to appearance rather than functionality. For example, the Windows Vista Start button is round rather than rectangular and is not labeled with the word *Start*; window frames and window-management buttons look different; and if your system supports Windows Aero, the window frames might be transparent. In addition, file system dialog boxes and some file system paths are different between the two platforms. For example, the *My Documents* folder in Windows XP is named *Documents* in Windows Vista.

In this section, we provide steps for navigating to or through menus and dialog boxes in Windows XP that differ from those provided in the exercises in this book. For the most part, these differences are small enough that you will have no difficulty in completing the exercises.

Managing the Practice Files

The instructions given in the "Using the Book's CD" section are specific to Windows Vista. The only differences when installing, using, uninstalling, and removing the practice files supplied on the companion CD are the default installation location and the uninstall process.

On a computer running Windows Vista, the default installation location of the practice files is *Documents\Microsoft Press\SPD2007_SBS*. On a computer running Windows XP, the default installation location is *My Documents\Microsoft Press\SPD2007_SBS*. If your computer is running Windows XP, whenever an exercise tells you to navigate to your *Documents* folder, you should instead go to your *My Documents* folder.

To uninstall the practice files from a computer running Windows XP:

1. On the Windows taskbar, click the **Start** button, and then click **Control Panel**.
2. In **Control Panel**, click (or in Classic view, double-click) **Add or Remove Programs**.
3. In the **Add or Remove Programs** window, click **Microsoft SharePoint Designer 2007 Step by Step**, and then click **Remove**.
4. In the **Add or Remove Programs** message box asking you to confirm the deletion, click **Yes**.

Using the Start Menu

Folders on the Windows Vista Start menu expand vertically. Folders on the Windows XP Start menu expand horizontally. However, the steps to access a command on the Start menu are identical on both systems.

To start Microsoft Office SharePoint Designer 2007 on a computer running Windows XP:

→ Click the **Start** button, point to **All Programs**, click **Microsoft Office**, and then click **Microsoft Office SharePoint Designer 2007**.

Navigating Dialog Boxes

On a computer running Windows XP, some of the dialog boxes you will work with in the exercises not only look different from the graphics shown in this book but also work differently. These dialog boxes are primarily those that act as an interface between SharePoint Designer and the operating system, including any dialog box in which you navigate to a specific location.

For example, to navigate to the *My Pictures* folder in Windows XP:

→ On the **Places** bar, click **My Documents**. Then in the folder content pane, double-click **My Pictures**.

To move back to the *My Documents* folder in Windows XP:

→ On the toolbar, click the **Up One Level** button.

Up One Level

Features and Conventions of This Book

This book has been designed to lead you step by step through all the tasks you are most likely to want to perform in Microsoft Office SharePoint Designer 2007. If you start at the beginning and work your way through all the exercises, you will gain enough proficiency to be able to create complex Web sites and pages. If you completed all the exercises and later need help remembering how to perform a procedure, the following features of this book will help you locate specific information:

- **Detailed table of contents.** Scan this listing of the topics and sidebars within each chapter to quickly find the information you want.
- **Chapter thumb tabs.** Easily locate the beginning of the chapter you want.
- **Topic-specific running heads.** Within a chapter, quickly locate the topic you want by looking at the running head of odd-numbered pages.
- **Detailed index.** Look up specific tasks and features and general concepts in the index, which has been carefully crafted with the reader in mind.
- **Companion CD.** Install the practice files needed for the step-by-step exercises, and consult a fully searchable electronic version of this book and other useful resources contained on this CD.

In addition, we provide a glossary of terms for those times when you need to look up the meaning of a word or the definition of a concept.

You can save time when you use this book by understanding how the *Step by Step* series shows special instructions, keys to press, buttons to click, and other functionality.

Convention	Meaning
(CD icon)	This icon indicates a reference to information stored on the book's companion CD.
USE	This paragraph preceding a step-by-step exercise indicates the practice files or programs that you will use when working through the exercise.
BE SURE TO	This paragraph preceding or following a step-by-step exercise indicates any requirements you should attend to before beginning the exercise or actions you should take to restore your system after completing the exercise.
OPEN	This paragraph preceding a step-by-step exercise indicates files that you should open before beginning the exercise.
CLOSE	This paragraph following a step-by-step exercise provides instructions for closing open files or programs before moving on to another topic.
1 **2**	Blue numbered steps guide you through hands-on exercises in each topic.
1 2	Black numbered steps guide you through procedures in sidebars and in expository text.
→	An arrow indicates a procedure that has only one step.
See Also	These paragraphs direct you to more information about a given topic in this book or elsewhere.
Troubleshooting	These paragraphs warn you of potential missteps that might prevent you from continuing with the exercise.
Tip **Note**	These paragraphs provide a helpful hint or shortcut that makes working through a task easier, or information about other available options.
Important	These paragraphs point out information that you need to know to complete a procedure.
(Save button) Save	The first time you are told to click a button in an exercise, a picture of the button appears in the left margin. If the name of the button does not appear on the button itself, it appears under the picture.
Enter	In step-by-step exercises, keys you must press appear as they would on a keyboard.
Ctrl + Home	A plus sign (+) between two key names means that you must hold down the first key while you press the second key. For example, "Press Ctrl + Home " means "hold down the Ctrl key while you press the Home key."
Program interface elements	In steps, the names of program elements, such as buttons, commands, and dialog boxes, are shown in black bold characters.
User input	Text that you are supposed to type is shown in blue bold characters.
Glossary terms	Terms explained in the glossary are shown in blue italic type in the chapters.

Using the Book's CD

The CD inside the back cover of this book contains documents that will provide you with additional information and it contains practice files you'll use as you work through the exercises in this book. The CD also contains site templates that you use to create sites. By using practice files and site templates, you won't waste time creating your own sample files and sites—instead, you can jump right in and concentrate on learning how to get the most of out of Microsoft Office SharePoint Designer 2007.

What's on the CD?

The following table lists the practice files and site templates necessary to complete the exercises, as well as sample site templates depicting the results of completed exercises, if the chapter includes them.

Chapter	Additional Information, Practice Files, and .stp Files
Chapter 1: Introducing SharePoint Designer	*Additional Documents\Microsoft Office and SharePoint Integration White Paper.doc*
	Additional Documents\SharePointProductsComparison.xls
	Additional Documents\SharePointSitesAndWorkspaces_ SG_E.ppt
	Additional Documents\WSSVersions.doc
Chapter 2: Working in SharePoint Designer	No practice files
Chapter 3: Customizing a Web Page	*Additional Documents\Microsoft_FrontPage_to_Expression_ Web.doc*
	CustomWebPage\CustomWebPage_Solution.stp
Chapter 4: Creating and Modifying Web Pages	*WebPages\WebPages_Solution.stp*
Chapter 5: Working with Lists and Libraries	*ListLib\ListLib_Solution.stp*
Chapter 6: Working with Data Views	*DataViews\DataView_Starter.stp*
	DataViews\DataView_Solution.stp

Chapter	Additional Information, Practice Files, and .stp Files
Chapter 7: Working with Data Sources	*DataSources\DataSources_Starter.stp* *DataSources\DataSources_Solution.stp* *DataSources\Shipments.xml*
Chapter 8: Using Controls in Web Pages	*Controls\Controls_Starter.stp* *Controls\Controls_Solution.stp*
Chapter 9: Working with Master Pages	*MasterPages\MasterPages_Starter.stp* *MasterPages\MasterPages_Solution.stp*
Chapter 10: Changing the Look and Feel of Pages by Using Cascading Style Sheets	*LookFeel\LookFeel_Starter.stp* *LookFeel\LookFeel_Solution.stp*
Chapter 11: Managing Web Content in a SharePoint Server Environment	No practice files
Chapter 12: Understanding Workflows	*Workflows\Workflows_Starter.stp* *Workflows\Workflows_Solution.stp*
Chapter 13: Building a Windows SharePoint Services Application	*BuildApps\BuildApps_Starter.stp* *BuildApps\BuildApps_Solution.stp* *Additional Documents\Application Templates Under the Hood.doc*
Chapter 14: Managing SharePoint Sites	No practice files
Chapter 15: Understanding Usability and Accessibility	*UsabilityAccessibility\Index.aspx*

In addition to the practice files, starting site templates, and sample solution site templates, the CD also includes exciting resources that will enhance your ability to get the most out of using this book and SharePoint Designer, including an electronic version of the book in PDF format.

Minimum System Requirements

To use this book, your client computer should meet the following requirements:

- **Processor.** Pentium 700 megahertz (MHz) or higher; 2 gigahertz (GHz) recommended.
- **Memory.** 512 megabytes (MB) of RAM; 1 gigabyte (GB) or more recommended.
- **Hard disk.** For the eBooks and downloads, we recommend 3 GB of available hard disk space with 2 GB on the hard disk where the operating system is installed.
- **Operating system.** Windows Vista or later, Windows XP with Service Pack 2 (SP2), or Windows Server 2003 with Service Pack 1 (SP1) or later. To complete the workflow exercises, you will need Microsoft .NET Framework 3.0, which is incorporated into Windows Vista, but not into Windows XP or Windows 2003.
- **Drive.** CD or DVD drive.
- **Display.** Monitor with 1024x768 or higher screen resolution and 16-bit or higher color depth.
- **Software.** Windows Internet Explorer 7 or later; or Microsoft Internet Explorer 6 with service packs.

> **Tip** Actual requirements and product functionality may vary based on your system configuration and operating system.

Step-by-Step Exercises

In addition to the hardware, software, and connections required to run SharePoint Designer, you will need the following to complete successfully the exercises in this book:

- Microsoft Office SharePoint Designer 2007
- 14 MB of available hard disk space for the practice files

Server Computer

To use this book, you must have access to a server running Windows SharePoint Services or SharePoint Server 2007. The server computer should meet the following requirements:

● **Operating system.** Windows Server 2003 SP1 or Windows Server 2003 x64 or Windows Small Business Server 2003; and the .NET Framework 3.0

● **Software.** Microsoft Windows SharePoint Services 3.0 or Microsoft Office SharePoint Server 2007

> **Note** The CD for this book does not contain the Windows Server 2003 operating system, or the Windows SharePoint Services or SharePoint Server software. You must have access to a working site before using this book. Windows SharePoint Services 3.0 can be downloaded from the Microsoft Download Center for no cost.

Installing the Practice Files

You must install the practice files on your hard disk before you can use them in the chapters' exercises. Follow these steps to prepare the CD's files for your use.

> **Important** Installing the practice files requires the privileges of a local system administrator.

To install the files from the CD:

1. Remove the companion CD from the envelope at the back of the book, and insert it into the CD drive of your computer.

   The Step By Step Companion CD License Terms appear. Follow the on-screen directions. To use the practice files, you must accept the terms of the license agreement. After you accept the license agreement, a menu screen appears.

   > **Important** If the menu screen does not appear, click the Start button and then click Computer. Display the Folders list in the Navigation Pane, click the icon for your CD drive, and then in the right pane, double-click the StartCD executable file.

2. Click **Install Practice Files**.

   If you are installing the practice files on a computer running Windows Vista, a File Download – Security Warning dialog box opens.

3. Click **Run**, and when an **Internet Explorer – Security** dialog box opens, click **Run**.

   The Microsoft Office SharePoint Designer Step By Step dialog box opens.

4. Click **Next** on the first screen, click **I accept the terms in the license agreement**, and then click **Next**.

5. If you want to install the practice files to a location other than the default folder (*Documents\Microsoft Press\SPD2007_ SBS*), click the **Change** button, select the new drive and path, and then click **OK**.

> **Important** If you install the practice files to a location other than the default, you will need to substitute that path within the exercises.

6. Click **Next** on the **Choose Destination Location** screen, and then click **Install** on the **Ready to Install the Program** screen to install the selected practice files. If a User Account dialog box opens stating that an unidentified program wants to access your computer, click **Allow**.

7. After the practice files have been installed, click **Finish**.

8. Close the **Step by Step Companion CD** window, remove the companion CD from the CD drive, and return it to the envelope at the back of the book.

Using the Practice Files

When you install the practice files and sample sites from the companion CD, the files are stored on your hard disk in chapter-specific subfolders under *Documents\Microsoft Press\SPD2007_SBS*.

Wherever possible, we start each chapter with a standard Windows SharePoint Services team site. It doesn't mean that if you follow all exercises in all chapters in sequence, you have to start with a new team site for every chapter—you can use the same site throughout the whole book. You should be a site owner of this site. During the exercises, you will be creating child sites below this team site and, for some chapters, you will be provided with a starter site template .stp file to use to create the child site.

The site template .stp files provided on the CD contain lists, libraries, files, and pages that you will use during the exercises. For chapters that require the creation of a site based on a site template, a Housekeeping segment in the beginning of each chapter lists the site template .stp files needed for that chapter. The text also explains any preparation you need to take before you start working through the chapter.

> **Important** Before you can use the practice files in this chapter, you need to install them from the book's companion CD to their default location. See "Using the Book's CD." You will need to create a practice site for this chapter based on site template *DataSources_ Starter.stp* in the practice file folder for this chapter.

If the chapter requires you to create a practice site, please refer to "Using the .stp Site Templates" later in this section for instructions to create a practice site.

Each exercise within a chapter is preceded by a Housekeeping segment that lists the practice files needed for that exercise. The text also explains any preparation you need to take before you start working through the exercise, as shown here:

> **USE** the *Shipments.xml* file. This practice file is located in the *Documents\Microsoft Press\ SPD2007_SBS\DataSources* folder. Also, use your own SharePoint site, instead of the *teams. consolidatedmessenger.com/DataSources* team site.
>
> **BE SURE TO** start SharePoint Designer before beginning this exercise.
>
> **OPEN** the *Shipments.xml* file.

You can browse to the practice files in Windows Explorer by following these steps:

Start

1. On the Windows taskbar, click the **Start** button, and then click **Documents**.
2. In your *Documents* folder, double-click **Microsoft Press**, double-click *SPD2007_SBS*, and then double-click a specific chapter folder.

Removing the Practice Files

You can free up hard disk space by uninstalling the practice files that were installed from the companion CD. The uninstall process deletes any files that you created in the *Documents\Microsoft Press\SPD2007_SBS* folder while working through the exercises.

Follow these steps:

Start

1. On the Windows taskbar, click the **Start** button, and then click **Control Panel**.
2. Under **Programs**, click **Uninstall a program**.
3. Click **Microsoft Office SharePoint Designer 2007 Step by Step**, and then click **Uninstall**.

   The Programs And Features dialog box opens.
4. Click **Yes**.

   The User Account Control dialog box opens.
5. Click **Allow**.

> **Important** Microsoft Product Support Services does not provide support for this book or its companion CD.

Using the .stp Site Templates

To create a practice site for a chapter based on a site template .stp file provided on the CD, perform the following steps.

> **BE SURE TO** verify that you have sufficient rights to upload a site template to a top-level site and to create a site in the site collection.
>
> **OPEN** in the browser the top-level SharePoint site to which you'd like to upload the site template .stp file. If prompted, type your user name and password, and then click OK.

1. Click **Site Action**, and then click **Site Settings** to display the Site Settings page.

   > **Tip** If you are using the .stp files on a SharePoint Server installation, clicking Site Settings will display a secondary menu. Click Modify All Site Settings to display the Site Settings page.

2. Under **Galleries**, click **Site templates** to display the Site Template Gallery page.

   > **Tip** If you see a Go To Top-level Site Settings link under Site Collection Administration, you are not on the top-level site administration page. A site template can only be uploaded to the Site Template Gallery on a top-level site. Click Go To Top-level Site Settings, and then repeat the previous step.

3. Click **Upload** to display the Upload Template: Site Template Gallery page.

4. Click the **Browse** button to open the **Choose File** dialog box.

5. Navigate to *Documents\Microsoft Press\SPD2007_SBS\XXX* where *XXX* is the folder associated with the chapter, click the .stp file that you want to use to create the new site, and then click the **Open** button.

6. Click **OK**.

   The Site Template Gallery: XXX page is displayed.

7. Click **OK** to redisplay the Site Template Gallery page.

   You can now create a new child site based upon the uploaded template.

8. Open in the browser the SharePoint site that you'd like to create the new practice site within.

9. Click **Site Actions**, and then click **Create** to display the Create page.

10. Under **Web Pages**, click **Sites and Workspaces** to display the New SharePoint Site page.

11. In the **Title** text box, type a logical name for the new site; you could simply provide the chapter name, for example DataViews.

12. Optionally, in the **Description** text box, type a description, for example SharePoint Designer SBS Chapter 6 Data Views.

13. In the **URL name** text box, repeat the same name as you typed in the **Title** text box.

14. In the **Template Selection** section, click the **Custom** tab, and then click the name of the template that you just uploaded, for example **DataViews Starter**.

15. In the **Permissions**, **Navigation**, and **Navigation Inheritance** sections, leave the default settings.

16. Click **Create**.

The home page of the new practice site is displayed.

> **CLOSE** the browser.

Removing the .stp Site Templates

To remove the chapter starter templates from the Site Template Gallery, perform the following steps.

> **BE SURE TO** verify that you have sufficient rights to delete a site template from the top-level Site Template Gallery.
>
> **OPEN** the top-level SharePoint site where you previously uploaded the site template STP files. If prompted, type your user name and password, and then click OK.

1. Click **Site Action**, and then click **Site Settings** to display the Site Settings page.

2. Under **Galleries**, click **Site templates** to display the Site Template Gallery page.

> **Note** If you see a Go To Top-level Site Settings link under Site Collection Administration, you are not on the top-level site administration page. A site template can only be uploaded to the Site Template Gallery on a top-level site. Click Go To Top-level Site Settings, and then repeat the previous step.

Edit

3. Click the **Edit** icon to display the details for the site template.

4. Click **Delete item** to remove the site template. You will be prompted to confirm your request. Click **OK** to complete the deletion and redisplay the Site Template Gallery.

5. Repeat the edit-and-delete steps to remove each site template that you no longer want available for the creation of practice sites.

CLOSE the browser.

Deleting a Practice Site

If you created a practice site that you no longer want, you can delete it. Perform the following steps to delete a practice site:

BE SURE TO verify that you have sufficient rights to delete a site.

OPEN in the browser the SharePoint site you want to delete. If prompted, type your user name and password, and then click OK.

1. On the **Site Actions** menu, click **Site Settings** to display the Site Settings page.

2. In the **Site Administration** section, click **Delete this site** to display the Delete This Site confirmation page.

3. Click the **Delete** button to delete the site.

Important Microsoft Product Support Services does not provide support for this book or its companion CD.

Getting Help

Every effort has been made to ensure the accuracy of this book and the contents of its CD. If you run into problems, please contact the appropriate source, listed in the following sections, for help and assistance.

Getting Help with This Book and Its CD

If your question or issue concerns the content of this book or its companion CD, please first search the online Microsoft Press Knowledge Base, which provides support information for known errors in or corrections to this book, at the following Web site:

www.microsoft.com/mspress/support/search.asp

If you do not find your answer in the online Knowledge Base, send your comments or questions to Microsoft Learning Technical Support at:

mspinput@microsoft.com

Getting Help with SharePoint Designer

If your question is about Microsoft Office SharePoint Designer, and not about the content of this Microsoft Press book, please search the Microsoft Help and Support Center or the Microsoft Knowledge Base at:

support.microsoft.com

In the United States, Microsoft software product support issues not covered by the Microsoft Knowledge Base are addressed by Microsoft Product Support Services. The Microsoft software support options available from Microsoft Product Support Services are listed at:

www.microsoft.com/services/microsoftservices/srv_support.mspx

Outside the United States, for support information specific to your location, please refer to the Worldwide Support menu on the Microsoft Help and Support Web site for the site specific to your country:

support.microsoft.com/common/international.aspx

Chapter at a Glance

Understand SharePoint Designer, **page 2**

Explore a SharePoint site, **page 10**

Understand the relationship between Windows SharePoint Services and SharePoint Server 2007, **page 14**

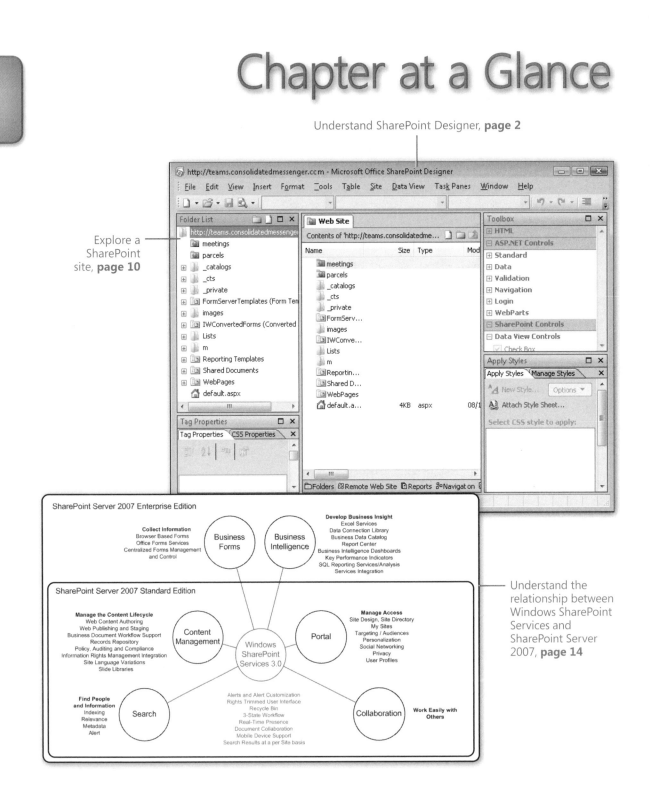

1 Introducing SharePoint Designer

In this chapter, you will learn to:

- ✔ Understand SharePoint Designer.
- ✔ Use SharePoint Designer to carry out common tasks.
- ✔ Understand Windows SharePoint Services.
- ✔ Explore a SharePoint site.
- ✔ Understand the relationship between Windows SharePoint Services and SharePoint Server 2007.
- ✔ Consider complications of upgrading customized SharePoint sites.

Microsoft Office SharePoint Designer 2007 is a powerful Web editing tool that you can use to create and customize any standards-compliant site. However, as its name reflects, the emphasis of this tool is on Microsoft Windows SharePoint Services and Microsoft Office SharePoint Server 2007 sites.

This book assumes that all readers are familiar with creating and modifying SharePoint sites in a browser. A few of you might be familiar with coding sites in Microsoft Visual Studio 2005, however, regardless of your current skill level, we are assuming that everyone wants to learn about the powerful capabilities of SharePoint Designer 2007. Throughout this book, we will point out which tasks can best be accomplished with a browser, Visual Studio and which can best be accomplished with SharePoint Designer.

These three tools represent a continuum of customization capability and the level of skills required. This ranges from a quick and simple ability to customize sites by using the browser to comprehensive customization with Visual Studio, which might require significant developer time. SharePoint Designer is in the middle of this continuum, allowing you to customize SharePoint quickly at the site level. You can choose to use SharePoint Designer in a more technical manner than the browser if you want, especially if you choose to modify the underlying code, but you can create sophisticated solutions without needing to do this.

In this chapter, you will learn what SharePoint Designer is and the common tasks you can accomplish by using it. You will see how SharePoint Designer works with Windows SharePoint Services 3.0 and SharePoint Server 2007. You will also learn about the relationship between Windows SharePoint Services 3.0 and SharePoint Server 2007 and explore a couple of sites. Finally, you will learn some of the complications you may experience if you upgrade sites that you customized using Microsoft Office FrontPage 2003.

> **Important** The exercises in this book use a fictitious business named Consolidated Messenger. In the scenarios, Consolidated Messenger is customizing two SharePoint environments, one for its intranet portal, *http://portal.consolidatedmessenger.com*, and another for its team collaboration sites, *http://teams.consolidatedmessenger.com*. Three people are involved in setting up and providing content for this environment: Peter Krebs, the owner of Consolidated Messenger; Bruce Gabrielle, managing director of parcels and packets; and Paula Flanders, Web designer.

> **Important** No practice files are required to complete the exercises in this chapter. For more information about practice files, see "Using the Book's CD" at the beginning of this book.

> **Troubleshooting** Graphics and operating system–related instructions in this book reflect the Windows Vista user interface. If your computer is running Windows XP and you experience trouble following the instructions as written, please refer to the "Information for Readers Running Windows XP" section at the beginning of this book.

Understanding SharePoint Designer

SharePoint Designer 2007 allows you to connect to a SharePoint Server 2007 site or a Windows SharePoint Services 3.0 site and renders the pages so that "what you see is what you get" (WYSIWG). This enables you to manipulate components by using toolbars similar to those in Microsoft Office applications, so that you can customize and develop business solutions based on Microsoft SharePoint Products and Technologies without needing to write code.

> **Tip** Windows SharePoint Services, SharePoint Server, and SharePoint Designer are known collectively as Microsoft SharePoint Products and Technologies.

A SharePoint site works in a different way than the other sites you may be familiar with. Instead of storing the site content in a folder on the Web server, such as *c:\inetpub\wwwroot*, the majority of the content is stored in a set of Microsoft SQL Server databases.

SharePoint Designer is based partially on FrontPage 2003 and partially on Microsoft Visual Studio 2005. FrontPage 2003 was developed by Microsoft based on technology purchased from Vermeer Technologies Inc. in early 1996. (In fact, Windows SharePoint Services was based on FrontPage Extensions and was originally called SharePoint Team Services.) You will still see evidence of the Vermeer Technologies name in some of the folder names SharePoint technologies use; for example, to access data by using SharePoint's *XML Web Services*, you need to connect to the *_vti_bin* virtual folder; more on this in Chapter 7, "Working with Data Sources." Windows SharePoint Services 3.0 and SharePoint Server 2007 are based on ASP.NET 2.0, which we'll describe in Chapter 4, "Creating and Modifying Web Pages."

At the same time that Microsoft introduced SharePoint Designer, it also introduced another product based on FrontPage and Visual Studio called Microsoft Expression Web. Both SharePoint Designer and Expression Web are designed for information workers and professional Web designers. These products are capable of creating pages that comply with standards, such as Web Content Accessibility Guidelines (WCAG). They also have a JavaScript editor and provide a Code view of each page, where you can enter client-side script helped by Microsoft *IntelliSense* support.

So what is the difference between the two products? When you open SharePoint Designer and Expression Web, (which is part of the Microsoft Expression Studio set of tools), they look very similar. The major differences between the current versions of these two products are as follows:

- You can edit SharePoint sites only by using SharePoint Designer. There are references to SharePoint components in the user interface of Expression Web, but these are dimmed, and if you open a SharePoint site, a dialog box warns you that Expression Web does not support the editing of sites based on Windows SharePoint Services or SharePoint Team Services.

- Expression Web provides 19 templates from which you can create sites. These templates use *Dynamic Web Templates (DWTs)*, originally known as Dreamweaver Web Templates, which are similar to the SharePoint master pages that you can use to give a site a generic look and feel. You can use DWTs on SharePoint sites, but because all other pages use master pages, you would be creating extra work for yourself.

As you can see, the differences between these two products are very small and you can use SharePoint Designer to customize sites that are not based on SharePoint technologies.

See Also To use SharePoint Designer to customize sites other than SharePoint sites, refer to *Microsoft Expression Web Step by Step*, by Chris Leeds (Microsoft Press, 2007).

Using SharePoint Designer to Carry Out Common Tasks

To organize a SharePoint site to meet the business needs of you and your coworkers, you can customize lists, libraries, and the pages of a SharePoint site by using a browser. With SharePoint Designer, you can carry out similar tasks, but you can also extend those customizations. SharePoint Designer complements your Web browser rather than replaces it.

Part of the SharePoint technologies ethos is to allow users to easily complete tasks that were traditionally completed by highly skilled technical users. Changes to sites were the domain of the IT department, the Web master, or the Web hosting company. This caused what became known as the *Web master bottleneck*; content on sites became dated and the number of visitors decreased. Microsoft has provided a number of tools that you can use to quickly and easily complete common tasks on a SharePoint site. SharePoint Designer is one such tool. However, you must ensure that the way you use these tools does not reinvent the Web master bottleneck, where the bottleneck now becomes you!

SharePoint Designer is a very powerful tool, and you can use it for many tasks, whether you are an administrator, developer, or an information worker. Just remember that in many cases, it is easier and quicker to use a Web browser. By transferring the necessary knowledge to another user who does not need to know how to use SharePoint Designer, you can remove yourself from the maintenance cycle, leaving you with more time to de-velop exciting solutions with SharePoint Designer. Use SharePoint Designer to produce solutions that are easily maintainable and supportable. Typically, you can achieve 75 per-cent of the necessary customizations of a SharePoint site by using a browser; 15 percent require the use of SharePoint Designer and 10 percent require a developer who is skilled in Visual Studio 2005.

Some of the most compelling uses of SharePoint Designer are as follows:

- Connecting to other data source connections, such as XML Web services, data-bases, and lists and libraries on other SharePoint sites. When the requirement is to show the same data over a large number of sites, you should consider using the SharePoint Server Business Data Catalog or Business Intelligence features.

- Using the Data View and Data Form Web Parts to create data driven solutions based on *XML* and *eXtensible Stylesheet Language Transformations (XSLT)* technologies, including creating custom views of business data exposed by the SharePoint Server Business Data Catalog (BDC). If you need to use either of these Web Parts on multiple sites, you can use techniques such as exporting and importing Web Parts or making them part of the *Web Part Gallery* to produce maintainable solutions, where you store the XSLT in a central document library and point these Web Parts to them. You can then centrally manage changes to the Web Parts you create without visiting every site that uses them.

- Controlling how other people use SharePoint Designer, by using the Contributor settings feature.

- Using Web Part connections to pass data from a Web Part on one page to one or more Web Parts on another page. With Web Part connections, you can manage the data displayed on a page in a dynamic and interesting way. Using a Web browser, you can connect only Web Parts that are placed on the same page.

- Prototyping a solution to justify business expenditure. You can quickly create solutions with SharePoint Designer to gather requirements and verify the business process the solution must meet, before submitting a proposal or requesting additional resources. You may need to involve a developer or an administrator so that the final solution is easily deployed and managed. You may not immediately identify that you are using SharePoint Designer as a prototyping tool, but if you have customized a site by using SharePoint Designer and then you receive requests to repeat the customization again and again on other SharePoint sites, you need to devise a solution that does not distract you from your other tasks.

- Performing one-off site customizations.

- Creating Workflows on a per lists or libraries basis by using the built-in Workflow Designer, without having to write server-side code or prototyping a workflow that will subsequently be created by a developer with Visual Studio skills.

- Customizing the site templates to meet the needs of specific business processes or sets of tasks in your organization, and then reusing them as a basis for future SharePoint sites.

Do not worry if this list means nothing to you. By the end of the book, you will understand what it means and should review this list of common tasks you can accomplish by using SharePoint Designer.

Understanding Windows SharePoint Services

The current version of Windows SharePoint Services, 3.0, is the third major upgrade of this product. The previous versions were Windows SharePoint Services 2.0, a component of Microsoft Server 2003, and SharePoint Team Services. Although you can use SharePoint Designer with either Windows SharePoint Services 3.0 or Windows SharePoint Services 2.0, you cannot use it with SharePoint Team Services. When we refer to Windows SharePoint Services in this book, we are referring to Windows SharePoint Services 3.0 unless otherwise stated.

> **Tip** You can download Windows SharePoint Services 3.0 from Microsoft's download site at:
>
> *www.microsoft.com/downloads/details.aspx?FamilyID=d51730b5-48fc-4ca2-b454-8dc2caf93951&DisplayLang=en*

> **Tip** To avoid confusion, use FrontPage 2003 to edit Windows SharePoint Services 2.0 sites so you don't try to use functionality available in SharePoint Designer that is not supported on Windows SharePoint Services 2.0 sites, such as master pages.

On the CD A comparison of Windows SharePoint Services 3.0 features and benefits with those of previous versions is provided in *WSSVersions.doc* on the book's companion CD.

Site Definitions

Previously in this chapter, we stated that SharePoint sites are different from traditional sites because they store the majority of their files in SQL Server content databases. In addition, when you create a page for a traditional site, you are creating a file; that is, each page has a corresponding HTML or ASP.NET (ASPX) file. This is not the case with SharePoint sites.

With Windows SharePoint Services, you can choose from a number of *site templates* to create a site incorporating pages, Web Parts, and other features that allow you to organize information, manage documents, and create workflows to support your business environment. When you create a SharePoint site from one of the built-in site templates, you *refer to* files stored on each Web server, in a subfolder, *TEMPLATE*, in the *12 hive*, which in a default install is *C:\Program Files\Common Files\Microsoft Shared\web server extensions\12*. You do not actually *create* any files. Each SharePoint site you create points to the same set of files in the *TEMPLATE* folder. All that is stored in the SQL Server content database is pointers to those files. As a result, a relatively small set of files can support a large number of SharePoint sites with many pages. The files in the TEMPLATE folder on the Web server are known as *site definitions*. There are 10 built-in site defini-tions, which form a good basis on which to create almost any SharePoint site. You should familiarize yourself with the features these site definitions offer so that you know which to use as a blueprint for your SharePoint site.

On the CD A PowerPoint presentation called "The SharePoint Server 2007 Sites and Workspaces Selection Guide" (*SharePointSitesAndWorkspaces_SG_E.ppt*) is on the book's companion CD.

When you create a site by using Windows SharePoint Services, you can immediately start to use that site. You do not need to create any new pages. You just need a Web browser or one of the Office programs.

On the CD A description of how different version of Office programs work together with versions of SharePoint technologies is provided in *Microsoft Office and SharePoint Integration White Paper.doc* on the book's companion CD.

After you create a SharePoint site, the site may not meet all your business needs as it is. You will probably need to modify the site's pages. Whether you use the Web browser or SharePoint Designer, your modifications are immediately visible to visitors to the site.

When you use SharePoint Designer to change a page that points to one of the site definition files, a copy of the page is modified and stored in the SQL Server con-tent database. The page no longer points to a site definition file, because by using SharePoint Designer, you have broken the link. Site definition pages modified by us-ing SharePoint Designer are known as *customized* pages, pages that point to files in the *TEMPLATE* folder are known as *un-customized* pages.

When you use a Web browser to modify a site definition page, the locations of those pages do not change. Therefore, if the page points to a file in the *TEMPLATE* folder on the Web server–that is, if it is an *un-customized* page–they remain in that folder–that is, they remain an *un-customized* page. The browser does not modify the physical file; instead, only the parts of the page you changed are stored in the SQL Server content database. When a user requests the page, SharePoint combines your changes with the file in the *TEMPLATE* folder, and sends the merged page to the user. If you had used SharePoint Designer to modify a site definition page, so that it is now stored in the SQL Server content database–that is, if it is now a *customized* page–and you modify the page by using the browser, it will remain in the SQL Server content database.

> **Tip** You can modify a site based on a site definitions, save your modified site, and use it as a template to create other sites. The term *site template* refers to both site definitions and these customized Web templates.

Site Collections

A SharePoint site always has one *top-level site* and, optionally, one or more *subsites*, also called *child sites*. This hierarchy resembles the hierarchy of folders in file systems, in that it is a tree-like structure. Such a hierarchy of SharePoint sites is called a *site collection*. You can use any of the 10 built-in site templates to create top-level sites as well as child sites within a site collection.

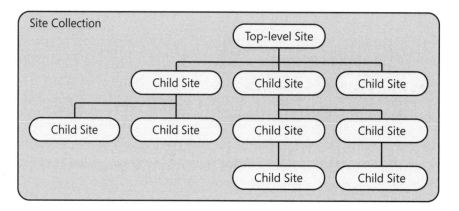

Typically, the top-level site of a SharePoint site collection is based on a team site template and is created for an entire team or department, with many visitors, who have read access, a limited number of members who contribute content, and one or two site collection owners. As child sites are created, the number of users who have access to the site just created, decreases and the number of members (those users who can create and update content) increases.

To identify the current site's position, SharePoint provides two sequences of links, known as *breadcrumbs*:

- *Global navigation breadcrumb*. Displayed on all pages at the top left of a page. Typically, this consists of one link, the link to the top-level site of a site collection. However, other links may be visible, such as a link to a portal site, and links to child sites that do not inherit the top link bar from their parent site.

- *Content navigation breadcrumb*. Displayed below the Home tab, shows the path from the last link on the global navigation breadcrumb to the location of the current page within the current site.

Global navigation breadcrumb

Content navigation breadcrumb

Portal > Teams > Data Views		Welcome Peter Krebs ▾	🌐

🌐 Controls   This List ▾   🔍

Home   **Site Actions** ▾

Data Views > Controls > Shared Documents
Shared Documents

View All Site Content	Share a document with the team by adding it to this document library.	
Pictures	New ▾ Upload ▾ Actions ▾ Settings ▾	View: **All Documents** ▾
▪ PictLib	Type Name Modified	⚪ Modified By
	...dRotator ! NEW ..OM	Peter Krebs

Sites Infrastructure

Within each SharePoint site, as within a folder of a file system, you can store files. How-ever, a SharePoint site provides an infrastructure that allows you to store more than just files; you can store other information such as tasks, contacts, events, calendars, *wikis*, and blog posts. The SharePoint site infrastructure includes the following components:

- *Libraries* SharePoint sites provide a number of libraries where you can store files. These include document, picture, and form libraries.

- *Lists* Lists, like libraries, hold information, examples of which are announcements, links, surveys, discussion boards, calendars, and tasks. In fact, libraries are just a specialized list.

- *Web Parts* Web Parts are reusable components that display information held in lists and libraries, as well as other content. This technology enables SharePoint sites to be flexible and highly customizable.

- *Recycle Bin* The Recycle Bin allows you to restore items, including files, list items, lists, and libraries that have been deleted from the site.

Each SharePoint site includes a set of built-in lists and libraries and, except for the Announce-ments list, these will be empty when you first create the site. The Announcement list con-tains a sample announcement to help you get started. Lists and libraries form the basis for the collaboration environment. You can tailor a list to meet your requirements by adding columns and list items.

You use libraries to store files. Storing files in SharePoint libraries provides the following benefits over storing files in file systems:

- Ability to associate custom properties, also known as metadata, with documents so that you can effectively store, organize, and retrieve documents.

- Use shared or personal views to sort and filter documents.

- Use document management features to check out and check in documents to avoid content loss.
- Use content approval so that users with the Manage Lists right can approve or reject which document is added to a library.
- Ability to combine workflows to facilitate business processes.

Exploring a SharePoint Site

There is no one interface for SharePoint technologies; instead, you can access a SharePoint site by using a Web browser, *My Network Places\Web* folder or compatible programs such as Office applications, including SharePoint Designer. You can choose the interface that suits the task you have to complete. However, depending on the program you choose, you may have a different view of the SharePoint site:

- If you use Windows Explorer, you will see only a small portion of the site's files and content, and you will not be able to view lists or their content.
- If you use a Web browser, you will see the lists and libraries that support the collaborative nature of SharePoint, together with their content.
- If you use SharePoint Designer, the product that provides the most comprehensive interface for the SharePoint infrastructure, you can also see site lists and libraries that you will not see elsewhere; however, you will see files but not their associated metadata, and you will not see list items.

> **Tip** Microsoft Visual Studio 2005 cannot access SharePoint content databases; nor can it render SharePoint sites as you would see them in a browser, as it can other Microsoft ASP. NET 2.0 sites. Therefore, to build solutions based on SharePoint technologies by using Visual Studio 2005, you need to write code. There is no WYSIWG method of achieving SharePoint site customization by using Visual Studio 2005.

> **Important** SharePoint permissions are used when accessing SharePoint resources in SharePoint Designer. For example, if you have permissions to edit a library or list on the SharePoint site, you can also edit the library or list within SharePoint Designer. SharePoint Designer can limit what you can do based on the permission level assigned to you. The introduction detailed the permissions you will need to complete all the exercises in this book.

See Also Because SharePoint Designer is a powerful tool, see Chapter 14, "Managing SharePoint Sites," for information about allowing users to access only a subset of its features.

In this exercise, you will start SharePoint Designer and explore a SharePoint site.

> **USE** the *teams.consolidatedmessenger.com* site (the top-level site of a SharePoint site based on the team site template) or whatever team site you want.

Start

1. On the taskbar, click the **Start** button, point to **All Programs**, click **Microsoft Office**, and then click **Microsoft Office SharePoint Designer**.

The SharePoint Designer program window opens, displaying a title bar that contains the program name and a site, if one is open. By default, SharePoint Designer remembers the last site you worked on and opens it when you open the program.

2. On the **File** menu, click **Open Site**.

The Open Site dialog box opens.

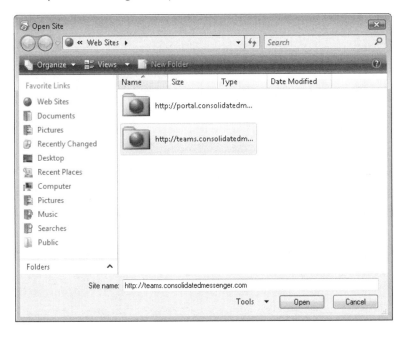

> **Tip** When you have a page from a SharePoint site open in the browser, you can also open the page and the SharePoint site itself in SharePoint Designer by clicking Edit With Microsoft Office SharePoint Designer on the File menu. To configure SharePoint Designer as your default HTML editor, in your browser, click Tools, and then click Internet Options. On the Programs tab of the Internet Options dialog box, click Microsoft Office SharePoint Designer in the HTML editor list.

3. In the **Site name** box, type http://teams.consolidatedmessenger.com, and click **Open**. If prompted, type your user name and password, and then click **OK**.

SharePoint Designer displays the contents of the site in the Folder List task pane and in the document window on the Web Site tab.

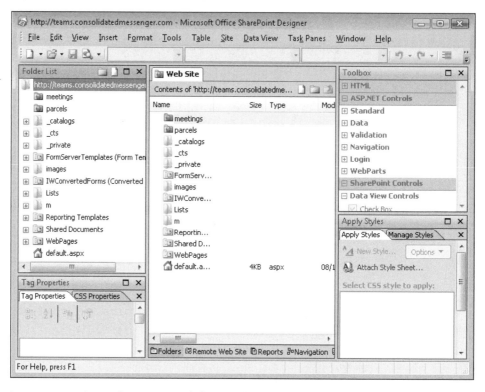

In our example, we have opened the top-level site of a site collection that is based on the team site template. The Folder List task pane displays child sites if they exist, folders, lists, libraries, and files. The icon that represents files is dependent on their extension. If you created a team site based on the team site template on a SharePoint Server installation, you may see additional libraries and lists.

In the Folder List task pane, special folders are listed, such as, _catalogs, _cts, _private, images, and Lists. The _catalog folder contains libraries such as those used to store Web Parts, and site and list templates, as well as master pages.

SharePoint has a number of other folders that start with an underscore, such as _layouts and _vti that contain images and pages that you can reference as links but whose contents are not listed in the Folder List task pane.

> **Important** Do not create folders for your private use with the names _layouts_, _wpresources_, or any names that begin with _vti_.

4. In the **Folder List** task pane, click the plus sign (**+**) to the left of **Lists**.

The *Lists* folder expands, and a SharePoint-specific subfolder appears for each list created for your site. You will not be able to see the columns or content of these lists. You must use the Web browser to see each individual *list item*.

5. Under the **Lists** top-level folder, expand the **Announcements** list.

The Announcements list expands, exposing an *Attachments* subfolder, if attachments are enabled, and a number of pages that correspond to views created for the list and forms to insert, edit, and display the properties of a list item.

6. Click the minus sign (**–**) to the left of the **Announcements** list.

The Announcements list collapses.

7. In the **Folder List** task pane, expand the **Shared Documents** folder.

The *Shared Documents* top-level folder expands and exposes a subfolder named *Forms* and all the documents users have uploaded into the library. (If this is a newly created team site, no documents are listed.) As with lists, you cannot see columns or the *metadata* in those columns in the Folder List task pane. You must use the Web browser to see the metadata associated with the documents.

8. Under the **Shared Documents** top-level folder, expand the **Forms** folder.

The *Forms* folder expands, exposing pages that correspond to views created for this library, including the Explorer view (*WebFldr.aspx*) and forms to manipulate metadata and upload documents. A file named *template.doc* is listed in the *Forms* folder. This file is used when you click New on the library's Action menu in the Web browser.

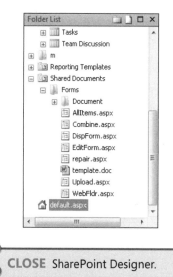

CLOSE SharePoint Designer.

Understanding the Relationship Between Windows SharePoint Services and SharePoint Server 2007

SharePoint technologies include Windows SharePoint Services, SharePoint Server, and SharePoint Designer. As we mentioned earlier, Windows SharePoint Services is a component of Windows Server 2003 and provides a collection of services that you can use to build sites, the function of which is to share information and collaborate with others. Windows SharePoint Services is a platform from which you can build applications. SharePoint Server is an application built on the Windows SharePoint Services 3.0 framework and, therefore, all the features of Windows SharePoint Services are available to SharePoint Server. SharePoint Server provides functionality that can aggregate information from a number of locations. It brings together functionality that was previously included in SharePoint Portal Server 2003 and Microsoft Content Management Server 2002, thereby providing Web solutions for Internet, extranet, and intranet sites.

Microsoft divides SharePoint Server functionality into six feature areas: Collaboration, Portal, Enterprise Search, Enterprise Content Management, Business Process, and Forms and Business Intelligence.

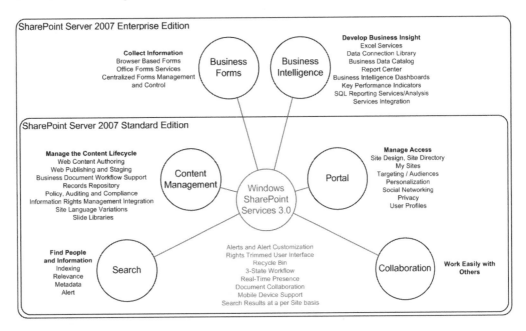

SharePoint Server 2007 is not a component of Windows Server 2003; it is a separate product and needs to be purchased. However, if you need only some of its features for your solution, then Microsoft does provide SharePoint Server 2007 in different editions:

- SharePoint Server 2007 Enterprise Edition
- SharePoint Server 2007 Standard Edition
- Office Forms Server 2007
- SharePoint Server 2007 for Search
- SharePoint Server 2007 for Internet, which is SharePoint Server 2007 Standard Edition licensed for use on the Internet

The edition of SharePoint Server 2007 you should use depends on your business requirements. You can use SharePoint Designer on all SharePoint Server editions.

On the CD A breakdown of the features of SharePoint Server 2007 and a comparison between the different SharePoint Server 2007 editions and SharePoint Portal Server 2003 is provided in *SharePointProductsComparison.xls* on the book's companion CD.

Because SharePoint Server 2007 is built upon Windows SharePoint Services, it comes with the same 10 built-in SharePoint site templates. With SharePoint Server 2007, you also have an additional 12 built-in site templates. However, not all the SharePoint Server–specific site templates can be used as a blueprint to create a site collection; similarly, there are some site templates that you cannot use to create child sites within a site collection. For example, the *Collaboration Portal* and *Publishing Portal* site templates can be used only when you create a site collection, because they create a hierarchy of sites, as you will see in the next exercise. Typically, you use the Collaboration Portal site template to create intranet sites, whereas you use the Publishing Portal site template to create Internet-facing sites. Both of these portal site templates make use of Web Content Management–enabled sites, which are referred to as *publishing sites*, where pages must go through an approval process before they are generally available.

In this exercise, you will start SharePoint Designer and explore a SharePoint Server site.

> **USE** the *portal.consolidatedmessenger.com* site, or whatever collaboration portal site you want.

> **Tip** The *portal.consolidatedmessenger.com* site was created by using the Collaboration Portal site template.

1. On the **Start** menu, point to **All Programs**, click **Microsoft Office**, and then click **Microsoft Office SharePoint Designer**.

   The SharePoint site you opened in the previous exercise is displayed.

2. On the **File** menu, click **Close Site**.

   The SharePoint site closes.

> **Tip** If a site is already open in SharePoint Designer when you open another site, SharePoint Designer opens the second site in a separate window. This can be confusing and can result in customizing the wrong site. We recommend that you have only one SharePoint Designer window open at a time.

3. On the **File** menu, click **Open Site**.

The Open Site dialog box opens.

4. In the **Site name** box, type http://portal.consolidatedmessenger.com, and click **Open**. If prompted, type your user name and password, and then click **OK**.

SharePoint Designer displays the contents of the site in the Folder List task pane and in the document window on the Web Site tab. Just as with Windows SharePoint Services, you can modify only one site at a time within a single SharePoint Designer program window. However, in the Folder List task pane, you will see the child sites beneath this site, such as, Docs, News, Reports, SearchCenter, and SiteDirectory. In the Folder List task pane, you will also see that many of the folders are the same as those you saw in the previous exercise, and they have the same functions.

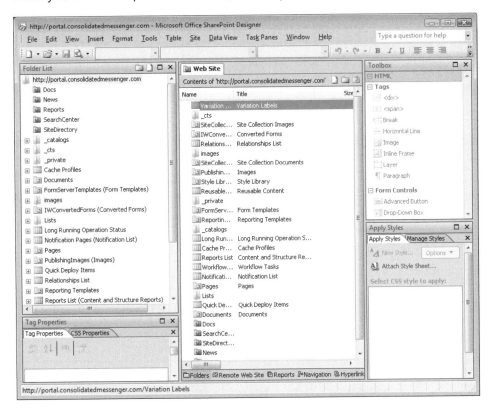

5. In the **Folder List** task pane, expand the **Pages** folder.

The *Pages* top-level folder expands and exposes a subfolder named *Forms* and a file named *Default.aspx*, which is the home page of the Collaboration Portal. You cannot edit the home page of a *publishing site* in SharePoint Designer. You must use a Web browser to do this; however, you can alter the layout of the page by using SharePoint Designer.

Notice the other libraries: PublishingImages, SiteCollectionDocuments, Site-CollectionImages, and Style Library. These, together with the Pages library, provide the Web Content Management functionality of this top-level site.

6. In the **Folder List** task pane, expand the **Lists** folder.

The *Lists* folder expands, and a subfolder appears for lists created on the site. However, not all lists within a SharePoint Server site are placed within the *Lists* folder; notice that lists such as *Quick Deploy Items*, *ReusableContent*, and *WorkflowTasks* are presented as top-level folders.

CLOSE SharePoint Designer.

Considering Complications of Upgrading Customized SharePoint Sites

Previously in this chapter, we stated that SharePoint sites are different from other sites because they store the majority of their files in SQL Server content databases and they use site definitions as templates for creating SharePoint sites. Site definitions have changed dramatically in Windows SharePoint Services 3.0, and, therefore, also in SharePoint Server 2007.

> **Note** If your company created custom site definitions in Windows SharePoint Services 2.0 or SharePoint Portal Server 2003, your company will need to upgrade those custom site definitions to include the new functionality. Creating new site definitions and the file that maps the old custom site definitions to the new custom site definitions is a task for the developer.

For example, a Windows SharePoint Services 2.0 team site is not the same as a Windows SharePoint Services 3.0 team site, but when you upgrade, the mapping process ensures SharePoint sites that you created from the team site definition includes the new Windows SharePoint Services 3.0 functionality, such as the Recycle Bin. However, even if you used the built-in site definitions in the previous version of SharePoint, there is a complication if you used FrontPage 2003 to customize any of your SharePoint sites.

This complication arises because when you use FrontPage 2003 to modify a site definition pages, then like with SharePoint Designer, the modified pages are stored in the SQL Server content database. In the previous version of SharePoint, different terms are used for this process. Pages stored in the SQL Server content database (that is, *customized pages* in SharePoint Designer terminology) were known as *un-ghosted* pages. Un-customized pages (that is, those pages that pointed to files on the Web server) were known as *ghosted* pages. The site definition mapping process that occurs during an upgrade of Windows SharePoint Services 2.0 or SharePoint Portal Server 2003 affects only ghosted pages. Un-ghosted pages are not upgraded and will not receive the new functionality.

If you are involved in the upgrade process or you are the owner of a Windows SharePoint Services 2.0 site, you can choose to do one of the following:

● Leave the customized page as a customized page, and it will always look like a Windows SharePoint Services 2.0 page. The upgrade process may make it look different from before, but you will not lose any of your customizations or data. However, if you have customized only one or two pages in a site, when you navigate to another page (for example, to the Site Settings page or to a list), you will see a Windows SharePoint Services 3.0 page.

● Reset the customized page back to the now-upgraded site definition un-customized page stored in the *TEMPLATE* folder in the 12 hive. You will lose all the customizations you made to the page, and you can decide whether to reapply that customization by using SharePoint Designer. This process can involve a great deal of time and effort. For example, if it takes 15 minutes to re-customize one page and as a site owner you have 100 pages, you need to allow 25 hours to re-customize these pages.

Some organizations may choose to reset all customized pages as part of the upgrade process; others may opt to let site owners decide what to do. You can reset pages to the site definition by using a browser or by using SharePoint Designer. You will learn how to do this in Chapter 3, "Customizing a Web Page."

> **Note** With SharePoint Designer, not only can you customize (un-ghost) pages (.aspx), but you can also customize master pages and cascading style sheet (.css) files, as you will see later in this book. At the time of this writing, it is unknown what affect customizing these files will have on the upgrade process to the next version of SharePoint.

Key Points

- Use SharePoint Designer to produce solutions that are easily maintainable and supportable.

- SharePoint Designer 2007 is a powerful site editing tool that you can use to create standards-compliant sites.

- You can customize SharePoint sites from a Web browser, SharePoint Designer, or Visual Studio 2005. Visual Studio does not provide a WYSIWYG interface to manipulate SharePoint components, whereas the other two products do.

- Windows SharePoint Services provides a powerful set of tools for information sharing and document collaboration, and a platform to build SharePoint-based solutions.

- The majority of the content of a SharePoint site is stored in a set of Microsoft SQL Server content databases.

- A SharePoint site consists of one or more site collections that contain one or more sites where information is stored in lists and libraries.

- SharePoint Server 2007 is a Windows SharePoint Services 3.0–based solution that consists of six features: Collaboration, Portal, Enterprise Search, Enterprise Content Management, Business Process, and Forms and Business Intelligence.

- Windows SharePoint Services, SharePoint Server 2007, and SharePoint Designer 2007 are collectively known as SharePoint Products and Technologies.

- Pages initially created in a SharePoint site point to site definition files in the *TEMPLATE* folder on the Web server, known as un-customized pages; however, when modified by using SharePoint Designer, they are stored in the SQL Server databases and are called customized pages.

- When upgrading customized Windows SharePoint Services 2.0 pages, you must decide whether to leave the customized pages so that they always look like Windows SharePoint Services 2.0 pages, or to reset them to un-customized Windows SharePoint Services 3.0 pages, thereby exposing the new functionality.

Chapter at a Glance

Use toolbars, **page 28**

Explore the SharePoint
Designer workspace,
page 24

Use task panes, **page 29**

Create a SharePoint
site hierarchy, **page 35**

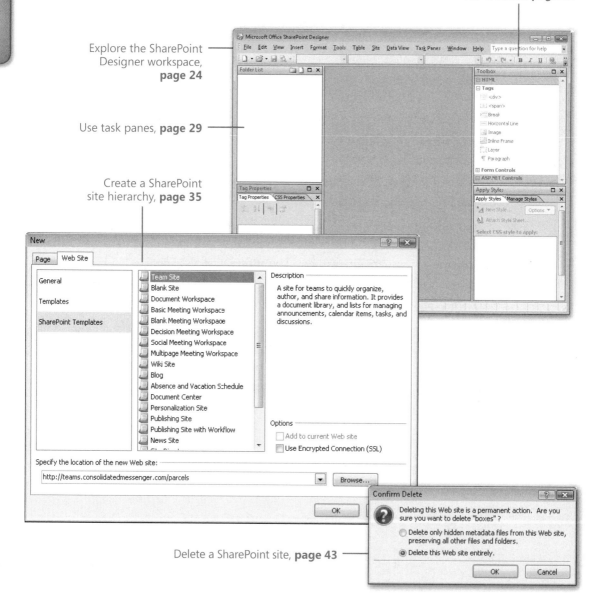

Delete a SharePoint site, **page 43**

2 Working in SharePoint Designer

In this chapter, you will learn to:

✔ Explore the SharePoint Designer workspace.

✔ Use toolbars.

✔ Use task panes.

✔ Create a SharePoint site hierarchy.

✔ Delete a SharePoint site.

After you start Microsoft Office SharePoint Designer 2007, you can interact with the program by using five interface elements: the document window, menu bar, toolbars, task panes, and context-sensitive menus. By using these five elements, you can create, modify, and delete SharePoint sites, connect to a variety of data sources (not just the data held within Microsoft SQL Server databases), create input forms, manage the validation of the data entry on these forms, and develop sophisticated business applications.

In this chapter, you will explore the SharePoint Designer 2007 workspace and learn about these five interface elements. You will also learn how to create and delete a SharePoint site.

Important No practice files are required to complete the exercises in this chapter. For more information about practice files, see "Using the Book's CD" at the beginning of this book.

Troubleshooting Graphics and operating system–related instructions in this book reflect the Windows Vista user interface. If your computer is running Windows XP and you experience trouble following the instructions as written, please refer to the "Information for Readers Running Windows XP" section at the beginning of this book.

Exploring the SharePoint Designer Workspace

When you start SharePoint Designer, you are presented with its workspace. The SharePoint Designer program window contains a number of elements. Initially these elements are in specific locations within the program window; however, you can move them to other areas of the program window or close them. You can customize the program window to assist you in creating solutions that meet your business needs.

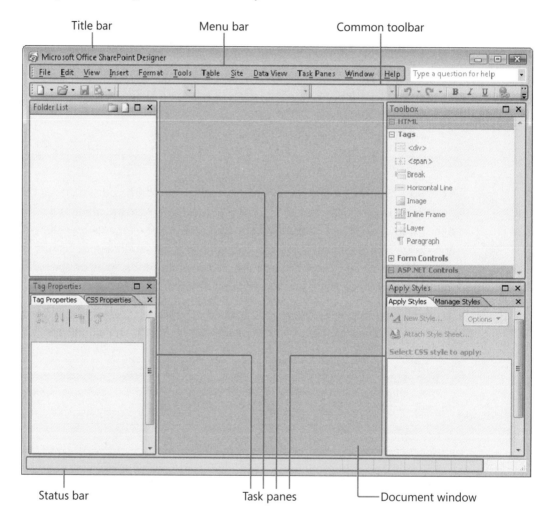

Important elements of the SharePoint workspace include the following:

- **Title bar.** This contains the program name and the site name, if one is open.

- **Menu bar.** The menu bar has 12 menus on it, many of which have a similar function to those you have used in other Office applications; for example, with the File menu, you can perform common file-based operations such as *New*, *Open*, *Save*, and *Save As*, and with the Edit menu, you can perform common word-processing operations such as cut, copy, paste, and delete text. You may not have seen these three new menu items before: Site, Data View, and Task Panes. You will use these menu items as you progress through this book.

- **Common toolbar.** This is one of 11 toolbars available to you. The Common toolbar appears by default under the menu bar and provides the common commands that you will use.

- **Document window.** When a site is open, this window contains the Web Site tab, which displays the contents of a site, and a tab for each page you open. In this window, you modify a page, either by manipulating the components or by writing code; therefore, this windows is also known as the *editing* window.

- **Task panes.** Task panes are placed in one of four areas within the SharePoint Designer program window. When you open SharePoint Designer, by default, six tasks panes are opened in four areas: the *Folder List* task pane opens in the upper left, the *Tag Properties* and *CSS Properties* task panes in the lower left, the *Toolbox* task pane in the upper right, and the *Apply Styles* and *Manage Styles* task panes in the lower right. You can open any of the 24 task panes by using the Task Panes menu item on the menu bar.

- **Status bar.** The status bar contains information such as estimating the time to download a page from a Web server, the size of the page, cascading style sheet version, and code errors.

You can change the way SharePoint Designer starts up by using the Applications Options dialog box, which you can open from the Tools menu. You use this dialog box to configure whether to open the last site automatically when SharePoint Designer starts and to show or hide the Status bar. Use the Proxy Settings option to alter the Internet Properties options of your browser, and the Configure Editors tab to associate file types with any editor on your computer. The default editor is used when you double-click a file in the Folder List task pane or when you right-click a file and click Open on the context-sensitive menu.

In this exercise, you will explore the SharePoint Designer workspace, open and close a SharePoint site, and review the startup settings of SharePoint Designer.

> **USE** the *teams.consolidatedmessenger.com* site (the top-level site of a site collection based on the team site template), or any team site you want.

Start

1. On the taskbar, click the **Start** button, click **All Programs**, click **Microsoft Office**, and then click **Microsoft Office SharePoint Designer**.

The SharePoint Designer program window opens.

> **Tip** By default, SharePoint Designer remembers the last site you worked on and opens it when you open the program. In this case, you may see a site listed in the Folder List task pane.

2. On the **File** menu, click **Open Site**.

The Open Site dialog box opens.

3. In the **Site name** text box, type http://teams.consolidatedmessenger.com, and then click **Open**. If prompted, type your user name and password, and click **OK**.

> **Important** SharePoint Designer uses the Internet Properties security settings of the browser to decide whether to prompt for credentials.

The contents of the SharePoint site are listed in the Folder List task pane and on the Web Site tab in the document window. At the bottom of the Web Site tab are the view buttons: Folders, Remote Web Site, Reports, Navigation, and Hyperlinks.

4. On the **Web Site** view bar, click **Navigation**.

> **Tip** An alternative is to click Navigation on the Site menu.

The Navigation view of the site appears. The Quick Launch link bar and the labels on the Quick Launch bar, such as Documents, Lists, Discussions, and Sites, are represented by boxes with globe symbols. There is also a box with a globe symbol that represents the SharePoint navigation bar. If this site had child sites and you had specified to display links to the child site on the top link bar of the parent site, you would see these links under the SharePoint navigation bar box.

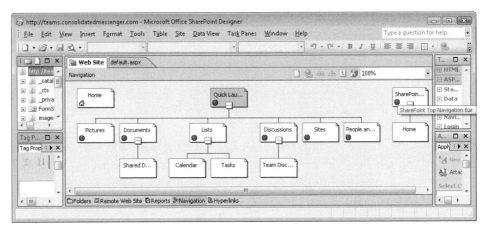

You can manage the Quick Launch bar and the SharePoint navigation bar by using this view unless the parent navigation was based on a site collection that used the Collaboration Portal or Publishing Portal site templates.

5. On the **Tools** menu, click **Application Options**.

The Application Options dialog box opens displaying the General tab where the Startup options are listed.

6. Click **OK**.

The Application Options dialog box closes.

BE SURE TO leave SharePoint Designer open if you are continuing to the next exercise.

Using Toolbars

SharePoint Designer consists of 11 built-in toolbars that provide you with a visual way of manipulating elements on your pages. Many of these toolbars are similar to the ones you use in other Microsoft Office applications, such as Standard, Formatting, Common, and Tables. A number of them are SharePoint Designer–specific: Code View, Dynamic Web Template, Master Page, Pictures, Positioning, Style, and Style Application. As with other Office applications, you can decide to show multiple toolbars simultaneously, and by default, SharePoint Designer will dock them under the menu bar. You can decide to dock them in other locations or to undock them completely and have them float over the program window. You can create your own toolbars and customize the existing toolbars.

In this exercise, you will customize the Common toolbar.

> **BE SURE TO** start SharePoint Designer if you exited after the last exercise. If SharePoint Designer opens a previous site, click Close Site on the File menu.

1. On the **View** menu, point to **Toolbars**, and then click **Customize** (or click **Customize** on the **Tools** menu).

   The Customize dialog box opens.

2. Click the **Commands** tab, and then in the right pane, under **Commands**, scroll down until you find **Close Site**.

Open

3. Drag **Close Site** next to the **Open** icon on the Common toolbar.

Close Site appears on the Common toolbar.

4. In the **Customize** dialog box, click the **Toolbars** tab, select **Common**, and then click **Reset**.

A dialog box prompts you to confirm that you want to reset the changes made to the Common toolbar.

5. Click **OK**.

The Close Site command disappears from the Common toolbar.

CLOSE the Customize dialog box, and then exit SharePoint Designer.

Using Task Panes

Task panes are helper windows that you can use to perform certain tasks, such as modifying HTML tag properties, adding ASP.NET controls and Web Parts to your pages, and managing *cascading style sheets*. You can open, close, and move task panes to the sides of the SharePoint Designer program window or make them float so that they appear in the middle of the program window. When you first open SharePoint Designer, only four task panes open and are placed on the right and left sides of the SharePoint Designer program window. Other task panes can be opened from the Task Pane menu. SharePoint Designer provides you with 24 task panes, listed in the following table.

Task pane	Description
Folder List	Displays the contents of a SharePoint site. Use this as you would Windows Explorer; that is, you can cut, copy, paste, rename, and delete files and folders between different sites and file systems. Any metadata associated with a file or folder are copied and are visible if the receiving document library has the same column name and type, but permissions and multiple versions are not transferred with the file.
Navigation	Displays a visual representation of the navigation structure of a SharePoint site in a tree-like view, similar to the Navigation view described earlier in this chapter, and includes the Quick Launch bar and SharePoint Top Navigation bar.
Tag Properties	Use to manipulate HTML tag properties, which are grouped into three categories: attributes, events, and misc(ellaneous).

(continued on next page)

Task pane	Description
CSS Properties	Use when working with cascading style sheets, particularly when manipulating cascading style sheet class, ID, or tag definitions. Use as an alternative to launching the Modify Style dialog box.
Layout Tables	Provides visual aids for designing and working with tables.
Apply Styles	Use to create new cascading style sheet styles and apply existing ones to elements within pages.
Manage Styles	Use to manage cascading style sheet styles that you have added to elements within pages.
Behaviors	Lists behaviors that you can add to pages. Behaviors are SharePoint Designer alternatives to writing JavaScript.
Layers	Use to insert and configure layers. A *layer* is the name given to an absolute positioned HTML division (DIV) tag. You use the DIV tag to group elements together so that you can format them with styles, or create animations or flyout menus.
Toolbox	Lists HTML tags, form controls, ASP.NET controls, and SharePoint controls that you can place on pages by dragging and dropping.
Data Source Library	Use to manage connections to data sources such as SharePoint lists and libraries (both for the current site and remote sites), Database Connections, XML files, and server-side scripts including RSS feeds, XML Web Services, Business Data Catalog, and Linked Sources, such as data sources that have similar columns and you would like to display the contents of these data sources together.
Data Source Details	Use to display or modify contents of the data sources defined in the Data Source Library task pane, by using either the *Data View Web Part (DVWP)* or *Data Form Web Part (DFWP)*.
Conditional Formatting	Use to format the data in a DVWP or DFWP based on criteria that you specify.
Find Data Source	Use to search data sources defined in the Data Source Library task pane.
Web Parts	Use to add Web Parts to pages from the site's Web Part Gallery or the Server Web Part Gallery; similar to the Add Web Part tool pane in the browser, but it does not expose the Close Web Part gallery.

Task pane	Description
Find 1	Use to search and replace text, code, and HTML within a page. This and the following task panes appear when you use the Find option on the Edit menu. You can find and replace text on one page, a number of pages, or the whole site. You can also find words in the code and regular expressions.
Find 2	Displays a second search task pane. Use when you want to leave the search results in the Find 1 task pane, but need to complete another search.
Accessibility	Use to check pages and sites against Web Content Accessibility Guidelines (WCAG) and Priority 1 and 2. This task pane appears when you use the Accessibility Reports option on the Tools menu.
Compatibility	Use to validate pages and sites for well-formed HTML/XTML or cascading style sheet versions. The Compatibility Checker currently supports CSS 2.1, 2.0, 1.0 and CSS IE6. This task pane appears when you use the Compatibility Reports option on the Tools menu.
Hyperlinks	Use to check and fix broken links.
CSS Reports	Use to check pages for cascading style sheet errors and highlight those cascading style sheet styles that are not used. This task pane appears when you use the CSS Reports option on the Tools menu.
Clip Art	Use to search for Clip Art.
Clipboard	Allows you to view up to 24 thumbnails of any item that can be cut or copied by an Office program (text, graphics, photographs, and more).
Contributor	Shows your contributor status and allows you to manage *Contributor Settings* if you are a site owner or administrator. Use Contributor Settings to control how SharePoint Designer is used to modify a SharePoint site.

The last option on the Task Pane menu, Reset Workspace Layout, allows you to restore the task panes to their default positions; that is, the Folder List task pane opens in the upper-left corner of the program window, the Tag Properties and CSS Properties task panes in the lower-left corner, the Toolbox task pane in the upper-right corner, and the Apply Styles and Manage Styles task panes in the lower-right corner.

In this exercise, you will view and manage task panes.

> **OPEN** the *teams.consolidatedmessenger.com* team site, or whatever site you want to use, and enter your credentials if prompted to do so.

1. On the **Edit** menu, click **Find**.

   The Find And Replace dialog box opens.

2. In the **Find what** text box, type **MasterPageFile**, and click **All pages** under **Find where**.

3. Select the **Match case** and **Find whole word only** check boxes under **Advanced**. Clear any other options that are selected under Advanced.

4. Click **Find All**.

   The Find And Replace dialog box closes, and the Find 1 task pane opens, docking at the bottom of the document window. The status bars of both the SharePoint Designer program window and the Find 1 task pane indicate the progress of the search. When complete, the Find 1 task pane status bar informs you that no occurrences of 'MasterPageFile' were found.

Find and Replace

5. In the **Find 1** task pane, click the **Find and Replace** button.

The Find And Replace dialog box opens.

6. Under **Advanced**, select **Find in source code** and click **Find All**.

The Find And Replace dialog box closes, and as before, the status bars indicate the progress of the Find process; the Find 1 task pane displays the results. In a newly created SharePoint site, each page refers to a master page. The number of pages returned in the results are dependent on the site template the site was created from and whether the site is created in a Windows SharePoint Services or SharePoint Server installation.

	Page	▼	Line	▼	Matched Text
	_catalogs/lt/Forms/AllItems.aspx [...	1			...@ Page language="C#" ="∼ma
	_catalogs/lt/Forms/DispForm.aspx...	1			...@ Page language="C#" MasterPageFile="∼ma
	_catalogs/lt/Forms/EditForm.aspx ...	1			<%@ Page language="C#" File="∼ma
	_catalogs/lt/Forms/Upload.aspx [1...	30			MasterPageFile="∼masterurl/default.master" File="∼ma
	_catalogs/masterpage/Forms/AllIt...	1			Inherits="Microsoft.SharePoint.W...
					...@ Page language="C#" MasterPageFile="∼ma

Found 80 occurrences of 'MasterPageFile' in 80 pages.

Next Result

7. In the **Find 1** task pane, click the **Next Result** button.

The first page in the results list opens in a new tab in the document window in Code view, with the first instance of the text you are looking for highlighted.

> **Tip** To continue searching the page for the next occurrence of the word, you would click the Next Result button; to find the previous occurrence of the search keyword, you would click the Previous Result button. When no more occurrences of the search keyword can be found on the current page, the next page in the results list opens in a new tab if the page is not already open. To open a specific page, double-click the page in the results list. To save your common find-and-replace searches, in the Find And Replace dialog box, click the Save Query button. To use a saved query, click the Open Query button.

8. On the **Task Panes** menu, click **Clipboard**.

The Clipboard task pane docks to the right edge of the SharePoint Designer program window.

9. Click **Task Panes**.

In the graphic shown on the next page, notice that the task panes displayed in the drop-down menu are grouped together, separated with a horizontal line. Task panes in the same group open in the same area of the SharePoint Designer program window. Task panes that open in the same area appear as tabs.

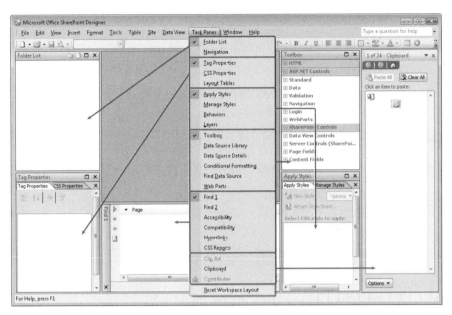

Close

10. In the lower-left corner of the **Find 1** task pane, click the **Close** button.

The Find 1 task pane closes.

> **Tip** Close task panes when you no longer need them, because they reduce the space available for the document window area.

11. In the lower-right task pane area, click the **Manage Styles** tab.

The title bar above the Manage Styles tab turns orange, indicating that the Manage Styles task pane has the focus.

12. Point to the orange **Manage Styles** task pane title. When the pointer changes to a four-headed arrow, drag the task pane to the lower left corner of the program window.

The lower-left task pane now contains tabs for Tag Properties, CSS Properties, Apply Styles, and Manage Styles.

> **Note** The Clip Art, Clipboard, and Contributor task panes cannot be moved or merged with the other task panes and will always open in a separate window docked at the right side of the SharePoint Designer program window.

13. Click the left arrow below the **Manage Styles** task pane title until you see the **Tag Properties** task pane.

14. On the **Task Panes** menu, click **Reset Workspace Layout**.

    SharePoint Designer displays the four default task panes in their original position.

CLOSE SharePoint Designer.

Creating a SharePoint Site Hierarchy

In Chapter 1, "Introducing SharePoint Designer," we described the basic concepts of sites, site collections, site definitions, and site templates. To recap, a site collection consists of one or more sites, where each site is created by using as a template a site definition or a customized site definition, both of which are commonly known as site templates.

The top-level site of a site collection is created when the site collection is created. A site collection can be created either by using the browser or programmatically. You cannot use SharePoint Designer, however, to create a site collection. You can use SharePoint Designer only to create child sites within a site collection.

See Also To create a site collection, refer to *Microsoft Office SharePoint Server 2007 Administrator's Companion*, by Bill English (Microsoft Press, 2007).

Microsoft Windows SharePoint Services and Microsoft Office SharePoint Server 2007 provide a number of built-in site definitions that you can use as a basis for the SharePoint sites you create. When you use the browser to create a site, these site definitions are grouped into at least two categories: Collaboration and Meetings. Other categories may appear if you have customized site definitions or site templates on your Web server.

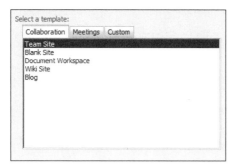

The 10 built-in site definitions are listed under their respective categories, in the following table.

Collaboration	Meeting
Team site	Basic Meeting Workspace
Blank site	Blank Meeting Workspace
Document Workspace	Decision Meeting Workspace
Wiki site	Social Meeting Workspace
Blog	Multipage Meeting Workspace

SharePoint Server 2007 installs an additional 12 site definitions. Some of these site definitions cannot be used to create sites that are top-level sites of a site collection and others can be used only as a template for child sites within a site collection. When you use the browser to create a site, these site definitions are grouped into two categories: Enterprise and Publishing. The following table lists the 12 built-in SharePoint Server site definitions under their respective categories, and specifies which you can use to create a top-level site collection or use as a basis for a child site of a site collection.

Enterprise	Top-level	Child	Publishing	Top-level	Child
Document Center	Yes	Yes	Collaboration Portal	Yes	No
Records Center	Yes	Yes	Publishing Portal	Yes	No
Personalization Site	No	Yes	Publishing Site	No	Yes
Site Directory	Yes	Yes	Publishing Site With Workflow	No	Yes
Report Center	Yes	Yes			
Search Center with Tabs	Yes	Yes			
Search Center	Yes	Yes			
My Site Host	Yes	No			

Microsoft has also released an additional 40 site templates for Windows SharePoint Services 3.0, known as the "*Fabulous 40*," which you can download from the Microsoft Download Center and use on both Windows SharePoint Services and SharePoint Server installations. Twenty of these site templates use the Blank site definition as a basis and were customized by using SharePoint Designer. The other 20 are new site definitions, which include new features. You can use the 40 site templates as well as the built-in site templates as a starting point to develop SharePoint-based solutions.

Publishing Site Templates

The site definitions *Report Center*, *Site Directory*, and *Search Center with Tabs* are categorized in the browser as Enterprise site templates; however, they should be classified as Publishing site templates as you will create publishing sites if you use them. A publishing site is a site that uses the SharePoint Server Web Content Management functionality; that is, pages requiring content approval before they are visible to a reader of the site.

See Also For information about publishing sites, see Chapter 11, "Web Content Management."

Publishing functionality is enabled on SharePoint Server sites when the Office SharePoint Server Publishing feature is activated. A *feature* is a new concept introduced with Windows SharePoint Services 3.0 that allows you to activate or deactivate functionality at a site, site collection, *Web application*, or *SharePoint Web farm*. The Office SharePoint Server Publishing feature is dependent on the activation of the Office SharePoint Server Publishing Infrastructure feature at the site collection level. Microsoft developed both these features, which are installed when SharePoint Server 2007 is installed on each Web front end. Site owners can activate features to extend the functionality of their sites. Therefore, it is possible to turn a SharePoint site, based on the team site definition, into a publishing site by activating the Office SharePoint Server Publishing feature.

When you create a site by using SharePoint Designer, the site templates are not categorized under the labels Collaboration, Meeting, Enterprise, Publishing, or Custom as they are when you use the browser. You cannot configure the site's name, permission inheritance, or whether to use the top link bar from the parent site. Neither can you categorize the new site within the Site Directory, if it is a child site of a Collaboration portal. So, after you have created the site in SharePoint Designer, you must remember to configure these and other site settings by using the browser.

The first task in developing a SharePoint-based solution when you use SharePoint Designer is to create a child site. The only value you need is the URL name, also known as the *internal* name. Use the best practices specified in the sidebar "Best Practices for Naming URLs," on the next page, when you specify the URL name. You cannot use SharePoint Designer to create a top-level site of a site collection.

Best Practices for Naming URLs

When you specify a *Uniform Resource Locator (URL)* for a SharePoint object, whether it is for a site or a list or library, do not use the following characters:

\ / : * ? " < > | # { } % & <TAB> " ! ~ +

SharePoint Designer will display a Warning dialog box if you use an illegal URL character; however, the message does not point specifically to the use of one of these characters.

See Also For more information about using these characters in URLs, see the Microsoft Knowledge Base article "Information about the characters that you cannot use in sites, folders, and files in SharePoint Portal Server 2003 or in SharePoint Server 2007," located at *support.microsoft.com/kb/905231/*.

Keep the name short and meaningful, and include terms that users enter as search query keywords. You will not be able to change the URL later. Be consistent in your naming conventions; for example, don't call a picture library *pictures* in one site and *images* in another. If your aim is to make the URL readable, then use an underscore in place of a space; if the URL consists of several words, capitalize the first character in each word. Although the space character is a legal URL character, there are several issues with having one or more spaces in the URL, such as the following:

- **Readability.** A space in the URL name is URL-encoded as %20. The resulting name is difficult for people to read. A site with a URL of *w s s*, would result in an encoded version of *w%20s%20s*, six extra characters.

- **URL length limitation.** A URL must contain no more than 260 total characters. SharePoint refers to every site, list, library, list item, or document as a URL. SharePoint prefixes the document name by the document library's URL, which is prefixed by the site's URL, and then by its parent's site's URL, and so on. In addition, when editing documents or list items, SharePoint appends the URL of the document library or list, so that when the user clicks on Save and Close, the browser redirects them back to the list or library the item was saved. If the URL of the list or library contains two spaces, then it would contain six extra characters. Then as the URL is appended to the URL for editing, that adds another six characters, making 12 extra characters. Therefore, if you consistently use long names, you'll eventually have problems, which is exaggerated if you use spaces.

● **Links in e-mails.** If you incorporate a URL in an e-mail, the e-mail program truncates the URL at the first space when sending the clickable link to the recipient, resulting in a broken link. When users click the link, they are taken to an invalid location in the browser and won't understand why they couldn't find the document.

In this exercise, you will create two SharePoint sites by using the menu bar and the context-sensitive menu. You will also customize the title of a SharePoint site.

BE SURE TO start SharePoint Designer before beginning this exercise. If a previous site opens, click Close Site on the File menu.

USE the *teams.consolidatedmessenger.com* site as the parent site for the new SharePoint team site, or use whatever top-level site you want.

1. On the **File** menu, click **New**.

The New dialog box opens.

2. Click the **Web Site** tab.

Your screen lists three categories of sites: General, Templates, and SharePoint Templates.

3. In the categories list, click **SharePoint Templates**, if it is not already selected.
The New dialog box displays no SharePoint Web templates.

4. Type http://teams.consolidatedmessenger.com/parcels in the **Specify the location of the new Web site** box, and then press [Enter]. If prompted, type your user name and password, and click **OK**.

> **Tip** When you create a site, you must specify a location that uses either *Hypertext Transfer Protocol (HTTP)* or *secure HTTP (HTTPS) with Secure Sockets Layer (SSL)*. You cannot specify a file system or use *File Transfer Protocol (FTP)* for the location of a SharePoint site.

SharePoint Designer communicates with the SharePoint site collection and retrieves a list of SharePoint site templates that you can use as a basis for your new SharePoint child site. These are displayed in the central pane of the New dialog box, also known as the *site type list*. The SharePoint templates listed are dependent on whether you are using Windows SharePoint Services or SharePoint Server, or whether your organization has created any site definitions. If you connect to another SharePoint site, you may see different SharePoint templates.

5. Click **Team Site** in the site type list, if it is not already selected.

In the right pane of the New dialog box, the Description section describes the purpose of the team site.

> **Important** After you create a site based on a site template, you cannot change the site template it is based on. If the functionality you require is not exposed with a SharePoint feature and you choose the wrong site template, you must delete the site and create it again.

6. Click **OK**.

The Create New Web Site dialog box opens.

The dialog box closes after the parcels team site is created. The contents of the parcels team site are listed in the Folder List task pane and in the document window under the Web Site tab.

7. In the **Folder List** task pane, right click the URL of the parcels team site, click **New**, and then click **Subsite**.

   The New dialog box opens, with the SharePoint Content tab active. If you display the New dialog box when a SharePoint site is open, you can use SharePoint Designer to create pages, child sites, and other SharePoint components, such as lists and libraries, by using one of the three tabs.

8. Type http://teams.consolidatedmessenger.com/parcels/boxes in the **Specify the location of the new Web site** box, and then click **OK**.

   A new SharePoint Designer program window opens, with the contents of the boxes team site listed in the Folder List task pane and in the document window under the Web Site tab.

9. On the **Site** menu, click **Administration**, and then click **Administration Home**.

   A browser window opens and displays the Site Settings page for the boxes team site. If prompted, type your user name and password, and then click **OK**.

Team Site > Site Settings

Site Settings

Site Information

Site URL:	http://teams.consolidatedmessenger.com/parcels/boxes/
Mobile Site URL:	http://teams.consolidatedmessenger.com/parcels/boxes/m/
Version:	12.0.0.4518

Users and Permissions	Look and Feel	Galleries	Site Administration	Site Collection Administration
▫ People and groups	▫ Title, description, and icon	▫ Master pages	▫ Regional settings	▫ Go to top level site settings
▫ Advanced permissions	▫ Tree view	▫ Site content types	▫ Site libraries and lists	
	▫ Site theme	▫ Site columns	▫ Site usage reports	
	▫ Top link bar		▫ User alerts	
	▫ Quick Launch		▫ RSS	
	▫ Save site as template		▫ Search visibility	
	▫ Reset to site definition		▫ Sites and workspaces	
			▫ Site features	
			▫ Delete this site	
			▫ Related Links scope settings	

> **Important** Only two links are specified in the Users And Permissions list. This indicates that the boxes team site is inheriting its permissions from its parent site, which in this case is parcels. To configure unique permissions, use the browser.

10. In the **Look and Feel** list, click **Title, description, and icon**.

The Title, Description, And Icon page appears. The name for the boxes team site is Team Site; boxes was used only to form the URL of the team site. To customize the site's title, description, or logo, you cannot use SharePoint Designer but must use the browser and the site's administrator pages.

11. In the **Title** text box, type Boxes Department, and then click **OK**.

The Site Settings page opens.

> **CLOSE** SharePoint Designer and all browser windows.

Deleting a SharePoint Site

If you no longer need or want a site then you can delete it. However, be warned—when you delete a site, it is not sent to the Recycle Bin. As we have seen earlier in this chapter, when you create a site by using SharePoint Designer, the title of the site is the name of the site template used to create the site. Therefore you could end up with many sites named *Team Site*, and it is only by looking at their URLs that you will be able to see which site they are, so always verify that you are deleting the correct site.

In this exercise, you will navigate from one SharePoint site to another site and delete a SharePoint site.

> **BE SURE TO** start SharePoint Designer before beginning this exercise.
> **USE** the sites created in the previous exercises.

1. On the **File** menu, point to **Recent Sites**, and then click **http://teams.consolidatedmessenger.com/parcels**. If prompted, type your user name and password, and then click **OK**.

The Folder List task pane displays the contents of the parcels team site and the boxes child site. Notice that the Folder List task pane displays the URL of the child site, rather than the title.

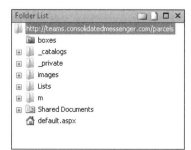

2. Double-click the **boxes** child site.

   A new SharePoint Designer program window opens with the contents of the boxes team site listed in the Folder List task pane and in the document window under the Web Site tab.

   > **Tip** You can customize only one site within each SharePoint Designer program window; however, when you have multiple SharePoint Designer program windows open, it is very easy to customize the wrong site. Therefore, customize one site at a time, and close all other SharePoint Designer program windows.

3. Right-click the boxes URL in the **Folder List** task pane, and click **Delete**.

   The Confirm Delete dialog box opens.

4. Click **Delete this Web site entirely**, and then click **OK**.

   The SharePoint Designer program window opens with no site open.

5. Return to the SharePoint Designer program window that displays the contents of the parcels team site.

   The boxes child site no longer appears in the Folder List task pane.

   > **Tip** If the boxes child site is still visible, click Refresh on the View menu.

   > **Warning** You cannot delete the top-level site of a site collection by using SharePoint Designer, nor can you delete a site that still contains child sites. If you try to do this, SharePoint Designer displays a warning.

   CLOSE all SharePoint Designer program windows. If you're not continuing directly to the next chapter, exit SharePoint Designer.

Key Points

- By default, SharePoint Designer remembers the last site you worked on and opens it when you start the program, but you can alter this setting on the General tab of the Application Options dialog box.

- The contents of the SharePoint site are listed in the Folder List task pane and on the Web Site tab in the document window. When you double-click a file in the Folder List task pane, the default editor is used to open the file. The default editor is specified on the Configure Editors tab of the Application Options dialog box.

- SharePoint Designer uses the security Internet Properties settings of your browser to decide whether to prompt for credentials.

- SharePoint Designer provides 12 built-in toolbars and 24 task panes that provide you with visual ways of manipulating elements on your pages.

- New to Windows SharePoint Services 3.0 is the concept of a feature: some can be activated at the site-collection level, whereas others can be activated on a site-by-site basis.

- You cannot change the site template that is used to create a SharePoint site after it is created. If the functionality you require is not exposed by a feature, you will have to delete the SharePoint Site and re-create it based on a different site template.

- URLs should not contain the characters \ / : * ? " < > | # { } % & <TAB> " ! ~. Nor should they contain spaces because these are encoded as %20. URLs must be fewer than 260 characters.

- You can delete child sites of a site collection by using SharePoint Designer; however, you cannot delete the top-level site of a site collection. Deleted sites are not sent to the Recycle Bin.

Chapter at a Glance

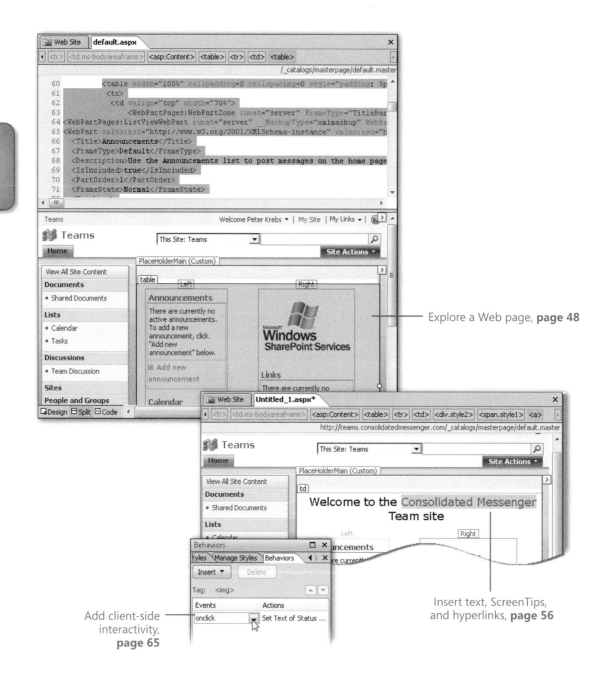

Explore a Web page, **page 48**

Insert text, ScreenTips, and hyperlinks, **page 56**

Add client-side interactivity, **page 65**

3 Customizing a Web Page

In this chapter, you will learn to:

✔ Explore a Web page.

✔ Insert text, ScreenTips, hyperlinks, Web components, and images.

✔ Add client-side interactivity.

✔ Create a table layout.

✔ Change the default page for a Web site.

✔ Reset to a site definition.

Microsoft SharePoint sites are designed to be flexible and highly customizable. The content of a site can be static or dynamic. Static content is typically stored on the page and is the same no matter which user requests that page. Dynamic content is stored separately from the page, and when a user requests a page, SharePoint then decides which content to include as a response to the user's request, dependent on any number of criteria, such as which security group the user is a member of. Most SharePoint pages contain both static and dynamic content.

When you use Microsoft Office SharePoint Designer 2007 to customize a SharePoint page, you can customize both static and dynamic content. When you use the browser, you can customize only the dynamic content. If you are a developer, you can use the SharePoint object model to perform advanced Web development customizations of both static and dynamic content. In any deployment, all three tools are likely to be used.

In this chapter, you will learn to create a page use the SharePoint Designer toolbar components to add static content, such as text, ScreenTips, hyperlinks, and an image. You will then add further static content by adding a Web component, use a behavior to add JavaScript to a page that adds text to the status bar and alter the layout of a table. You will see how each site has a home page, the default page. Using this page, you'll see the differences between *customized* and *un-customized* SharePoint pages, and how to reset a customized page to site definition.

> **Important** No practice files are required to complete the exercises in this chapter. For more information about practice files, see "Using the Book's CD" at the beginning of this book.

> **Troubleshooting** Graphics and operating system–related instructions in this book reflect the Windows Vista user interface. If your computer is running Windows XP and you experience trouble following the instructions as written, please refer to the "Information for Readers Running Windows XP" section at the beginning of this book.

Exploring a Web Page

When you open a page, SharePoint Designer 2007 provides you with the following three views of your page:

- *Design view* displays the page as it would appear in a browser and provides a WYSIWYG editing environment. To identify the page elements, such as borders, margins, and padding, you can use SharePoint Designer 2007 visual aids.

- *Code view* displays the HTML tags, client-side script, such as JavaScript, and controls that SharePoint uses to display content, such as the name of the site, and the Search box. The code elements are color-coded to make it easier for you to identify text that users would see in their browser from the code surrounding the text. Each line of code is numbered so that error messages can reference them, and you can quickly identify problems.

- *Split view* divides the document window horizontally and displays the Code view at the top and Design view at the bottom.

Because you can use any of these three views to edit a page, when you display a page in the document window, it is sometimes called the *editing window*.

> **Caution** You should not use SharePoint Designer to directly edit pages within the file system on a SharePoint Web server; doing so will corrupt the files and adversely affect your SharePoint installation. You should always open a SharePoint site and edit pages from the site over HTTP.

The page you see in your browser when you request a page from a Microsoft Windows SharePoint Services 3.0 site is the combination of two Microsoft ASP.NET pages: a *master page* and a *content page*.

A master page is a special ASP.NET 2.0 page that you can use to share code between pages. It provides a site with a consistent appearance and navigation for each page within a site. You cannot view a master page in your browser, but you can view and customize a master page by using SharePoint Designer.

When you open a content page in Design view, the merged view of the two pages is displayed, and the name of the master page that is applied to the page is displayed in the upper-right corner of the page. In this view, you can edit only the code that the content page contains. You will see a no-entry symbol if you point to code that the master page contains. In the Code view of a content page, you see only the code that the content page contains. An example of a content page is the *home page* of a SharePoint site, which is named *default.aspx*. The home page is the page that renders in your browser if you type the URL of a site and do not specify a specific page.

When you use a browser to request a page from a Microsoft Office SharePoint Server 2007 Web publishing site, it can be a combination of three ASP.NET pages: a master page, a page layout, and a content page. (In this scenario, the content page is referred to as a publishing page.) Alternatively, the page your browser requests could also be a combination of only two ASP.NET pages: a master page and a content page. (In this scenario, the content page is referred to as a non-publishing page.) In this chapter, you will explore and customize a non-publishing page, in particular the content pages of a SharePoint team site. We describe customizing master pages in Chapter 9, "Working with Master Pages," and customizing publishing pages in Chapter 11, "Managing Web Content in a SharePoint Server Environment."

> **Tip** SharePoint Designer has references to publishing such as Publish Selected Files, Don't Publish, and Publish Site. These functions refer to non-SharePoint sites and not to the Web Content Management publishing feature of SharePoint Server 2007.

When you type text on a page, SharePoint Designer applies a set of default text attributes. You can change these default settings by using the Page Editor Options dialog box.

In this exercise, you will review the Page Editor Options to configure the Design and Code views and then explore a content page.

USE the *http://teams.consolidatedmessenger.com* site, or whatever team site you want.
BE SURE TO start SharePoint Designer before beginning this exercise.
OPEN the site in SharePoint Designer.

1. On the **Tools** menu, click **Page Editor Options**.

   The Page Editor Options dialog box opens with the General tab active. This tab contains a number of settings that affect the Code view. You can also change these options from the Code View toolbar. The default settings make it easy for you to work with code and find errors.

2. Click the **Default Fonts** tab.

   The default setting is to use the Unicode (UTF-8) language, which is the World Wide Web Consortium (W3C) recommendation. Depending on the size of your monitor, you may want to change the font size of the Code view.

> **Tip** Do not change the Design view font. Microsoft Internet Explorer and Firefox use Times New Roman as their default font, and you will want the view of a page in Design view to reflect the rendering of the page within the browser.

3. Click **OK** to close the **Page Editor Options** dialog box.

4. In the **Folder List** task pane, double-click **Default.aspx**.

The home page of the team site opens as a second tab in the document window.

Views   Visual Aids status

> **Tip** You can switch between tabs by pressing Ctrl+Tab or Ctrl+Shift+Tab.

The title bar of the SharePoint Designer program window contains the URL of the page, and the relative address of the master page applied to this content page is displayed at the top of the Design view below the Quick Tag Selector. The page contains two Web Part zones, denoted by two blue borders labeled at the top as Left and Right.

> **Tip** *Web Part zones* are containers for Web Parts. On a SharePoint team site, the Left zone contains the Web Parts named Announcements and Calendar, and the Right zone contains the Site Image and the Links Web Parts. The use of Web Parts and Web Part zones is discussed in Chapter 4, "Creating and Modifying Web Pages."

The SharePoint Designer program window status bar identifies whether visual aids are turned on or off. If your page is displayed in a grid-like manner showing margins and table cells, then the visual aids feature is turned on.

5. On the **View** menu, point to **Visual Aids**, and then click **Show**.

The status of visual aids is reversed; in other words, if they were previously turned on, then the SharePoint Designer program window status bar now indicates Visual Aids: Off.

6. Move the pointer over the page to where the pointer shape changes from an arrow to the no-entry icon.

No-Entry

A no-entry icon denotes content that is merged from the master page. You will not be able to click or enter text at the location where the no-entry icon appears.

7. Click **Home**.

A purple border labeled *PlaceHolderHorizontalNav (Master)* surrounds the Home tab, a chevron icon appears to the left of the tab, and the Quick Tag Selector disappears. The PlaceHolderHorizontalNav (Master) is a SharePoint control merged from the master page that dynamically creates the contents for the horizontal navigation bar when a page is rendered.

8. Click below and outside of the **Left** Web Part zone.

A purple border labeled *PlaceHolderMain (Custom)* surrounds both the Web Part zones. A dotted border, labeled *td*, surrounds the Left Web Part zone, and the <td> tag is active on the Quick Tag Selector. The previous six tags are displayed using a black font; the others use a grey font. The Tag Properties task pane displays the <td> tag properties. Those attributes that have values are at the top of the task pane in bold royal blue.

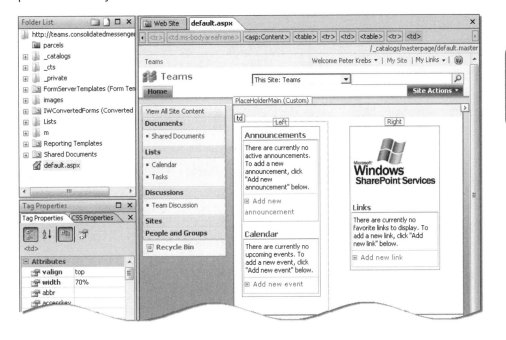

> **Tip** If the Quick Tag Selector does not appear, click Quick Tag Selector on the View menu.

The SharePoint control, PlaceHolderMain, is defined in the <asp:Content> tag, which is the last tag on the Quick Tag Selector that uses a black font and is where you place most of your text for default.aspx content pages. The <td> tag denotes that the Left Web Part zone is placed within an HTML table cell.

9. Press <kbd>Esc</kbd> twice.

The first time, the table cell that contains the Left Web Part zone is highlighted. The second time, the table containing the table cell is highlighted. The content of the Tag Properties task pane changes as you move to different tags. The Esc key navigates you to the parent HTML tag container.

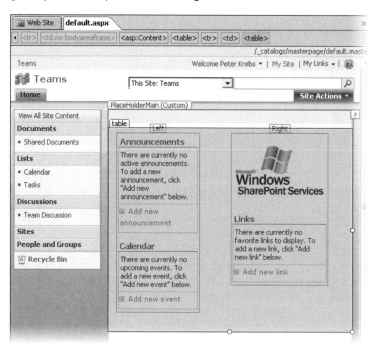

Tip Because SharePoint sites contain a number of controls, it can be difficult to position your cursor exactly where you want it. Use the Esc key together with the Up Arrow, Down Arrow, Left Arrow, and Right Arrow keys to navigate around the page.

⊟ Split

10. At the bottom of the default.aspx document window, click **Split**.

The document window divides horizontally and displays the Code view in the upper pane and the Design view in the lower pane. The table is highlighted in both the Design and Code views.

> **Tip** You can switch between views by pressing Ctrl+Page Up or Ctrl+Page Down.

11. Right-click the **default.aspx** tab, and then click **Close**.

The home page of the team site closes, leaving the Web Site tab displayed in the document window.

Inserting Text, ScreenTips, and Hyperlinks

You can type new text on a page in Design view. This text is static content that SharePoint Designer saves within the Web page file. You can also choose to insert text from a file, or to copy and then paste text from a file into your Web pages. The standard Windows application shortcuts for copy, cut, paste, and undo work in SharePoint Designer, as they do in any other Microsoft program. Generally, you will want to paste the contents of a file as text and add your own formatting, because the formatting from other file formats may be verbose and may not generate the most efficient Web format.

You can add other components, such as images, hyperlinks, and *ScreenTips*, directly to the page. ScreenTips are useful because they provide information when users point to hyperlinks.

In this exercise, you will create a new page based on the home page of a team site. You will then add text and quickly format it by using the Common toolbar. After adding a hyperlink to the text and associating a tooltip with the hyperlink, you will configure the hyperlink so that a new browser window opens when a user clicks the hyperlink.

> **USE** the *http://teams.consolidatedmessenger.com* site, or whatever team site you want.
> **OPEN** the site in SharePoint Designer.

1. In the **Folder List** task pane, right-click **Default.aspx**, and then click **New From Existing Page**.

   A new document window opens with the tab labeled *Untitled_1.aspx*.

2. At the bottom of the document window, click **Design**, click the Web Part zone labeled **Left**, and then click the ⬅ key twice.

   On the Quick Tag Selector, the <td> tag is highlighted in orange.

3. Within the table cell, type Welcome to the Consolidated Messenger Team sites, and then press [Enter] to move to a new line.

   An asterisk appears on the Untitled_1.aspx tab, indicating that the page has changed but that you have not saved your changes. This type of page is commonly referred to as a *dirty page*.

   > **Tip** If you want to use all the text in a file in a page, insert the entire file. On the Insert menu, click File. With SharePoint Designer, you can insert text of the following formats: HTML, Rich Text Format, Text Files, Word Perfect, Word 2007 Document, Word 97-2003 Document, and Works 6.0-9.0.

Font Size

Center

4. Select the text **Welcome to the Consolidated Messenger Team sites**. On the Common toolbar, click the **Font Size** arrow, and then click **medium (14pt)**.

5. On the Common toolbar, click the **Center** button.

6. Select the text **Consolidated Messenger**, and on the **Insert** menu, click **Hyperlink**.

   The Insert Hyperlink dialog box opens.

7. In the **Insert Hyperlink** dialog box, click the **ScreenTip** button.

   The Set Hyperlink ScreenTip dialog box opens.

8. In the **ScreenTip** text box, type Consolidated Messenger Intranet site, and then click **OK** to close the Set Hyperlink ScreenTip dialog box.

9. In the **Address** text box of the **Edit Hyperlink** dialog box, type
   http://portal.consolidatedmessenger.com
   and then click the **Target Frame** button.

   The Target Frame dialog box opens.

10. In the **Common targets** list box, select **New Window**, and then click **OK**.

    The Target Frame dialog box closes, and the bottom of the Edit Hyperlink dialog box displays Target Frame: _blank.

11. In the **Insert Hyperlink** dialog box, click **OK**.

    The Insert Hyperlink dialog box closes. The text *Consolidated Messenger* is highlighted, and on the Quick Tag Selector, the orange <a> tag appears.

Save

12. On the Common toolbar, click the **Save** button.

The Save As dialog box opens with the *http://teams.consolidatedmessenger.com* team site selected.

13. In the **File name** text box, type home.aspx, and then click **Save**.

The Save As dialog box closes, the tab label changes to home.aspx with no asterisk, and in the Folder List task pane, home.aspx is listed in the root of the site.

CLOSE the home.aspx page.

Inserting Web Components

Web components, also called *webbots*, are prepackaged blocks of HTML that add functionality to your page without the need for you to write code. Not all Web components are supported on SharePoint sites, including Table Of Contents for the Web Site, Included Content based on date and time, List and Document views, and Web Search. Web components do not produce standards-compliant, cross-platform code, and for this reason the ability to insert Web Components does not exist in Microsoft Expression Web. For a similar reason, DHTML Effects were removed from both Expression Web and SharePoint Designer. Different technologies are available now that you can use to achieve similar results, such as using Really Simple Syndication (RSS) feeds in place of the MSN and MSNBC Web Components.

On the CD   The file *Microsoft_FrontPage_to_Expression_Web.doc* on the book's companion CD, provides resources and suggestions for achieving functionality similar to that provided by Web components.

In this exercise, you add a Marquee Web Component to a Web page. This component makes the text scroll horizontally across the screen. Some Web designers believe that adding dynamic effects to a page can make them more interesting and can be used to highlight information. Over usage of such an effect can also have a negative image.

> **USE** the SharePoint team site you modified in the previous exercise.
>
> **OPEN** the team site in SharePoint Designer, if it is not already open.

1. In the **Folder List** task pane, right-click **home.aspx**, and then click **Check Out**.

   A green check mark appears to the left of home.aspx in the Folder List task pane.

   > **Tip** Always check out pages before you modify them. This prevents other users from making changes at the same time.

2. In the **Folder List** task pane, double click **home.aspx**.

   The page opens as a second tab in the document window.

3. On a new line under the words **Welcome to the Consolidated Messenger Team sites**, type Parcels Boxes Letters, and then press ⌷Enter⌷ to move to a new line.

4. Select the words **Parcels Boxes Letters**, and on the **Insert** menu, click **Web Component**.

   The Insert Web Component dialog box opens.

5. Under **Component Type**, click **Dynamic Effects**, and under **Choose an effect**, click **Marquee**.

6. Click **Finish** to close the **Insert Web Component** dialog box.

   The Marquee Properties dialog box opens.

7. Click **OK** to close the **Marquee Properties** dialog box.

8. In the document window, click the words **Parcels Boxes Letters**.

   A black border surrounds the words, and the orange marquee tag appears on the Quick Tag Selector.

   > **Warning** The Marquee effect uses the <marquee> tag that was introduced by Microsoft as an extension to the HTML 3.2 specification and is not included in any of the HTML or XHTML W3C specifications. You can use it on a SharePoint site, but it may not scroll if you use a browser other than Internet Explorer.

9. In the **Folder List** task pane, right-click **home.aspx**, and click **Check In**.

   A SharePoint Designer window opens asking if you want to save changes.

10. Click **Yes**.

    The green check mark to the left of home.aspx in the Folder List task pane disappears.

Preview

11. On the Common toolbar, click the **Preview** button.

A browser window opens.

12. If prompted, type your user name and password, and then click **OK**.

The home.aspx page is displayed with the words *Parcels Boxes Letters* scrolling from the right to the left.

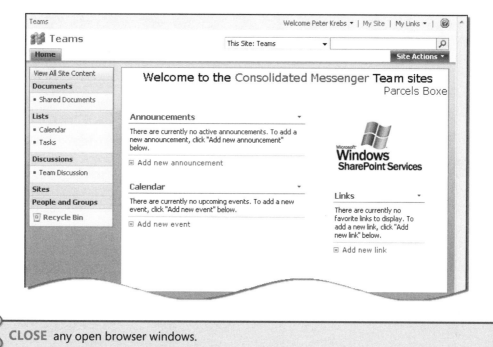

CLOSE any open browser windows.

Important The Design view of SharePoint Designer cannot render the marquee tag as you would see it in a browser. There may be other aspects of a page that are not the same when you view them in the browser; therefore, as you make changes to a page, you should constantly review the page in a browser and test the functionality of your changes. Every browser is different, so you should also test your page in the set of browsers with resolutions commonly used by visitors to your sites. If you have multiple browsers installed on your computer, you can use the Preview arrow to preview a page in a specific browser at a particular resolution.

Inserting Images

SharePoint Designer provides a number of tools to manage the graphics that you include on pages, such as the following:

- **Image conversion.** When you insert an image into a page that is not a GIF or JPEG, by default SharePoint Designer converts the file to GIF or JPEG format depending on the number of colors in the original image. After you insert an image, you can resize it in SharePoint Designer by changing its properties in the Picture Properties dialog box.

- **Auto Thumbnail.** You can tell SharePoint Designer to create a small version of an image, a thumbnail, and link it to the full-sized image that it represents, by right-clicking an image, and clicking Auto Thumbnail. Alternatively, select the image and press Ctrl+T.

> **Tip** You can configure the settings for both these image manipulation options by using commands located on the Picture and AutoThumbnail tabs of the Page Editor Options dialog box.

For prototyping purposes or for images on team sites, the SharePoint Designer image manipulation capabilities should be adequate, but if you are producing a public-facing site, you may want to obtain a third-party image editing tool. Ideally, you should resize images before inserting them into pages, because when you resize an image by using HTML tag attributes, the original image is downloaded to the user's computer, even though the browser renders the image at a smaller size.

In this exercise, you will insert an image into a page and then resize the image.

> **USE** the SharePoint team site you modified in the previous exercise.
> **OPEN** the site in SharePoint Designer, if it is not already open, and display the *home.aspx* page.

1. Place the insertion point on a new line, and then on the **Insert** menu, point to **Picture**, and click **Clip Art**.

   The Clip Art task pane docks at the right edge of the SharePoint Designer program window.

2. In the **Clip Art** task pane, under **Results should be,** click the arrow to the right of **All media file types**, and then clear the **Clip Art, Movies**, and **Sounds** check boxes.

3. In the **Search for** text box, type people, and then click **Go**.

> **Tip** If a Microsoft Clip Organizer dialog box opens, asking whether you want to include thousands of additional clip art images and photos from Microsoft Office Online when you search, click No.

A number of picture thumbnails appear in the Clip Art task pane.

4. Point to each image to read its tooltip. Click the image that displays the tooltip **businesses, businesswomen**.

The Accessibilities Properties dialog box opens.

5. In the **Alternate Text** box, type People make the team. Then click **OK**.

The image is inserted into the page.

> **Tip** Alternate text allows you to type text that displays if the image does not load or if users are unable to see images. Append a period to the end of the words you enter so that users who listen to screen readers are able to understand your pages more easily, especially when two alternative text tags are next to each other.

6. Click the image that you inserted. On the **Quick Tag Selector**, click the arrow to the right of the orange **<img>** tag, and then click **Tag Properties**.

A Picture Properties dialog box opens with the General tab active.

7. Click the **Appearance** tab. In the **Width** text box type 200, and then click **OK**.

The Picture Properties dialog box closes and the image resizes.

8. Right-click the **home.aspx** tab, and then click **Save**.

The Save Embedded Files dialog box opens.

9. Click **Change Folder**.

The Change Folder dialog box opens.

10. Double-click **images**, and then click **OK**.

The images folder is shown in the Folder column to the right of the image file name.

11. Click **Rename**, type people.jpg as the name of the image file, and then click **OK**.

> **Tip** You can use the Picture File Type button on the Save Embedded Files dialog box to convert image files to a different image format.

The Save Embedded Files dialog box closes and the asterisk disappears from the home.aspx tab.

Close

12. In the **Clip Art** task pane, click the **Close** button.

Adding Client-Side Interactivity

Behaviors are blocks of code that add functionality to your page without the need for you to write code. They consist of an action and an event. The event triggers the action. Behaviors affect all components between a set of HTML tags; therefore, you cannot associate them with a specific Web Part or a Web Part zone. When you add a behavior to a number of words within a paragraph, you need to add HTML tags to separate the words from the rest of the paragraph; for example, use the <span> tag.

Use the Behaviors task pane to insert and manage behaviors. In this task pane, clicking the Insert button lists behaviors based on the CSS schema setting on the Authoring tab of the Page Editor Options dialog box. You can apply one or more behaviors to any component on your page. The order of the behaviors can be changed by using the Up or Down buttons in the Behavior task pane.

When you insert a behavior, SharePoint Designer retrieves code from files located on your computer and copies it into the Web page. The default location of these files is *C:\Program Files\Microsoft Office\Templates\1033\Behaviors12\ACTIONS*. If you have never coded before, you can use the code that behaviors produce as an introduction.

In this exercise, you will add an action to an image so that a message is displayed in the status bar of the browser window when the pointer passes over the image.

> **USE** the SharePoint team site you modified in the previous exercise.
> **OPEN** the site in SharePoint Designer, if it is not already open, and display the *home.aspx* page.

1. Click the *people* image that you inserted into the page in the previous exercise. Then on the **Format** menu, click **Behaviors**.

The Behaviors task pane opens, displaying Tag: <img> beneath the Insert button. This indicates the content on which the behavior will be performed.

2. In the **Behaviors** task pane, click **Insert**, point to **Set Text**, and then click **Set Text of Status Bar**.

   The Set Text Of Status Bar dialog box opens.

3. In the **Message** textbox, type People make the team, and then click **OK** to close the **Set Text of Status Bar** dialog box.

   The action that appears in the Behaviors task pane uses an Onclick event.

> **Note** In Design view, it is not obvious that a page contains behaviors; also, the Behaviors task pane shows behaviors only after you have clicked a component on a page that you have associated with a behavior.

4. In the **Behaviors** task pane, point to the **onclick** event, click the arrow that appears, and then click **onmouseover**.

5. At the bottom of the document window, click **Split** to display the HTML code that associates the image with the **Set Text of Status Bar** behavior.

   The code looks something like this:

   ```
   <img alt="People make the team." src="images/people.jpg" width="200"
   height="280" onmouseover="FP_setStatusBarText('People make the team')">
   ```

6. Point to **FP_setStatusBarText**, press ⌃, and then click to jump to the JavaScript code for the behavior.

   The code looks something similar to this:

   ```
   <script type="text/javascript">
   var navBarHelpOverrideKey = "wssmain";
   Function FP_setStatusBarText(txt) {//v1.0
     Window.status=txt;
   }
   ```

Design

Preview

7. At the bottom of the document window, click **Design**.

8. On the Common toolbar, click the **Preview** button.

   A dialog box opens, warning you that you have not saved your changes.

9. Click **Yes**.

   A browser window opens.

10. If prompted, type your user name and password, and then click **OK**.

    The home.aspx page is displayed.

11. Point to the image.

    People make the team is displayed in the browser status bar and as a tooltip.

CLOSE the browser.

Creating a Table Layout

SharePoint Designer provides you with three main methods of manipulating tables: the Table menu, the Table button on the Common toolbar, and the Layout Tables task pane. You can use tables to help you lay out a page or to present data in a tabular format. Most SharePoint pages use tables to lay out a grid to position various elements, such as text, graphics, and controls. In fact, most pages contain many tables; several are nested within other tables, with empty cells to separate areas of the page. To modify the built-in pages that are installed with Windows SharePoint Services or SharePoint Server 2007, you need to be familiar with manipulating tables.

> **Note** Using tables to lay out a page is a legacy mechanism. If you were to create a new site that is not based on SharePoint technologies, you would consider creating all new pages by using cascading style sheet–based layouts. You could create new SharePoint pages that use cascading style sheets to control the layout of the page, but as soon as you attach a master page, table elements will be returned to the browser. SharePoint Designer provides you with nine cascading style sheet–based layouts for creating new pages. We discuss the use of cascading style sheet in SharePoint sites in Chapter 10, "Changing the Look and Feel of Pages by Using Cascading Style Sheets," and Chapter 15, "Understanding Usability and Accessibility."

In this exercise, you create a new table layout and turn on visual aids so that you can see the outline of that table. You will then format the table and add content.

> **USE** the SharePoint team site you modified in the previous exercise.
>
> **OPEN** the site in SharePoint Designer, if it is not already open, and display the *home.aspx* page.

1. On the **View** menu, point to **Visual Aids**, and then click **Show**.

   Visual Aids: On appears in the SharePoint Designer status bar.

Table

2. Place the insertion point on a new line below the image. On the Common toolbar, click the **Table** button. Select three rows and three columns, and then release the mouse button to insert the table on the page.

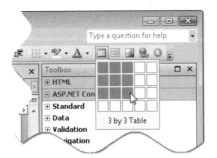

3. Right-click one of the table cells, and then click **Table Properties**.

   The Table Properties dialog box opens.

4. In the **Background** section, in the **Color** list, click **yellow**, and then click **OK** to close the **Table Properties** dialog box.

5. Select the top two cells on the left, right-click, point to **Modify**, and then click **Merge Cells**, so that the first row now contains two cells.

6. In the first cell of the first row, type Worldwide sending options and in the second cell of the first row, type Guaranteed Delivery.

7. In the first cell of the second row, type Zone 1, press [Tab], type USA zip codes, press [Tab], and then type Delivery by 5:30 pm next working day.

8. In the first cell of the third row, type Zone 2, press [Tab], type International, press [Tab], and then type Delivery 2-5 working days.

> **Tip** On a SharePoint site, you usually enter the above data in a list and add a List View Web page in a Web Part zone on the home page.

Worldwide sending options	Guaranteed Delivery
Zone 1 USA zip codes	Delivery by 5:30 pm next working [td]y
Zone 2 International	Delivery 2-5 working days

9. On the Common toolbar, click the **Save** button.

Save

CLOSE the *home.aspx* page.

Changing the Default Page for a Web Site

When you customize a non-publishing page, your changes are immediately visible to visitors to that page. When the page you need to customize is the home page of a site, you may not want your changes to be immediately visible. If you do not have the SharePoint Server's Web Content Management functionality available to you, an alternative to modifying the home page is to create a new page based on the home page, complete the customization on the new page, and then make the new page the home page for the site.

In this exercise, you will change the default page for a site and then test that the change was implemented successfully.

> **USE** the SharePoint team site you modified in the previous exercise.
>
> **OPEN** the site in SharePoint Designer, if it is not already open.

1. In the **Folder List** task pane, right-click **home.aspx**, and then click **Set as Home Page**.

   The Confirm Rename warning box opens.

   ```
   Confirm Rename                                        ? X
   ⚠  Are you sure you want to rename "default.aspx", the home page
      of your web site?

   ☐ Don't show me again.        [ Yes ]        [ No ]
   ```

2. Click **Yes**.

   A Rename dialog box opens.

   ```
   Rename                                                ? X
   ❓  There are 3 pages that have hyperlinks to this page.

       Do you want to update these pages so that the hyperlinks will not
       be broken?

              [ Yes ]       [ No ]       [ Cancel ]
   ```

3. Click **Yes**.

   In the Folder List task pane, home.aspx now appears as *default.aspx*, and the original default.aspx is named *default-old.aspx*.

4. Right-click **default.aspx**, and then click **Preview in Browser**. If prompted, type your user name and password, and then click **OK**.

   The home page of the site is displayed.

5. On the Quick Launch bar, under **Documents**, click **Shared Documents**.

   The default view of the Shared Documents library is displayed.

6. Click the **Home** tab.

   The home page of the site is displayed again.

> **CLOSE** the browser.

Resetting to a Site Definition

As we described in Chapter 1, "Introducing SharePoint Designer," when you create a site based on a site definition you do not create and save any pages in the SQL Server content databases. The content databases contain only pointers to files on the Web server and such pages are known as *un-customized* pages. Therefore, if you create 100 team sites, the home page of all these team sites all point to and share one file, the default.aspx file that is stored in the *TEMPLATE* folder on the Web servers. This is different from other site solutions where each site would have its own unique copy of its home page. This makes SharePoint sites very efficient as a Web solution, because on most occasions when a user requests a page, it is cached in the memory of the Web server.

When a user requests a page, such as the home page for a team site, the following things happen:

- The master page and the default.aspx page are retrieved from the *TEMPLATE* folder and loaded into the memory of the Web server, if they are not there already.

- The team site properties are retrieved from the content database, such as the site title, site logo, permissions, the lists and libraries that the site contains, and whether they should be shown on the Quick Launch bar.

- The default.aspx page properties are retrieved from the content database, such as its title, the Web Part zones it contains, and whether there are any Web Parts in these zones.

- The Web Parts properties that populate the Web Part zones are retrieved from the content database, together with any associated data.

- The master page, default.aspx page, and all the data retrieved from the content database, taking in account the security settings of the user, are merged to form one HTML page that is sent to the user.

When you use SharePoint Designer to edit an *un-customized* page, a copy of the site definition file is stored in the SQL Server content database where your unique customizations can be retained. The page is now known as a *customized* page. All subsequent requests for that page result in retrieving the page from the SQL Server content database. Any time you save a page in SharePoint designer, whether you modify it or not, it will always be saved to the SQL Server content databases.

> **Note** The response time—that is, the time between requesting a page and the time when the page is rendered in your browser—is greater for a customized page than an un-customized page, because the customized page has to be retrieved from the SQL Server content database. However, due to the caching improvements in ASP.NET 2.0, the performance impact of using customized pages compared with un-customized pages is small. However, the real difference is that if the pages are modified on the server by the SharePoint administrator, customized pages will not pick up those changes.

SharePoint Designer provides warning dialog boxes and visual indicators when you save an un-customized page and create a customized page. It also provides you with a means of resetting your customized page so that it points back to the un-customized page in the *TEMPLATE* folder on the Web servers. You can reset pages to site definition files in both Windows SharePoint Services sites and SharePoint Server sites.

You cannot reset a page back to a site definition if the page was not created by customizing an instance of a site definition file, because when a page was created from an existing page or a blank page, or was created in another program and then imported into the site, the page has no association with the site definition files. Site definition files include master pages, cascading style sheet files, list forms, and pages that are used by libraries when creating a new document. Any of these pages can be customized and then reset back to the site definition.

In this exercise, you will customize a page and then reset it back to its site definition.

> **USE** the SharePoint team site you modified in the previous exercise.
> **OPEN** the site in SharePoint Designer, if it is not already open.

1. In the **Folder List** task pane, double-click **default-old.aspx**.

   The page opens in the document window, with a tab labeled *default-old.aspx*.

2. Place the cursor between the two Web Part zones, type Customized, and then click the **Save** button.

   A Site Definition Page warning dialog box opens.

3. Click **Yes**.

In the Folder List task pane to the left of default-old.aspx, a blue circle with an inner white character *i* appears. This indicates that this page was an un-customized page pointing to a file on the Web server, but is now stored in the SQL Server content database.

4. In the **Folder List** task pane, right-click **default-old.aspx**, and then click **Reset to Site Definition**.

   A Site Definition warning dialog box opens.

5. Click **Yes**.

   In the Folder List task pane, the blue information icon to the left of default-old. aspx disappears and a copy of the customized default-old.aspx file, named *default-old_copy.aspx*, with a blue information icon appears. The default-old.aspx page in the document window refreshes and the customizations you completed earlier in this exercise are lost.

   Note The current default.aspx for this site is stored in the SQL Server content database, but is not a *customized* page as it does not have a blue information icon (it was created from an existing page), and cannot be reset to a site definition.

   CLOSE all open pages within the document window. If you are not continuing to the next chapter, exit SharePoint Designer.

Key Points

- SharePoint Designer provides you with three views of a page: Design, Code, and Split.

- You should not use SharePoint Designer to edit pages on a SharePoint Web server file system. You should always open a SharePoint site and edit pages from the site over HTTP.

- A non-publishing page is the combination of two ASP.NET pages: a master page and a content page.

- The Design view of a content page shows the merged view of the master page and the content page, whereas the Code view shows only the code of the content page.

- A SharePoint Server publishing page is a combination of three ASP.NET pages: the master page, a page layout, and a content page. You cannot modify a publishing content page by using SharePoint Designer; you must use the browser. However, you can modify the master page and page layout by using SharePoint Designer.

- In the Page Editor Options dialog box, you can configure picture conversion formats, auto thumbnail creation, and settings for the Design and Code views.

- Visual aids make it easier to work with page elements.

- SharePoint Designer saves all pages to the SQL Server content databases. You can reset pages back to site definition pages if they originally pointed to them.

Chapter at a Glance

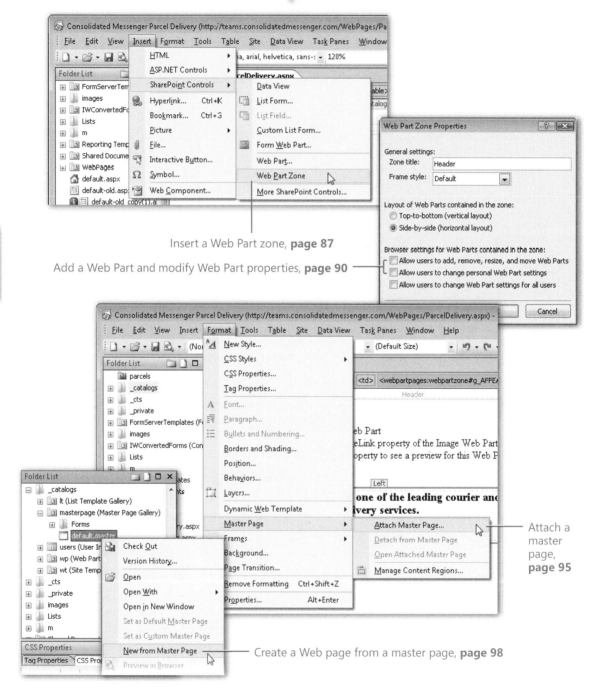

Insert a Web Part zone, **page 87**

Add a Web Part and modify Web Part properties, **page 90**

Attach a master page, **page 95**

Create a Web page from a master page, **page 98**

4 Creating and Modifying Web Pages

In this chapter, you will learn to:

- ✔ Create a Basic Meeting Workspace site.
- ✔ Create a Web Part page by using a browser.
- ✔ Create an ASP.NET page.
- ✔ Insert a Web Part zone.
- ✔ Add a Web Part and modify Web Part properties.
- ✔ Attach a master page.
- ✔ Create a Web page from a master page.
- ✔ Delete a Web page.

With Microsoft Office SharePoint Designer 2007, you can create a number of different file formats, some of which you may not consider to be pages; for example, text and cascading style sheet files, and others you may not have heard about before reading this book.

In Chapter 3, "Customizing a Web Page," you learned how to customize a nonpublishing page, which merges together a master page and a content page. In particular, you investigated the home page of a SharePoint team site.

In this chapter, you'll investigate the differences between pages on the SharePoint team site and a Basic Meeting Workspace site, and how to create content pages for both collaboration and Meeting Workspace sites by using SharePoint Designer. In this chapter, you will use both the browser and SharePoint Designer to create Web Part pages. You'll learn that Web Part pages are just Microsoft ASP.NET 2.0 content pages and that any SharePoint content page can contain one or more Web Parts. You'll also learn how to change the appearance of pages by adding and removing Web Part zones, the containers for Web Parts, as well as adding and removing Web Parts.

> **Important** No practice files are required to complete the exercises in this chapter. For more information about practice files, see "Using the Book's CD" at the beginning of this book.

> **Troubleshooting** Graphics and operating system–related instructions in this book reflect the Windows Vista user interface. If your computer is running Windows XP and you experience trouble following the instructions as written, please refer to the "Information for Readers Running Windows XP" section at the beginning of this book.

Creating a Basic Meeting Workspace Site

In Chapter 2, "Working in SharePoint Designer," you created a site hierarchy by using the team site definition, and in Chapter 3, you explored the home page of a team site. Before we create a new page, we are going to explore a different-looking SharePoint page, the home page of a SharePoint Basic Meeting Workspace site. The Meeting Workspace does not contain a Quick Launch bar and uses a second row of tabs, called *Pages*, which you can manipulate in the browser by using the Add Pages and Manage Pages options on the Site Action menu. These additional pages are stored in a hidden document library called *pages (Workspace pages)*.

> **Tip** Don't confuse the *pages (Workspace pages)* document library on a meeting workspace site with the *Pages* document library on a publishing site, which is not hidden and is Web Content Management–enabled. They are completely different document libraries, and do not share the same functionality.

Using the browser, you can add only 10 of these Meeting Workspace pages before a message is displayed stating that you have reached the maximum number of pages for the workspace and that you must delete a page before a new one can be added. This is a limitation of the browser interface; you can create additional Meeting Workspace pages by using SharePoint Designer.

Before you create a Meeting Workspace page, as with any site, you must familiarize yourself with that site.

Both the team site home page and the Basic Meeting Workspace home page are ASP. NET 2.0 content pages but associated with different master pages. When you opened the team site home page in Chapter 2, the name of the master page was *default.master*, whereas sites based on Meeting Workspace site definitions use a master page named *MWSDefault.master*.

The team site home page and the Basic Meeting Workspace home page have a main content region, PlaceHolderMain, which contains Web Part zones and Web Parts. However, the Meeting Workspace contains the following two additional regions in which you can add content:

● The PlaceHolderLeftNavBar content region, which is located to the left of the page (where the Quick Launch bar is situated on a team site). This region includes a Web Part zone labeled MeetingNavigator that contains the Meeting Series List View Web Part (LVWP).

● The PlaceHolderTitleInTitleArea content region, which includes a Web Part zone labeled Meeting Summary, that also contains an instance of the Meeting Series LVWP.

In this exercise, you will create a Basic Meeting Workspace site by using SharePoint Designer, and you will then explore the home page.

> **Note** Creating a Meeting Workspace by using SharePoint Designer does not tie it directly to any event; therefore, the Meeting Series LVWP does not display any data. If you create a Meeting Workspace by using Microsoft Office Outlook or from a Calendar Event, the two LVWPs contain a link for each meeting event.

USE the SharePoint team site, or whatever team site you want.

BE SURE TO start SharePoint Designer before beginning this exercise.

OPEN the site in SharePoint Designer, and close any pages that might be open in the document window.

New Document

1. On the Common toolbar, click the **New Document** arrow, and then in the list, click **Web Site**.

Page...
Web Site...
SharePoint Content...
HTML
ASPX
CSS
Workflow...
Folder
Create from Dynamic Web Template...
Create from Master Page...

The New dialog box opens.

2. In the left-most pane of the **New** dialog box, click **SharePoint Templates** if it is not already selected, and then click **Basic Meeting Workspace**.

> **Note** As SharePoint Designer retrieves a list of site definitions from the Web server for this particular site collection, you may be prompted for your user name and password. The list of site definitions returned depend on how the server administrator has configured your installation. You may see a different site definitions, especially if you modify a number of sites within a different of site collections.

3. In the **Specify the location of the new Web site** text box, type
http://teams.consolidatedmessenger.com/meetings
and then press Enter. If prompted, type your user name and password, and click **OK**.

The Create New Web Site dialog box briefly appears and then a new SharePoint Designer program window opens displaying the *meetings* child site. The title of the site is taken from the name of the site template.

4. In the **Folder List** task pane, double click **default.aspx**.

The home page of the *meetings* site opens as a second tab in the document window.

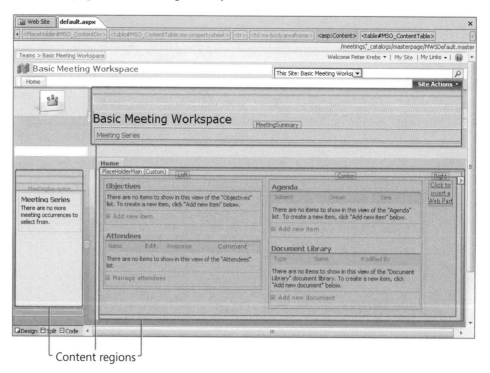

Content regions

As with the team site home page, the main content of the page is held within the PlaceHolderMain (Custom) content region, which for this home page contains three Web Part zones denoted by two blue borders, labeled at the top as Left, Center, and Right. The relative address of the master page is listed in the upper-right corner of the page.

5. In the **Folder List** task pane, right-click **pages (Workspace Pages)**, and then click **Properties**.

The Document Library Properties dialog box opens.

6. Click the **Settings** tab of the **Document Library Properties** dialog box, and notice that the **Hide from browsers** check box is selected.

Tip To administer the Workspace Pages document library you need to access the library's Settings page. Click the Security tab, and then click Manage Permissions Using The Browser. On the breadcrumb of the Permissions page that opens, click Settings. The Customize Workspace Pages page opens, from which you can manage the settings for this document library.

CLOSE the meeting site and the browser.

See Also For more information about creating Meeting Workspaces, see Chapter 8, "Working with Meeting Workspaces," and Chapter 11, "Using Windows SharePoint Services with Outlook 2007," of *Microsoft Windows SharePoint Services 3.0 Step by Step* by Olga Londer, Bill English, Todd Bleeker, and Penelope Coventry (Microsoft Press, 2007).

Creating a Web Part Page by Using a Browser

When a SharePoint site is created, it contains a number of page, most of which contain Web Parts. You can create additional pages, known as *Web Part Pages*. You can only use the browser to create Web Part Pages, and when you create these pages they are stored and accessed via document libraries.

When you use SharePoint Designer to create an ASP.NET page, you are not limited to storing them in a document library; as you will see later in this chapter, you can store pages in the root of the site or in a folder. However, if you plan to create a large number of pages, you should create a document library specifically for this purpose. You can use this document library to store both the pages you create using SharePoint Designer and those you create using the browser. Then users who need to access or customize the pages by using the browser do not need to know which method you used to create the pages, and you can use the document management features of SharePoint to manage the pages.

When you create Web Part Pages, you use one of eight built-in Web Part Page templates stored on each Web server as a basis. Web Part Pages are ASP.NET pages associated with a master page and pre-populated with a number of empty Web Part zones, each with a unique name. Each template has a different column and zone layout so that you can choose the one that best suits your needs. When you create a page based on one of these Web Part Page templates, you create an un-customized page; that is, no page is stored in the Microsoft SQL Server content database—there is simply a pointer to the Web Part Page template on the file system.

Each template contains one Web Part that you can modify to display a title, caption, description, and icon. You can you add one or more Web Parts to one or more zones that the template contains as you modify the page. Information concerning Web Parts that you add to Web Part zones and their properties is stored in the SQL Server content database, but in a separate table from the table, that stores the page. Therefore, when you insert or modify a Web Part, the page can still point to the Web Part Page template in the *TEMPLATE* folder on the Web server. (This is true for any page created from a site definition file.)

SharePoint Designer does not provide a separate method of saving Web Part modifications; you have to save the page for SharePoint Designer to save the modifications to the Web Part. Saving the page results in a customized page, even though you have not modified the page's static content. If you do not want to save the page in the SQL Server content database (that is, if you want your page to remain an un-customized page), you can use the Revert To Site Definition option without losing any Web Part modifications.

In the following exercise, you will create a document library in which to store Web Part pages. You will also create a Web Part page and modify Web Part properties.

> **USE** the SharePoint team site you modified in the previous exercise.
> **OPEN** the SharePoint site in a browser.

> **Important** In this exercise, you need a site created from the team site template. Do not use a site pages on a Meeting Workspace site template.

1. Click **Site Actions**, and then click **Create**.

   The Create Page Web page is displayed.

2. Under **Libraries**, click **Document Library**.

   The New page is displayed.

3. In the **Name** text box, type WebPages.

   > **Tip** The name that you type in the Name text box is used to create the URL, as well as the title of the document library and title of the page. For details about good naming conventions, see the sidebar "Best Practices for Naming URLs" in Chapter 2.

4. In the **Document Template** area, in the **Document template** list, click **Web Part Page**.

5. At the bottom of the page, click the **Create** button.

   The All Documents view of the new Web Part Pages document library is displayed.

6. Click the **New** button.

   The New Web Part Page page is displayed.

7. In the **Name** text box, type WebShipping.

8. In the **Layout** area, in the **Choose a Layout Template** list, click **Header, Right Column, Body**, and at the bottom of the page, click **Create**.

   The new Web Part page is displayed with three distinct Web Part zones: Header, Body, and Right Column. The page is empty except for the top link bar, the breadcrumb, and the Site Actions link. No Web Parts are placed within the Web Part zones.

9. Open the *teams.consolidatedmessenger.com* team site in SharePoint Designer. In the **Folder List** task pane, expand the **WebPages** document library to display its contents.

WebShipping.aspx should appear.

10. Double-click **WebShipping.aspx**.

The WebShipping page opens in the document window. The main PlaceHolderMain content region contains the Header, Body, and Right Column Web Part zones. The PlaceHolderPageTitleInTitleArea content region contains a fourth Web Part zone labeled *TitleBar*, which includes the Web Part Page Title Bar Web Part.

> **Tip** If you cannot see the names of the content regions, verify that Visual Aids are on and the Template Region Labels option on the Visual Aids menu is selected.

11. In the **Web Part Page Title Bar Web Part**, right-click **WebShipping**, and then click **Web Part Properties**.

The Web Part Page Title Bar dialog box opens.

12. In the **Title** text box, place the cursor between **Web** and **Shipping** and press `Space`, then click **OK**.

The dialog box closes, and an asterisk appears on the WebShipping.aspx tab.

> **Tip** In the browser, you can modify the Web Part Page Title Bar Web Part by clicking the Edit Title Bar Properties link when the page is in Edit mode.

Save

13. On the Common toolbar, click the **Save** button.

The Site Definition Page Warning dialog box opens, stating that saving your changes will customize a page from the site definitions.

14. Click **Yes**.

The dialog box closes, and in the Folder List task pane, a blue information circle appears to the left of WebShipping.aspx.

15. In the **Folder List** task pane, right-click **WebShipping.aspx**, and then click **Reset to Site Definition**. When the Site Definition Page Warning dialog box appears, click **Yes**.

In the Folder List task pane, the blue information icon to the left of WebShipping disappears and WebShipping_copy.aspx appears with a blue information icon. The *WebShipping.aspx* page in the document window refreshes, showing that your modification to the Web Part properties remain.

> **CLOSE** the *WebShipping.aspx* page.

Creating an ASP.NET Page

All built-in Web Part Pages consist of an ASP.NET page with Web Part zones. If you want to create a Web Part page similar to the ones created using the browser, then in SharePoint Designer, you could copy an existing page, as you did in Chapter 3, or you need to create an ASP.NET page, associate a master page and insert Web Part zones and Web Parts, using as many Web Part zones as you want in the layout of your choice. All built-in Web Part Pages use tables, but if you are concerned about accessibility, you may want to use tables of HTML *<div>* tags to lay out the pages you create from scratch. Because you can insert more than one Web Part per Web Part zone, it is common practice to insert one Web Part zone to a table cell or *<div>* tag.

See Also For more information about page accessibility, see Chapter 15, "Understanding Usability and Accessibility."

In this exercise, you will create a new ASP.NET page with a table layout.

> **USE** the SharePoint team site you modified in the previous exercise.
> **OPEN** the site in SharePoint Designer, if it is not already open.

New Document

Save

1. On the Common toolbar, click the **New Document** button.

   A new file named *Untitled_1.aspx* opens.

2. On the Common toolbar, click the **Save** button.

   The Save As dialog box opens.

3. Double-click **WebPages**. In the **File name** text box, type ParcelDelivery.aspx.

4. Click **Change title**.

   The Set Page Title dialog box opens.

5. If prompted, type your user name and password, and then click **OK**.

6. In the **Page title** text box, type Consolidated Messenger Parcel Delivery.

Set Page Title	? ✖
Page title:	
Consolidated Messenger Parcel Delivery	
The title of the page is displayed in the title bar of the browser.	
	OK Cancel

7. Click **OK** to close the **Set Page Title** dialog box, and then click **Save** to close the **Save As** dialog box.

8. On the **Table** menu, click **Layout Tables**.

   The Layout Tables task pane appears in the lower left of the SharePoint Designer program window.

9. In the **Layout Tables** task pane, under **Table layout**, scroll down and click **Header, Body, Footer, and Right**.

Layout Tables	☐ ✖
operties \ Layout Tables	◀ ▷ ✖
Height: ___ (450)	
Alignment:	
≡ ≡ ≡	
☐ Auto-scale cells with table	
Set Page Margins...	
Table layout	
Header, Body, Footer, and Right	

Table markers appear in the page body, designating a table 635 (525+110) pixels wide by 611 (83+472+56) pixels high. The green lines indicate the outer edge of the table, and the internal blue lines indicate the cell layout of the table.

Inserting a Web Part Zone

With Web Part zones, users can manipulate the content of a page by using a browser. You can insert Web Part zones into ASP.NET pages. If an ASP.NET page is associated with a master page, and therefore would be classified as a content page, then Web Part zones can be inserted only into content regions on such content pages. You cannot insert Web Part zones into master pages. Developers or Web designers can use Microsoft Visual Studio 2005 to define Web Part zones in pages stored in the 12 hive on a Web server; or you can use SharePoint Designer to insert a Web Part zone into a new or existing page and then save the page in the SQL Server content database.

You can insert only Web Parts into Web Part zones; you cannot insert text or images. Web Part zones have properties that affect the presentation of the Web Parts they contain, and they control the actions users are allowed to perform using the browser. These properties are detailed in the table on the next page.

Web Part zone property	Description
Zone title	Used when storing Web Part information in the SQL Server content database. You should give each zone a meaningful and consistent title; for example, don't name the Web Part zone in a left cell *First* on one page and *Left* on another. This is particularly important if you create Web Part zones on page layouts in publishing sites.
Frame Style	The default frame style for all Web Parts in the zone. This setting can be overridden by the Web Part Frame Style property.
Layout of Web Parts contained in the zone	Allows you to choose between Top-To-Bottom (Vertical Layout) or Side-By-Side (Horizontal Layout).
Browser settings for Web Parts contained in the zone	Allows you to restrict the modification of the page by browser users. By clearing the three check boxes, you effectively remove the ability to customize any Web Parts placed in the zone by using the browser.

In this exercise, you will insert two Web Part zones.

> **USE** the SharePoint team site you modified in the previous exercise.
>
> **OPEN** the site in SharePoint Designer, if it is not already open, and display the page on which you would like to insert a Web Part zone.

1. Position the insertion point in the top cell.

> **Tip** To see the table cells, turn on Visual Aids: on the View menu, point to Visual Aids and click Show.

2. On the **Insert** menu, point to **SharePoint Controls**, and then click **Web Part Zone**.

   A Web Part zone labeled *Zone 1* appears in the top cell, and an orange tag, named *webpartpages:webpartzone*, appears in the Quick Tag Selector.

3. Right-click **Zone 1**, and then click **Web Part Zone Properties**.

 The Web Part Zone Properties dialog box opens.

4. In the **Zone title** text box, type Header, click **Side-by-side (horizontal layout)**, and then below **Browser settings for Web Parts contained in the zone**, clear the three check boxes.

5. Click **OK** to close the **Web Part Zone Properties** dialog box.

6. Position the insertion point in the left cell under the header cell. Then on the **Insert** menu, point to **SharePoint Controls**, and click **Web Part Zone**.

7. Double-click **Zone 1** to open the **Web Part Zone Properties** dialog box. In the **Zone title** text box, type Left.

8. Click **OK** to close the **Web Part Zone Properties** dialog box.

9. On the Common toolbar, click the **Save** button.

Adding a Web Part and Modifying Web Part Properties

Managing Web Parts in SharePoint Designer is very similar to managing Web Parts by using the browser. In the browser, when you edit a page and add a Web Part, you can choose the Advanced Web Part Gallery And Options to open the Add Web Parts tool pane. SharePoint Designer has a similar interface: the Web Parts task pane. The only difference is that, in the browser, you are presented with three galleries, whereas in SharePoint Designer, you see only two because *Closed Web Parts* are displayed on the page as an opaque image, instead of being listed in the Closed Gallery as they are in the browser. (A Web Part gallery is a collection of Web Parts.)

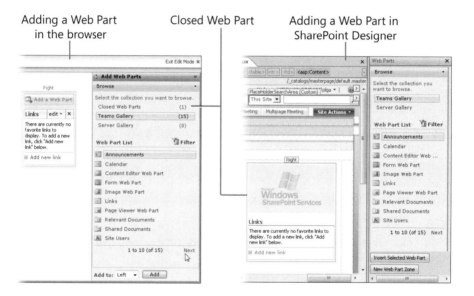

In SharePoint Designer, the two galleries are as follows:

- **[site name] Gallery.** In our example, this is *Teams Gallery*. The number of Web Parts listed in the [site name] Gallery varies based on the definition of the site and the features that are activated on that site. The Web Parts listed in this gallery can be managed at the site collection level, where it is known as the Web Part Gallery.

- **Server Gallery.** This gallery contains Web Parts that a SharePoint Administrator has added to the server farm by using the command-line tool stsadm. This gallery is sometimes referred to as the central Web Part Gallery.

The Web Parts in the galleries act as templates from which you create instances of these Web Parts on your page. The template of the Web Part remains in the galleries for you to use again. You can configure each instance of a Web Part differently; in fact, as soon as you add an instance of a Web Part to a page, you should alter the title of the Web Part to reflect its use.

You can add the same Web Parts to a page by using either SharePoint Designer or the browser. There are two types of Web Parts:

- *List View Web Parts (LVWPs)*. Web Parts that display the contents of lists and libraries. Each time the data within the list or library changes, the changes are reflected in the LVWP. You will see LVWPs for lists and libraries for the site you have open in SharePoint Designer, and you will see LVWPs for lists or libraries created in other sites.

- **Built-in Web Parts.** A Microsoft Windows SharePoint Services 3.0 installation has eight built-in Web Parts: Content Editor Web Part (CEWP), Form Web Part, Image Web Part, Page Viewer Web Part, Relevant Documents, Site Users, User Tasks, and XML Web Part. Microsoft Office SharePoint Server 2007 includes more than 50 additional built-in Web Parts, including Business Data List, Content Query Web Part (CQWP), Current User Filter, Excel Web Access, Key Performance Indicators, Search Box, and SQL Server 2005 Analysis Services cubes. A detailed description of these Web Parts is outside the scope of this book.

See Also For more information about Web Parts, see Chapter 29, "Microsoft Office SharePoint Server 2007 Web Parts," in *Microsoft Office SharePoint Server 2007 Administrator's Companion*, Bill English, 2007.

Using SharePoint Designer, you can also create a *Data View Web Part (DVWP)*, also known as a *Data Form Web Part (DFWP)*, which you can use to display and modify lists and libraries, as well as other data sources.

See Also For more information about the Data View Web Part, see Chapter 6, "Working with Data Views."

Web Parts are further classified by their location, as follows:

- *Dynamic Web Parts.* These Web Parts are placed in Web part zones by using either SharePoint Designer or the browser. (When using the browser, you can add Web Parts only to Web Part zones.) Dynamic Web Parts are stored separately from the page, and only when a user requests the page is the SQL Server content database queried to find out the number of dynamic Web Parts, what they are, and in which Web Part zone they should be placed. They are then merged with the master page and content page.

- *Static Web Parts.* These Web Parts are placed outside of Web Part zones by using SharePoint Designer. They cannot be customized by using the browser. Static Web Parts are stored as part of the page and can be added to both master pages and content pages.

In this exercise, you will add, modify, and delete a Web Part.

> **USE** the SharePoint team site you modified in the previous exercise.
> **OPEN** the site in SharePoint Designer, if it is not already open, and display the *ParcelDelivery.aspx* page.

1. In the **Header** Web Part zone, click **Click to insert a Web Part**.

   The Web Parts task pane opens.

Four-Way Arrow Pointer

Add Pointer

2. Point to the icon to the left of the **Image Web Part**. You may need to click the Next link in the Web Parts task pane if you cannot see the Image Web Part.

   The mouse pointer changes to a four-headed arrow.

3. Drag the Web Part to the **Header** Web Part zone.

   As you move the Web Part, the pointer changes to an arrow with a plus sign (+) enclosed in a square. SharePoint Designer redisplays the page with the Image Web Part placed in the Header Web Part zone.

4. Double-click the **Image Web Part** to open the **Image Web Part** dialog box.

5. In the text box below **Image Link**, type /_layouts/images/homepage.gif, and in the **Alternative Text** text box, type Consolidated Messenger Teams logo.

> **Tip** You do not have to type the URL of the image file. You can click the ellipsis button below Image Link to open the Edit Hyperlink dialog box, from which you can navigate to the image file that you want to use.

6. Expand the **Appearance** section. Then in the **Title** text box, type Teams Logo.

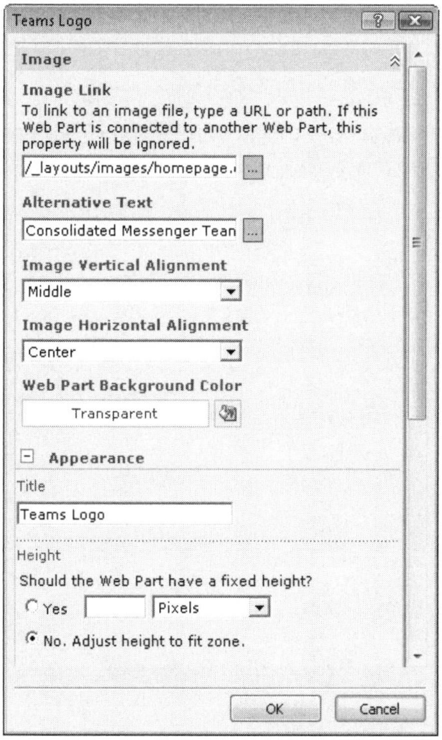

7. Click **OK** to close the **Image Web Part** dialog box.

   The Image Web Part displays the Microsoft Windows SharePoint Services logo.

8. Drag a second **Image Web Part** on top of the first Image Web Part.

   The two Web Parts should display side by side.

9. Click the **Left** Web Part zone. In the **Web Parts** task pane, click **Content Editor Web Part**. Then at the bottom of the **Web Parts** task pane, click **Insert Selected Web Part**.

10. In the **Content Editor Web Part**, select the text **To add content, select this text and replace it by typing or inserting your own content**, type Consolidated Messenger is one of the leading courier and parcel delivery services, and then press Enter to move to a new line.

11. Select the sentence you just typed, and on the Common toolbar, in the **Styles** list, click **Heading 3**.

Center

12. On the Common toolbar, click the **Center** alignment button.

> **Tip** You can use the Common toolbar buttons and Design view to edit the contents of the Content Editor Web Part in a WYSIWYG manner. To enter HTML source code or JavaScript, use Code view.

13. Right-click the **Content Editor Web Part**, and then click **Web Part Properties** to open the **Content Editor Web Part** dialog box.

14. Expand the **Appearance** section, and in the **Title** text box, type Who Are We.

15. In the **Chrome Type** list, click **None**.

16. Click **OK** to close the **Content Editor Web Part** dialog box.

Save

17. On the Common toolbar, click the **Save** button, and then press F12. If prompted, type your user name and password, and click **OK**.

A browser window opens, with Consolidated Messenger Parcel Delivery in the program window title bar and displaying the *ParcelDelivery.aspx* page. There is no SharePoint look and feel to the page.

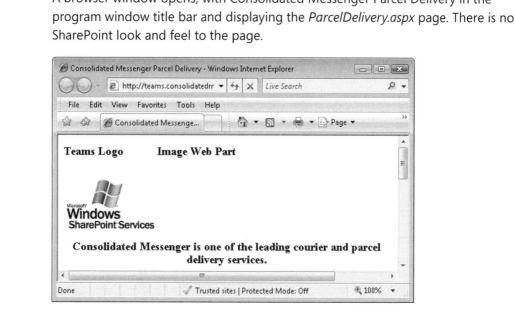

CLOSE the browser.

Attaching a Master Page

In the previous exercises, you created an ASP.NET page and added Web Part zones and Web Parts to it, but it did not contain any SharePoint site navigation nor did it inherit any look and feel from the SharePoint site. You can envisage the page we created as just the content page. It is not associated with a master page, which is the page that defines the common user interface and code.

In this exercise, you will attach a master page to an existing page.

USE the SharePoint team site you modified in the previous exercise.

OPEN the site in SharePoint Designer, if it is not already open, and display the *ParcelDelivery.aspx* page.

1. On the **Format** menu, point to **Master Page**, and then click **Attach Master Page**.

   The Select A Master Page dialog box opens.

2. In the **Select a Master Page** dialog box, click **Default Master Page (~masterurl/default.master)**.

3. Click **OK** to open the **Match Content Regions** dialog box.

4. Click **OK** to accept the default of associating all the code within the HTML body tags of the current page, ParcelDelivery.aspx, to the content region, PlaceHolderMain on the master page.

SharePoint Designer redisplays ParcelDelivery.aspx, which now has a SharePoint look and feel.

5. On the Common toolbar, click the **Save** button and then press [F12] to review the page in the browser.

Save

> **Tip** If you have a site based on HTML or ASPX pages, you can convert the site into a SharePoint site by copying the pages into libraries, folders, or the root directory of a SharePoint site. Then rename any files that have an HTM or ASP extension to ASPX, and attach the master page to them as described in this exercise.

CLOSE the browser.

Creating a Web Page from a Master Page

You can use several different methods to create an ASP.NET page within SharePoint Designer. However, because the page will be part of a SharePoint site, you will most likely want to keep the same navigation elements and look and feel as other pages. This is achieved by linking the content page with a master page. In Chapter 3, you created a new ASP.NET page by copying an existing page that is associated with a master page and then customizing it. In this chapter, you first created an ASP.NET page by using the browser, which again is automatically associated with a master page, and then in the previous exercise, you attached a master page to an ASP.NET page.

You can also create a content page from a master page. As we have seen in previous exercises, most customizations, Web Part zones, and Web Parts are stored within one or more content regions. When you create a content page from a master page, you can't make any changes to the content regions. To make changes to the content, you must make the content regions editable.

In this exercise, you will create a content page from a master page and then make the PlaceHolderMain content region editable.

> **USE** the SharePoint team site you modified in the previous exercise.
>
> **OPEN** the site in SharePoint Designer, if it is not already open, and close any pages or task panes that are open in the document window.

1. In the **Folder List** task pane, expand the **_catalogs** folder, and then expand the **masterpage (Master Page Gallery)** document library to display its contents.

   The default.master file should appear.

2. Right-click **default.master**, and then click **New from Master Page**.

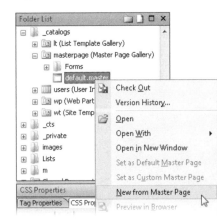

A new file, with a tab label of *Untitled_1.aspx*, appears in the document window. An asterisk to the right of the label name indicates that the page is not yet saved.

3. Right-click the **untitled_1.aspx tab**, and then click **Save**.

   The Save As dialog box opens showing the *teams.consolidatedmessenger.com* site contents.

4. In the **File name** text box, type ShippingAdvice.aspx, and then click **Save**.

   The tab is renamed to *ShippingAdvice.aspx*, and in the Folder List task pane, the file appears in the root of the site.

5. On the **View** menu, point to **Toolbars**, and then click **Master Page** to open the floating Master Page toolbar.

6. On the Master Page toolbar, click the **Regions** arrow, and then in the list, click **PlaceHolderMain**.

   The PlaceHolderMain (Master) content region on the *ShippingAdvice.aspx* page is highlighted.

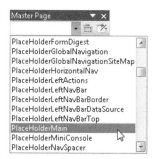

7. Close the Master Page toolbar.

Chevron

8. Click the chevron to the right of the **PlaceHolderMain** content region, and in the **Common Content Tasks** list, click **Create Custom Content**.

The content region is renamed *PlaceHolderMain (Custom)*, thereby making this content region editable. You can now insert text, Web Part zones, and Web Parts into this area of the *ShippingAdvice.aspx* content page.

Save

9. Click the **Save** button.

Deleting a Web Page

As you develop your solutions and experiment with SharePoint Designer, you will create pages that after some time you will no longer need. SharePoint Designer, like other Microsoft Office products, allows you to easily delete a page when you no longer need it.

In this exercise, you will delete a page and then restore it from the Recycle Bin.

> **USE** the SharePoint team site you modified in the previous exercise.
>
> **OPEN** the site in SharePoint Designer, if it is not already open, and display the *ShippingAdvice.aspx* page.

1. In the **Folder List** task pane, right-click **ShippingAdvice.aspx**, and then click **Delete**.

   The Confirm Delete dialog box opens.

2. Click **Yes** to close the **Confirm Delete** dialog box.

   ShippingAdvice.aspx is no longer listed in the root of the site.

3. On the **Site** menu, click **Recycle Bin**.

   A browser window opens and displays the Recycle Bin for the team site.

4. If prompted, type your user name and password, and then click **OK**.

5. Select the **ShippingAdvice.aspx** check box, and then click **Restore Selection**.

6. Click **OK** in the Windows Internet Explorer dialog box.

The Recycle Bin page is redisplayed, where *ShippingAdvice.aspx* is no longer listed.

7. Return to SharePoint Designer, and press F5.

In the Folder List task pane, *ShippingAdvice.aspx* is listed.

CLOSE the browser windows. If you're not continuing directly to the next chapter, exit SharePoint Designer.

Key Points

- The Meeting Workspace uses a master page, named MWSDefault.master, and stores pages in a hidden document library named pages (Workspace pages).

- In the browser, you can create a Web Part Page based on one of the eight built-in Web Part Page templates.

- In SharePoint Designer, you can create an ASP.NET page and then attach a master page to give it the look and feel of the SharePoint site.

- You can create a content page from a master page, but you can add content to the page only if you make at least one PlaceHolderMain content region editable.

- Web Part zones can be inserted only in content regions on content pages; they cannot be inserted on master pages.

- There are two types of Web Parts: List View Web Parts and built-in Web Parts. List View Web Parts display the contents of SharePoint lists and libraries.

- Web Parts can be inserted outside Web Part zones on content pages and master pages on by using SharePoint Designer. These are known as static Web Parts.

- Web Parts inserted into Web Part zones are known as dynamic Web Parts. Details of dynamic Web Parts are stored in the SQL Server database separate from content pages and master pages.

- Any pages or files you delete in SharePoint Designer are stored in the Recycle Bin, from which you can restore them.

Chapter at a Glance

Create a list, **page 104**

Customize a List View Web Part, **page 112**

Create List View pages, **page 118**

Modify a built-in List Form page, **page 121**

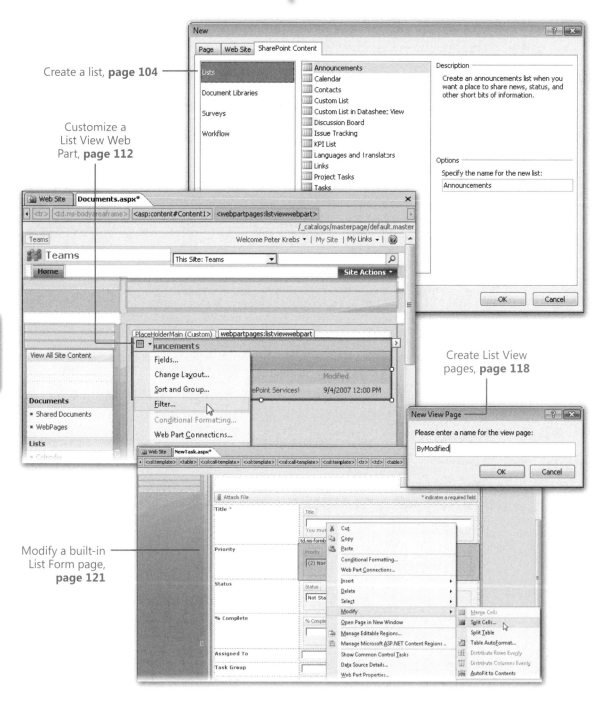

5 Working with Lists and Libraries

In this chapter, you will learn to:

✔ Create a list.

✔ Create and customize a List View Web Part.

✔ Modify a built-in List View page.

✔ Create a List View page.

✔ Modify a built-in List Form page.

Lists and libraries are central components to both Microsoft Windows SharePoint Services and Microsoft Office SharePoint Server 2007 sites. Lists are containers for items that have similar columns or metadata, security settings, and user interfaces for viewing and managing the items. You can use lists to manage and display information for collaboration purposes. Libraries are specialized lists, where each list item refers to one document. Libraries have strong document management features. Lists and libraries are core to the SharePoint infrastructure and are used to store internal data, not visible through the browser, that enables you to build Windows SharePoint Services applications.

In this chapter, you will learn to identify when to use the browser and when to use Microsoft Office SharePoint Designer 2007 to manipulate lists and libraries. You will consolidate your understanding of lists and libraries, as well as reinforce the link between a list or a library and the List View Web Part. You will also learn how to create *views*, and how to modify the pages that allow you to display, edit, and create new list items.

> **Important** No practice files are required to complete the exercises in this chapter. For more information about practice files, see "Using the Book's CD" at the beginning of this book.

> **Troubleshooting** Graphics and operating system–related instructions in this book reflect the Windows Vista user interface. If your computer is running Windows XP and you experience trouble following the instructions as written, please refer to the "Information for Readers Running Windows XP" section at the beginning of this book.

Creating a List

Just as you base a new site on a site template, you base a new list or library on a *list template*. When you select a list template, you are either referring to files on the file systems of the SharePoint Web servers or to a template file in the List Template Gallery, which is stored in the Microsoft SQL Server database.

Windows SharePoint Services and Office SharePoint Server 2007 provide a number of built-in list definitions that you can use as a basis for SharePoint lists and libraries. When you use the browser, the list definitions are grouped into four categories: Libraries, Communications, Tracking, and Custom Lists. When you use SharePoint Designer 2007, Windows SharePoint Services provides the first 15 list definitions, described in the following table. An additional list, Import Spreadsheet, is available only when you use a browser and not when use SharePoint Designer.

Category	List	Description
Libraries		
	Document Library	The most commonly used library. Supports versioning, checking in, checking out, and workflow.
	Form Library	Provides special storage and handling capabilities for XML-based business forms that require a Windows SharePoint Services–compatible XML editor, such as Microsoft Office.
	Wiki Page Library	Provides an interconnected collection of Wiki pages. Wiki page libraries support pictures, tables, hyperlinks, and Wiki linking.
	Picture Library	Provides special capabilities for working with image files (such as thumbnails), download options, and a slide show. Requires a Windows SharePoint Services–compatible image editor, such as Microsoft Office Picture Manager.

Category	List	Description
Communications		
	Announcements	Provides a place to share news, status, and other brief pieces of information that have date and time expiration support.
	Contacts	Provides contact management features, integrated with Windows SharePoint Services–compatible contact programs, such as Microsoft Office Outlook.
	Discussion Board	Provides newsgroup/bulletin board–style discussions, including the ability to display only approved posts.
Tracking		
	Links	Manages hyperlinks.
	Calendar	Previously known as an events list. Allows you to provide calendar-based views of upcoming meetings, deadlines, and other important events. Provides two-way synchronization with Outlook 2007.
	Tasks	Manages work items or team activities that can be integrated with a workflow.
	Project Tasks	An enhanced Tasks list. Supports Gantt views and integration with Microsoft Office Project.
	Issue Tracking	Provides the management structure for a set of issues or problems, including an issue history, which you can view as the issue is changed.
Custom Lists		
	Survey	Provides a Web-based questionnaire.
	Custom List	Provides a list with a minimum number of columns. You specify your own columns.
	Custom List in Datasheet View	Provides a custom list whose default view is a spreadsheet-like environment, convenient for data entry, editing, and formatting.
	Import Spreadsheet	Creates a custom list from a Windows SharePoint Services–compatible spreadsheet program, such as Microsoft Office Excel. Particularly useful when you want to create a list that has the same columns and content as an existing spreadsheet.

SharePoint Server 2007 provides an additional six built-in lists, as described in the following table.

Category	List	Description
Library	Report Library	Simplifies the creation, management, and delivery of pages, documents, and key performance indicators (KPIs) that communicate metrics, goals, and business intelligence information.
	Translation Management Library	Allows you to organize documents in multiple languages and to manage document translation tasks.
	Data Connection Library (DCL)	Facilitates the sharing of files that contain information concerning external data connections. Designed for use with Excel, Microsoft Office InfoPath, and SQL Reporting Services.
	Slide Library	Facilitates the sharing of Microsoft Office PowerPoint slides, and provides special features for finding, managing, and reusing slides.
Custom Lists	Languages and Translators	Allows the system to track how documents should be translated from one language to another and by whom. Used in combination with the Translation Management Library.
	KPI List	Tracks and displays a set of goals, with colored icons communicating the degree to which the goals have been achieved.

After you create a list or library, you can perform tasks such as the following:

- View, add, modify, or delete list items, documents, or metadata.
- Modify list-level or item-level permissions.
- Add, delete, or modify *columns*. Columns are referred to as fields in SharePoint Designer.
- Add, delete, or modify *content types*.
- Create views to allow multiple perspectives on the list's or library's data.
- Create a list template from a list, including its content.

You cannot create or modify list items or the metadata associated with documents by using SharePoint Designer; nor can you create or modify list permissions, content types, columns, or *site columns*, or create list templates. You must use the browser or develop code to complete these tasks.

Content Types and Site Columns

Content types and site columns are new mechanisms introduced with Windows SharePoint Services 3.0. Content types are more powerful than site columns.

- **Content types** are designed to help users define a reusable collection of settings that can include columns, workflows, and other attributes. They can be associated with their own document template, and with their own workflow and retention policies, as well as settings for the document information panel (DIP). As a result, they support a number of business scenarios, such as a expenses approval process.

- **Site columns** are reusable columns that can be used across multiple sites, lists, and libraries, thereby decreasing the amount of re-work you would need to do if you want to create consistent metadata across sites, lists and libraries. All columns in a content type must be a site column.

Windows SharePoint Services and SharePoint Server come with a set of default content types and site columns, instances of which are created for each new site collection. Many content types reference one or more site columns, and all default lists and libraries are associated with a content type. Content types are created in a hierarchical structure, where each content type can act as a basis for creating new content types. For example, all default document libraries are associated with the *Document* content type, which defines the *Name* column. The *Document* content type is based on the *Item* content type, which defines the *Title* column, and in turn, the *Item* content type is based on the *System* content type that is the top of the content type hierarchy.

You can create content types and site columns at the site collection level or site level. When created at the site collection level, they can be used by lists and/or libraries or by any site within the site collection hierarchy. When created at the site level, they can be used only by lists and libraries within that specific site. In addition, you cannot use the *Document* content type in lists; nor can you use the *List* content type in document libraries.

When you create a Windows SharePoint Services–based application, you should consider using content types and site columns as they provide an extremely powerful mechanism to organize and standardize your company's data. They reduce the amount of re-work you would otherwise need to complete to achieve this consistency. Both Windows SharePoint Services and SharePoint Server use them extensively and you will see a specific implementation of their use in Chapter 11, "Managing Web Content in a SharePoint Server Environment."

In this exercise, you will create a Wiki Page library and an Issue Tracking list, change the default settings of the list and library, and then view the site in a browser.

> USE the *teams.consolidatedmessenger.com*, or any team site you want.
> BE SURE TO start SharePoint Designer before beginning this exercise.
> OPEN the site in SharePoint Designer.

New Document

1. On the Common toolbar, click the **New Document** arrow, and then click **SharePoint Content**.

   The New dialog box opens. SharePoint Designer contacts the open SharePoint site and populates the SharePoint Content tab with components that you can create on that site; therefore, the number of list templates that you can use will vary from server to server.

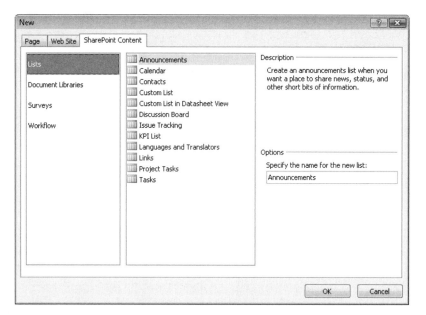

2. Click **Document Libraries**, and then click **Wiki Page Library**.

   In the rightmost area of the New dialog box, under Description, a brief description of Wiki Page libraries appears.

3. Under **Options**, type WikiPages, and then click **OK** to close the **New** dialog box.

   The name that you type under Options is used to create the URL as well as the title of the library.

See Also For information about good naming conventions, see the sidebar "Best Practices for Naming URLs" in Chapter 2, "Working in SharePoint Designer."

The WikiPages library appears at the bottom of the Folder List task pane.

> **Tip** If want to change the URL of a list or library, in the Folder List task pane, right-click the list or library, and then click Rename. All references to the old URL will be replaced with the new URL. However, if users have bookmarked or created hyperlinks to the list or library, these will continue to point to the old URL.

4. Right-click **WikiPages**, and then click **Properties**.

   The Document Library Properties dialog box opens.

5. On the **Settings** tab of the **Document Library Properties** dialog box, in the **Name** text box, type Shipping Information.

   This text will appear in the title area of the browser window.

6. In the **Description** text box, type This wiki page library contains a set of wiki pages that describes how to ship packages to almost anywhere in the world, easily.

7. Select the **Require content approval for submitted items** check box.

8. In the **Use version history** list, click **Major and minor (draft) versions**, and in the **Make drafts visible to** list, click **Users who can edit items**.

9. Click **Apply**.

10. On the **Supporting Files** tab, in the **Default view page** list, click **WikiPages/Forms/RecentChanges.aspx**.

11. Click **OK** to close the **Document Library Properties** dialog box.

The Name text appears in brackets to the right of WikiPages.

12. In the **Folder List** task pane, right-click **Lists**, point to **New**, and then click **SharePoint Content**.

The New dialog box opens.

13. Click **Issue Tracking**, and under **Options**, type Issues.

14. Click **OK** to close the **New** dialog box.

Issues appear under Lists in the Folder List task pane.

> **Tip** When you use any of the built-in list definitions as the basis for a list, the list is al-ways created under the Lists folder. For consistency, you should do the same. Libraries are traditionally created in the root of the site, although there is no reason they could not also be placed in a folder. If you create a list in the root of the site, you can later move the list by dragging it to the Folder List task pane, without it affecting the URL.

15. Right-click **Issues**, and then click **Properties**.

The List Properties dialog box opens.

16. On the **Settings** tab, clear the **Enable attachments** check box, and then click **OK** to close the **List Properties** dialog box.

A Microsoft Office SharePoint Designer dialog box opens, warning you that if any files are attached to list items, disabling attachments will result in their deletion.

17. Click **OK**, and then press ⌴F12⌴.

A browser window opens displaying the All Issues view of the Issues list. Links to both the WikiPages and the Issues list are displayed in the Quick Launch bar.

CLOSE the browser window.

Creating a List View Web Part

A List View Web Part (LVWP) is a Web Part that displays the contents of a list or library. Using SharePoint Designer to add an LVWP and modify the Web Part settings is very similar to using the browser. The default settings and the look and feel of the LVWP are slightly different in SharePoint Designer, which adds column headings to the LVWP. So if you want to keep a consistent look and don't want to have to spend time reconfiguring the default settings, you should use the browser to add the LVWP and then open the page in SharePoint Designer to complete your modifications.

In this exercise, you will create an Announcements LVWP.

USE the site you modified in the previous exercise.
OPEN the site in SharePoint Designer, if it is not already open.

New Document

1. On the Common toolbar, click the **New Document** button.

A new file named *untitled_1.aspx* opens.

Save

2. On the Common toolbar, click the **Save** button to open the **Save** dialog box. In the **File name** text box, type Documents.aspx, and then click **Save**.

The untitled_1.aspx tab is renamed as *Documents.aspx*.

3. On the **Insert** menu, point to **SharePoint Controls**, and then click **Web Part**.

The Web Parts task pane opens.

4. Click **Announcements**, and then click **Insert Selected Web Part**.

The Announcements LVWP is created on the page and the <webpartpages: listviewwebpart> tag is highlighted in orange on the Quick Tag Selector. The Announcements List View Web Part has a text-based look and feel. In a newly created team site, one list item is displayed: "Get Started with Windows SharePoint Services!"

5. On the **Format** menu, point to **Master Page**, and then click **Attach Master Page**.

6. Click **OK** to close the **Select a Master Page** dialog box, and then click **OK** to close the **Match Content Region** dialog box.

The *Documents.aspx* page is redisplayed, and the Announcements LVWP appears with a look and feel that is consistent with all the other Web Parts displayed on the site.

7. On the Common toolbar, click the **Save** button.

Customizing a List View Web Part

All Web Parts, including the LVWP, share a common set of properties that control appearance, layout, and advanced characteristics such as whether the Web Part can move to a different Web Part zone. You configured many of these settings in Chapter 4, "Creating and Modifying Web Pages."

LVWPs have other configurable settings, such as which columns are displayed, the sort order of the list items, whether the list items are filtered, and whether items with the same value are grouped in their own section.

In this exercise, you will modify the Announcements LVWP to display announcements whose expiration dates are not set or have not expired. You will also modify the Announcement LVWP to show no more than five announcements.

> **USE** the site you modified in the previous exercise.
>
> **OPEN** the site in SharePoint Designer, if it is not already open.

List View Options

1. Open the **Documents.aspx** page, and in the **Announcements** LVWP, click **Announcements** to display the **List View Options** smart tag.

2. Click the **List View Options** smart tag arrow, and then click **Filter**.

The Filter Criteria dialog box opens.

3. Click **Click here to add a new clause**.

4. Click the **Field Name** arrow, and in the list, click **Expires**.

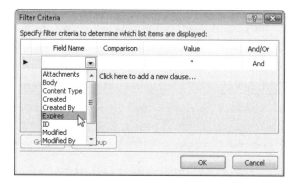

5. Under **Comparison**, click **Equals**, click the arrow that appears, and then click **Is Null**.

6. Under **And/Or**, click **And**, click the arrow that appears, and then click **Or**.

7. Click **Click here to add a new clause**, click the arrow that appears under **Field Name**, and then click **Expires**.

8. Under **Comparison**, click **Equals**, click the arrow that appears, and then click **Greater than or Equal**.

Field Name	Comparison	Value	And/Or
Expires	Is Null	"	Or
Expires	Greater Th...	'[Current Date]'	And
	Click here to add a new clause...		

Tip To delete a filter criterion, click the arrow to its left to select the entire criteria line, and then press the Delete key.

9. Click **OK** to close the **Filter Criteria** dialog box.

10. Click the **List View Options** smart tag, and then click **Change Layout**.

   The List View Options dialog box opens.

11. Click **Full toolbar**, and then click **Summary toolbar** in the list.

12. On the **Paging** tab, click **Limit the total number of items displayed to**, and then type 5 in the text box.

13. Click **OK** to close the **List View** dialog box.

14. Click the **List View Options** smart tag, and then click **Web Part Properties**.

The Announcements dialog box opens.

15. In the **Chrome Type** list, click **Title only**, and then click **OK** to close the **Announcements** dialog box.

The Announcements List View Web Part is redisplayed showing the title of the Announcements list with no toolbar under it.

Modifying a Built-In List View Page

Views are Microsoft ASP.NET 2.0 pages that use an LVWP to display all or a subset of the contents of a list or library based on specific criteria defined by the metadata. They allow you to display information in different formats without having to enter the information more than once, thereby enabling you and other users to find information easily. When a list or library is created, instances of view pages that point to files in the *TEMPLATE* folder on the Web servers. They contain one Web Part zone named *Main* and one LVWP. In SharePoint Designer, you can see the instances of these pages immediately below the list container, whereas in libraries, you can see them in the Forms folder.

Using SharePoint Designer or the browser, you can modify the LVWP of view pages, and you can add other Web Parts to the Main Web Part zone. SharePoint Designer provides additional customization options, such as inserting and customizing static text and images, adding additional Web Part zones, and adding Web Parts outside Web Part zones by using techniques described in previous chapters.

In this exercise, you will modify the All Items view of a Tasks list.

USE the site you modified in the previous exercise.
OPEN the site in SharePoint Designer, if it is not already open.

1. In the **Folder List** task pane, expand the **Lists** folder, and then expand the **Tasks** list to display its contents.

   The Tasks list contains six view pages: active.aspx, AllItems.aspx, byowner.aspx, duetoday.aspx, MyGrTsks.aspx, and MyItems.aspx. The other three pages—DispForm.aspx, EditForm.aspx, and NewForm.aspx—are not view pages, but are used to display the metadata for a list item, modify the metadata for a list item, and create a new list item, respectively.

List View Options

2. Open **AllItems.aspx**. In the **Tasks** LVWP, click **Tasks** to display the **List View Options** smart tag.

3. Click the **List View Options** smart tag, and then click **Fields**.

   The Displayed Fields dialog box opens.

4. Under **Available Fields**, hold down the [Ctrl] key and select the **Start Date** and **Task Group** fields. Then click **Add**.

   The two fields appear under Displayed Fields.

5. Click **Start Date**, and then click **Move Up** twice so that **Start Date** is above **Due Date**.

Displayed Fields dialog box:

> Displayed Fields   ? ⌧
>
> Choose the fields to display.
>
> Available fields: Displayed fields:
>
> Content Type   [Add >>]   Attachments
> Created   Title (linked to item with edit m
> Created By   [<< Remove]   Assigned To
> Description   Status
> Edit (link to edit item)   Priority
> ID   [Move Up]   Start Date
> Modified   Due Date
> Modified By   [Move Down]   % Complete
> Title   Task Group
> Title (linked to item)
> Type (icon linked to document
> Version
>
> ◄ ▬▬ III ▬▬ ►   ◄ ▬▬ III ▬▬ ►
>
>   ☐ Show field totals
>
>   [OK]   [Cancel]

6. Click **OK** to close the **Displayed fields** dialog box.

The AllItems.aspx page is redisplayed with the Start Date column visible in the Tasks LVWP.

> Teams > Tasks
>
> **Tasks**
>
>   PlaceHolderBodyRightMargin (Master)
>
> PlaceHolderMain (Custom) rack of work that you or your team Main to complete.
>   WebPartPages:ListViewWebPart
>
> 📋 w ▾   Actions ▾   Settings ▾
>
> 🗑 Title   Assigned To   Status   Priority   Start Date   Due Date   % Complete   Task Group
> There are no items to show in this view of the "Tasks" list. To create a new item, click "New" above.

Save

7. On the Common toolbar, click the **Save** button.

The Site Definition Page Warning dialog box opens, stating that saving changes will customize the page from the site definition.

8. Click **Yes**.

A blue information circle appears to the left of the AllItems.aspx page in the Folder List task pane.

> **Tip** You can retain the view page as an uncustomized page by resetting the page to the site definition. You will not lose any modifications as long as they were limited to customizing Web Parts within Web Part zones. Resetting the view page back to its site definition creates a copy of the page that is visible in the views list in addition to the page you reset, so either delete the copy or move it to some other container.

Creating a List View Page

The built-in list views that are associated with a list or library may not meet all your needs. You can use the sort and filter option on a column of a list view, but this is only a temporary solution because the next time you use the list or library, your sort or filter choices are not remembered. Using both the browser and SharePoint Designer however, you can create new list views, thereby retaining your choices. In addition, by creating list views other formatting options are available, such as the order and visibility of columns, grouping list items together in either an expanded or collapsed manner, and limiting the number of list items displayed.

In this exercise, you will create a new view for a library to display documents grouped by the person who last modified them and sorted on the modification date and file size. You will then make this view the default view.

> **USE** the site you modified in the previous exercise.
> **BE SURE TO** use a document library that contains several files, preferably uploaded or modified by different users.
> **OPEN** the site in SharePoint Designer.

1. In the **Folder List** task pane, right-click **Shared Documents**, point to **New**, and then click **Document Library View Page**.

   The New View Page dialog box opens.

   > **Tip** You can also create a view by using the Page tab in the New dialog box. Click List View Pages, and then click Document Library View Page Wizard.

2. In the **Please enter a name for the view page** text box, type ByModified.

The name that you type for the view page forms part of the URL.

See Also For information about good naming conventions, see the sidebar "Best Practices for Naming URLs" in Chapter 2.

3. Click **OK** to close the **New View Page** dialog box.

   In the Folder List task pane, under the Forms folder in Shared Documents, the *ByModified.aspx* view page appears, and the view page opens in the SharePoint Designer document window, with ByModified in the View list.

List View Options

4. In the **Shared Documents** LVWP, click **Shared Documents** to display the **List View Options** smart tag.

5. Click the **List View Options** smart tag, and then click **Sort and Group**.

   The Sort And Group dialog box opens.

6. Under **Sort order**, click **Name (for use in forms)**, and then click **Remove**.

7. Under **Available fields**, click **Modified By**, and then click **Add**.

8. Repeat step 7 to add **Modified** and **File Size**.

9. Click **Modified By**, and in the **Group Properties** section, select the **Show group header** check box, and click **Expand group by default** if it is not already selected.

10. Click **Modified**, and in the **Sort Properties** section, click **Descending**.

11. Click **OK** to close the **Sort and Group** dialog box.

12. In the **Folder List** task pane, right-click **Shared Documents**, and then click **Properties**.

The Document Library Properties dialog box opens.

13. On the **Supporting Files** tab, in the **Default view page** list, click **Shared Documents/Forms/ByModified.aspx**.

14. Click **OK** to close the **Document Library Properties** dialog box.

The *ByModified.aspx* page is redisplayed with the documents grouped by Modified By.

Save

15. Click the **Save** button.

The Site Definition Page Warning dialog box opens, stating that saving changes will customize the page from the site definition.

16. Click **Yes**.

A blue information circle appears to the left of the *ByModified.aspx* page in the Folder List task pane.

17. Press F12.

A browser window opens displaying the ByModified view of Shared Documents.

18. If prompted, type your user name and password, and then click **OK**.

19. On the Quick Launch bar, under **Documents**, click **Shared Documents**.

The ByModified view of Shared Documents is displayed.

Modifying a Built-In List Form Page

Lists and libraries, when created, provide a number of built-in view pages. They also provide built-in pages to create new list items, edit, and display existing list items; up-load documents create a new document and edit and display metadata associated with documents. These pages are known as *form pages*. Like view pages, form pages consist of one Web Part zone named *Main* and one Web Part. However, whereas view pages use an LVWP, form pages use a Web Part named the *List Form Web Part (LFWP)*.

Although form pages are Web Part pages, you cannot modify them by using the browser. Also in SharePoint Designer, unlike the LVWP on list views, the LFWP on form pages does not provide the List View Options smart tag, so you cannot control the order in which fields are displayed or whether a field should appear. To create a tailored data entry form, you must use SharePoint Designer and the *Custom List Form*. However, your Web-based modifications will not restrict users who use the Datasheet view of the form or who alter properties in Microsoft Office applications. You will need to either customize those other data entry methods or educate your users concerning the differences.

See Also For information about how to use controls to provide additional data integrity checks for the data entry form, see Chapter 8 "Using Controls in Web Pages."

You can add a Custom List Form to a page only by using SharePoint Designer. After you have added this Web Part, you can modify it by using the browser; however, SharePoint Designer provides a WYSIWYG method of manipulating this Web Part, whereas the browser does not.

The Custom List Form is a version of the Data Form Web Part (DFWP), which is new to Windows SharePoint Services 3.0. It has its origin in the Data View Web Part (DVWP), which was available in Windows SharePoint Services 2.0. With the DFWP, you can create solutions for viewing and managing data that resides both internally and externally to SharePoint sites.

See Also   For information about the DFWP, see Chapter 6, "Working with Data Views."

In this exercise, you will explore the LFWP and create a Custom List Form.

USE the *teams.consolidatedmessenger.com* team site and the Tasks library, or you can use whatever site and list or library you want.

OPEN a SharePoint site in SharePoint Designer.

1. In the **Folder List** task pane, expand the **Lists** folder library, and then expand the **Tasks** list to display its contents.

2. Right-click **NewForm.aspx**, and click **Copy**. Then right-click **Tasks**, and click **Paste**.

   The NewForm_copy(1).aspx file appears under the Tasks list.

3. Right-click **NewForm_copy(1).aspx**, click **Rename**, and then type NewTask.aspx.

4. Double-click **NewForm.aspx** to open it in the document window.

   The Form Web Part contains sample fields and not the fields from the Tasks list.

5. In the **Main** Web Part zone, right-click **Tasks**, and then click **List Form Properties**.

   The List Or Document Library Form dialog box opens, where you can change the list or library that this page is associated with, change the purpose of the form from inserting a new list item to viewing or modifying list item metadata, and indicate whether the standard toolbar should be shown.

6. Click **Cancel** to close the **List or Document Library Form** dialog box.

7. In the **Main** Web Part zone, double-click **Tasks** to open the **Tasks** dialog box, where you can customize the Web Part, appearance, layout, and advanced property settings.

8. Click **Cancel** to close the **Tasks** dialog box.

9. With the **Tasks List Form** Web Part still selected, press ⌨Del.

   The Web Part is deleted, leaving an empty Web Part zone. In the Quick Tag Selector, the <WebPartPages:WebPartZone#Main> tag is highlighted in orange.

10. On the **Insert** menu, point to **SharePoint Controls**, and then click **Custom List Form**.

   The List Or Document Library Form dialog box opens.

> **Tip** You can create a new page and add a List Form or a Custom List Form from the menu that appears when you click SharePoint Controls on the Insert menu. These Web Parts are not available from the Web Part task pane.

11. In the **List or document library to use for form** list, click **Tasks**.

   The Task content type is automatically selected in the Content Type To Use From Form list.

12. Click **OK** to close the **List or Document Library Form** dialog box.

The Custom List contains fields from the Task list, and the Common Data View Tasks list is displayed.

13. In the Form Web Part, click the **Priority** arrow, and then in the Quick Tag Selector, click the **td.ms-formbody** tag.

The table cell that contains the Priority list is selected.

14. In the Form Web Part, right-click **td.ms-formbody**, point to **Modify**, and then click **Split Cells**.

The Split Cells dialog box opens.

15. In the **Number of columns** text box, type 3, and then click **OK**.

Two new cells appear to the right of the Priority list.

16. On the **View** menu, point to **Visual Aids**, and then click **ASP.NET Non-visual Controls** if not already selected.

> **Tip** If ASP.NET Non-visual Controls is grayed out you will need to turn Visual Aids on first and then repeat step 16.

17. Click the **Status** text label, and then click **H3.ms-standardhe**, which appears above **Status**.

A four-way arrow appears.

18. While holding down the mouse button, drag **H3.ms-standhe** to the cell to the right of the **Priority** list.

19. Under the **Status** list, point to **[Field Description]** so that the mouse point changes to a four-way arrow and while holding down the mouse button, drag **[Field Description]** to the last cell in the row above its current location.

Four-Way
Arrow Pointer

20. Point to the **Status** list so that the mouse pointer changes to a four-way arrow, and while holding down the mouse button, drag the **Status** list to the left of **[Field Description]** in the last cell in the row above.

This row should now contain the Priority and the Status lists, plus two text labels and two Field Descriptions. The row that formerly contained the Status text label and the list is now empty.

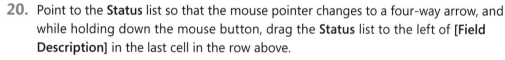

21. Right-click the empty row, point to **Delete**, and then click **Delete Rows**.

Save

22. On the Common toolbar, click the **Save** button.

   The Site Definition Page Warning dialog box appears, stating that saving changes will customize the page from the site definition.

23. Click **Yes**.

   A blue information circle appears to the left of the NewTask.aspx page in the Folder List task pane.

24. In the **Folder List** task pane, right-click **Tasks**, and then click **Properties**.

   The List Properties dialog box opens.

25. Click the **Supporting Files** tab of the **List Properties** dialog box.

26. In the **Content type specific forms** list, click **Task**. To the right of the **New item form** text box, click **Browse**.

   The Current Web Site dialog box opens.

27. Click **NewTask.aspx**, and then click **OK** to close the **Current Web Site** dialog box.

   NewTask.aspx now appears in the New Item Form box of the List Properties dialog box.

![List Properties dialog box showing the Supporting Files tab with Default view page Lists/Tasks/AllItems.aspx, Content type specific forms Task, Display item form Lists/Tasks/DispForm.aspx, New item form Lists/Tasks/NewTask.aspx, and Edit item form Lists/Tasks/EditForm.aspx]

28. Click **OK** to close the **List Properties** dialog box.

29. In the **Folder List** task pane, click **Tasks**, and then press F12, and click **Yes** to save your changes.

   A browser window opens displaying the All Items view of the Tasks list.

30. If prompted, type your user name and password, and then click **OK**.

31. On the toolbar, click **New** to display the **New Item** page.

`New ▾`

In the address of the browser, the NewTask.aspx page should be referenced.

> **CLOSE** the browser window. Close all open pages in the documents, saving any if necessary, and then if you're not continuing to the next chapter, exit SharePoint Designer.

Key Points

- Windows SharePoint Services and SharePoint Server provide a number of built-in list definitions that you can use as a basis to create lists or libraries with SharePoint Designer.

- In SharePoint Designer, you cannot create or modify list items or metadata associated with documents. Nor can you create or modify list permissions, content types, columns, or site columns, or create list templates. You must use the browser or develop code to complete these tasks.

- To maintain the same look and feel as other Web Parts and to save time, create LVWPs by using the browser, and then use SharePoint Designer to complete your customizations.

- LVWPs are like any other Web Part in that you can add them to master pages, both in Web Part zones and outside Web Part zones. LVWPs share a common set of Web Part properties that control appearance, layout, and advanced characteristics. They also have other configurable settings, such as which columns to display and the sort order of the list items.

- View pages and form pages both consist of one Main Web Part zone and one Web Part. In the case of a view page, the Web Part is an LVWP, and in the case of a form page, it is an LFWP.

- You can create a tailored data entry form by using the Custom List Form, which is a version of the DFWP.

Chapter at a Glance

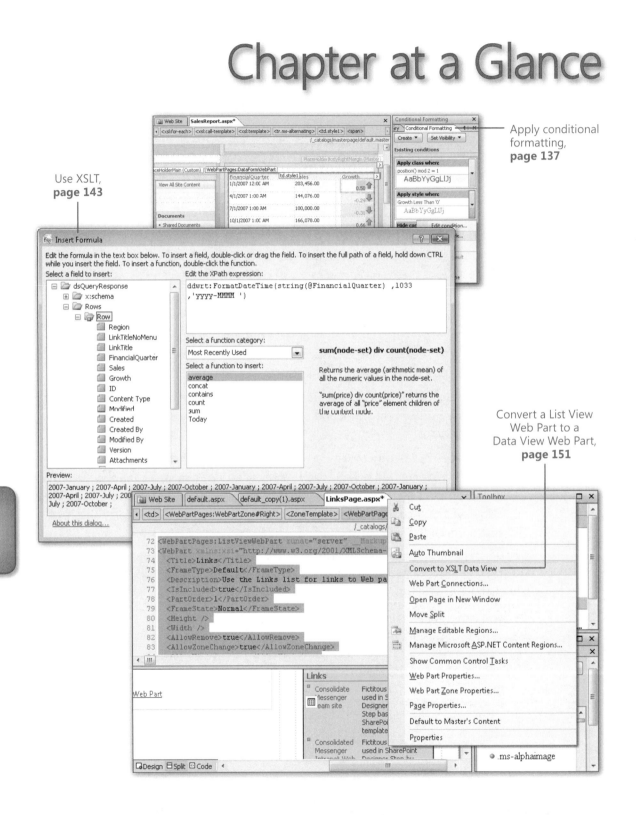

Apply conditional formatting, **page 137**

Use XSLT, **page 143**

Convert a List View Web Part to a Data View Web Part, **page 151**

6 Working with Data Views

In this chapter, you will learn to:

- ✔ Create and customize Data Views.
- ✔ Apply conditional formatting.
- ✔ Use XSLT.
- ✔ Allow insertions, deletions, and updates.
- ✔ Use CAML.
- ✔ Convert a List View Web Part to a Data View Web Part.
- ✔ Deploy Web Parts.

In the previous chapter, you created a custom list form, which added a SharePoint control named the *Data Form Web Part* (DFWP) to your Web page. You also saw how easy it is in Microsoft Office SharePoint Designer 2007 to manipulate this Web Part. In the previous version of Windows SharePoint Services, the DFWP was known as the *Data View Web Part* (DVWP) or Data Views, because at that time, the Web Part allowed you only to view data. The DFWP SharePoint control not only allows you to view data, but it can provide you with a form for entering data into a variety of data sources, such as Microsoft SQL Server databases, XML files, and Web services, as well as data held in SharePoint lists and libraries. The data from these data sources is exposed as XML data, to which the DFWP applies an Extensible Stylesheet Language for Transformations (XSLT) to present the data as HTML. The terms *Data View Web Part* or *Data Views* are still used to refer to the DFWP SharePoint control.

> **Tip** XSLT is a language for formatting the presentation of XML data. Like XML, XSLT is both human-readable and computer-readable and is an open standard.

Using Data Views, you can display, edit, and modify list item data in a more flexible manner than when you use the List View Web Part (LVWP). You can use Data Views in many business scenarios where traditionally a developer created a custom Web Part. Even if you find that the DFWP control does not meet all your business requirements, it is still a superb prototyping tool to obtain business signoff.

In this chapter, using lists and libraries as your data source, you will create and modify Data Views. You will format the data based on specific criteria defined by the metadata, and work with the XSLT. You will learn how to convert an LVWP to a DVWP and review the XSLT that is generated to match the Collaborative Application Markup Language (CAML) that the LVWP uses to render the contents of the list. You will also learn how to deploy the DVWP to other sites.

Important Before you can use the practice files in this chapter, you need to install them from the book's companion CD to their default location. You will need to create a practice site for this chapter based on the site template *DataView_Starter.stp* located in this chapter's practice file folder. Then when you perform the exercises in this chapter, remember to use your SharePoint site location in place of *teams.consolidatedmessenger.com*.

For more information about practice files, see "Using the Book's CD" at the beginning of this book.

Troubleshooting Graphics and operating system–related instructions in this book reflect the Windows Vista user interface. If your computer is running Windows XP and you experience trouble following the instructions as written, please refer to the "Information for Readers Running Windows XP" section at the beginning of this book.

Creating Data Views

The Data View Web Part (DVWP) is a very flexible Web Part that you can create only by using Office SharePoint Designer 2007. Like other Web Parts, DVWPs follow these rules:

- They can be placed inside and outside Web Part zones.
- They have the standard properties shared by all Web Parts, such as Title, Height, Width, and Frame State.
- Depending on the settings of the Web Part zone properties, they can be relocated to other Web Part zones by using the browser.

- Web Part properties can be accessed through the browser Web Part tool pane.

- When inside a Web Part zone, they support personal and shared views.

Additionally, you can edit the XSL and the parameters passed to the XSL without needing to open the page in SharePoint Designer.

In this exercise, you will create a DVWP that displays the contents of a list.

USE your own SharePoint site location in place of the *teams.consolidatedmessenger.com* team site.

BE SURE TO start SharePoint Designer before beginning this exercise. Turn off ASP.NET Non-visual Controls, if they are still on, by using the View, Visual Aids menu.

OPEN the DataViews child site in SharePoint Designer.

1. In the **Folder List** task pane, expand the **WebPages** folder, and then double-click **Products.aspx** to open the page in the document window.

2. Click the **Main** Web Part zone. Then on the **Data View** menu, click **Insert Data View**.

A Data Form Web Part control is added to the Web Part zone and the Data Source Library task pane opens, where the lists for the Web site are displayed under the Current Site section. The number of lists displayed should match the number in brackets to the right of the SharePoint Lists header and should match the number of lists that you can see in the Folder List task pane. Lists configured to be hidden from the browser are not listed in the Data Source Library task pane.

3. In the **Data Source Library** task pane, expand **SharePoint Libraries** to display non-hidden libraries contained in this Web site.

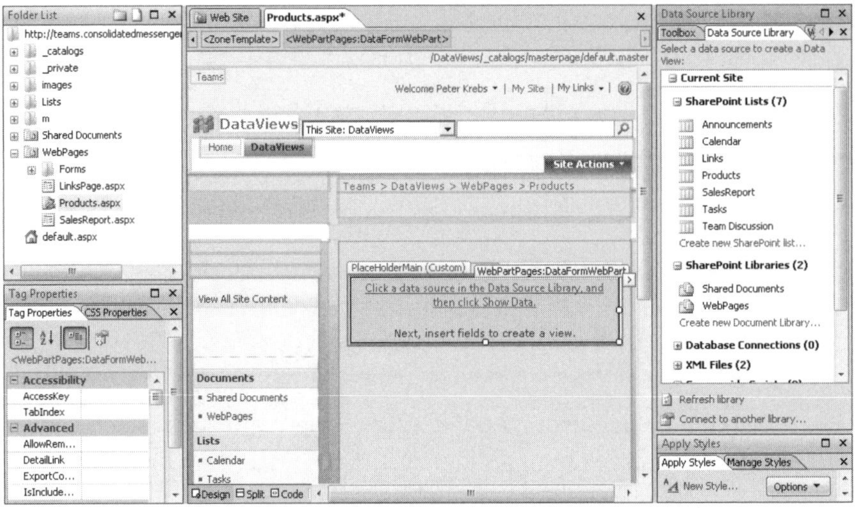

4. In the **Data Source Library** task pane, under **SharePoint Lists**, drag **Products** into the **DataFormWebPart** control.

Within the DataFormWebPart control, an HTML table appears with Title, Modified By, and Modified columns, together with the list data in the body of the table as HTML rows and cells. The Data Source Details task pane opens, and to the right of Row, [1/17] denotes that the list contains 17 list items. The 1 indicates that the value of the first item is displayed below Row.

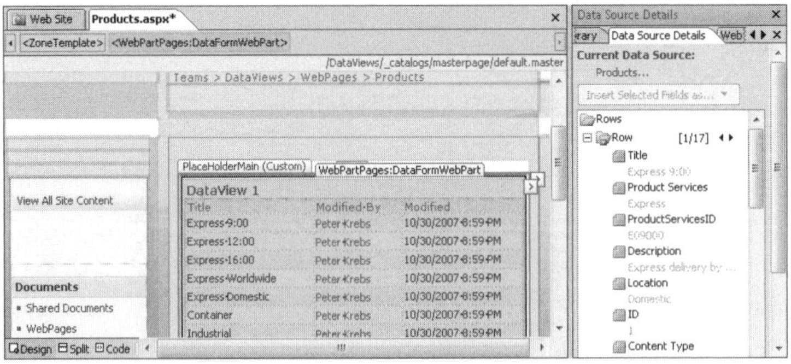

Tip Unlike when adding an LVWP, when you create a Data View, no criteria is used to display the list items. If you want to mimic the configurations of an LVWP, it is easier to add an LVWP and convert it to a Data View. You will see the step to do this later in this chapter.

Next

5. In the **Data Source Details** task pane, to the right of **Row**, click the **Next** arrow to view the second list item value.

The text in the square brackets to the right of Row indicates you are now viewing the second of 17 list items.

> **Tip** You can use the Next and Previous arrows to review the contents of the list without displaying the list in a browser.

Save

6. On the Common toolbar, click **Save** button and then press ⌷F12⌷.

The page opens in the browser.

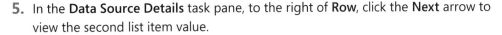

CLOSE the browser.

Customizing Data Views

Data Views provide virtually limitless possibilities for formatting data. Like LVWPs, Data Views do not contain data; they point to data stored elsewhere. When you request a page, SharePoint queries the SQL Server content database for the properties of the Data View to find the location of the data. Then the Microsoft Windows SharePoint Services Data Retrieval Service obtains the data as XML, and SharePoint dynamically transforms the data to HTML as described by the XSLT in the Data View. SharePoint Designer displays the returned XML data in the Data Source Details task pane and in the Design View. You can use the Design view as a visual XSLT editor, so you can manipulate the

XML data in the Data View Web Part using the same editing techniques that you used for editing static HTML in Chapter 3, "Customizing a Web Page." As you format the data in one of the HTML cells, the affect cascades to other cells within the same column.

You can modify the DVWP in many of the same ways that you can modify the LVWP, such as specifying which fields to display; filtering, sorting and grouping data items; displaying data items in sets, or limiting the number of items to be displayed. With the DVWP, you have more sophisticated sorting and grouping options and additional layout styles; however, you cannot use the Datasheet view for DVWPs.

An XML Primer

XML is a language for defining and representing data of all kinds, where data is stored as text rather than in binary format. XML is an open standard that many vendors support. In contrast to HTML, XML tags describe only the data itself, not how the data should be displayed. You can choose the tag names as long as the XML data is well formed; that is, as long as it obeys the following set of rules:

- One root element contains all other elements.
- Each element must have matching opening and closing tags.
- Elements must use consistent capitalization; that is, they are case sensitive.
- Elements must be nested correctly; that is, no elements overlap.
- Element attribute values must be enclosed in quotes with no repeating attributes in an element.

The root element in the following XML data is *Invoices*. *InvoiceNo* is known as an attribute and *Company* and *Net* are child elements. The content of the *Company* element is Adventure Works, whereas the element *Net* has no content.

```
<?xml version="1.0" encoding="UTF-8" ?>
<Invoices xmlns="http://consolidatedmessenger.com/finance">
    <Invoice InvoiceNo="143">
        <Company>Adventure Works</Company>
        <Net></Net>
        <![CDATA[
            function tax(){ window.open('TBD'); }
        ]]>
    <Invoice>
</Invoices>
```

When an XML document contains data that does not follow the XML rules (for example, if you want to include HTML or code in the XML document), you should include the data in an XML CDATA section to indicate that it should not be parsed as XML.

In this exercise, you will manipulate a Data View in Design view so that SharePoint Designer will generate the necessary XSLT. In the process, you will investigate the customizing capabilities that the Data View has in addition to those of the LVWP.

> **USE** the site you modified in the previous exercise.
>
> **OPEN** the site in SharePoint Designer, if it is not already open, and display the *Products.aspx* file.

Chevron

1. Click the chevron to the right of the **DataFormWebPart** control to display the **Common Data View Tasks** list.

> **Tip** To hide the Common Data View Tasks list, click the chevron again.

2. Click **Edit Columns**.

   The Edit Columns dialog box opens.

3. Under **Displayed Columns**, click **Modified By**, and then click **Remove** twice.

4. Under **Available fields**, click **Description**, and while holding down the [Ctrl] key, click **Product Services** and **ProductServicesID**. Then click **Add**.

5. Under **Displayed Columns**, click **Product Services**, and then click **Move Up** twice.

6. Click **OK** to close the **Edit Column** dialog box.

7. In the **Common Data View Tasks** list, click **Sort and Group**.

   The Sort And Group dialog box opens.

8. Under **Available fields**, click **Product Services**, and then click **Add**.

9. Under **Group Properties**, click **Show group header**, and then click **Advanced Grouping**.

The Advanced Grouping dialog box opens.

10. Select the **Show column totals per group** check box, and then click **OK** to close the **Advanced Grouping** dialog box.

11. Click **OK** to close the **Sort and Group** dialog box.

    The page is redisplayed, with group headings added and the list items sorted.

12. In the first cell of the DataFormWebPart control, right-click **Air and Ocean**, point to **Delete**, and then click **Delete Columns**.

The Product Services field is removed from the DataFormWebPart control.

13. In the group heading, click **Product Services**, and then press [Del].

    Product Services is removed from each group heading.

14. Press [Del] four times to remove the colon (:) and additional spaces.

15. In the field heading row, click **Description**, and on the Quick Tag Selector, click the preceding **<tr>** HTML tag.

16. On the Common toolbar, click **Bold**.

B

Bold

17. In the field heading row, place the insertion point between **Product** and **Services**, and then press [Space]. Repeat to insert a space between **Services** and **ID**.

18. On the Common toolbar, click the **Save** button, and then press [F12] to review the Products page in the browser. If prompted, type your user name and password, and then click **OK**.

Save

19. Close the browser, and then close the Products page so that it is not displayed in the document window.

CLOSE the browser and the *Products.aspx* file.

Applying Conditional Formatting

The Data View offers a feature known as *conditional formatting* that you can use to alter the appearance of a set of cells or rows based on criteria that you specify. Within a Data View, you can apply conditional formatting to an HTML tag, a data value, or a range of text. The criteria you specify do not have to be based on the field being formatted. You can also show or hide data based on criteria. However, it is more efficient to add a filter to hide an entire row than to use conditional formatting, because with filters, the data retrieval engine returns only the data you need, thereby reducing the amount of data that is retrieved from the SQL Server database and the processing by the Web servers to render the page.

In this exercise, you will create a Data View based on Sales figures that are stored in a list. You will then show or hide a red or green arrow depending on the sales growth for each quarter.

> **USE** the site you modified in the last exercise.
>
> **OPEN** the site in SharePoint Designer, if it is not already open.

1. In the **Folder List** task pane, expand **WebPages**, and double-click **SalesReport.aspx** to open the page in the document window.

2. Click the **Main** Web Part zone, and on the **Data View** menu, click **Insert Data View**.

   The Data Source Library task pane opens.

3. Click **SalesReports**, and then click **Show Data**.

   The Data Source Details task pane opens.

4. While holding down the Ctrl key, click **FinancialQuarter**, **Sales**, and **Growth**. Then click **Insert Select Field as**, and click **Multiple Item View**.

An HTML table appears in the DataFormWebPart control with the FinancialQuarter, Sales, and Growth columns in the order you selected them.

5. In the **Folder List** task pane, expand the **Images** folder, and then drag **GreenUpArrow.bmp** into a data cell to the right of **0.50**.

   The Accessibility Properties dialog box opens.

6. In the **Alternate Text** text box, type Green Up Arrow, and then click **OK** to close the **Accessibility Properties** dialog box.

   A green upward-pointing arrow appears in all cells of the Growth column.

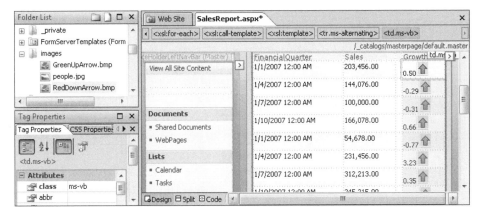

7. In the **images** folder, drag **RedDownArrow.bmp** next to **GreenUpArrow.bmp**.

   The Accessibility Properties dialog box opens.

8. In the **Alternate Text** text box, type Red Down Arrow, and then click **OK** to close the **Accessibility Properties** dialog box.

   A red downward-pointing arrow appears in all cells of the new column.

9. Right-click a red down arrow image, and then click **Conditional Formatting**.

   The Conditional Formatting task pane opens.

> **Tip** You can also click Conditional Formatting in the Common Data View Tasks list to display the Conditional Formatting task pane.

10. Click **Create**, and then click **Hide Content**.

The Condition Criteria dialog box opens.

11. Click in the cell below **Field name**, click the arrow that appears, and then click **Growth**.

12. Under **Comparison**, click **Equals**, click the arrow that appears, and then click **Greater Than or Equal**.

13. Click **OK** to close the **Condition Criteria** dialog box.

The red down arrow icon disappears when the value in the Growth column is positive. In the Conditional Formatting task pane, a Hide Content When condition appears, displaying the criteria Growth Greater Than Or Equal 0'.

14. Right-click a green up arrow image. In the **Conditional Formatting** task pane, click **Create**, and then click **Hide** content.

15. In the **Condition Criteria** dialog box, click the cell below **Field name**, click the arrow that appears, and then click **Growth**.

16. Under **Comparison**, click **Equals**, click the arrow that appears, and then click **Less Than**.

17. Click **OK** to close the **Condition Criteria** dialog box.

The green down arrow icon appears when the value in the Growth column is positive. In the Conditional Formatting task pane, a second Hide Content When condition appears, displaying the criteria.

> **Tip** The Hide Content condition is exactly the opposite of the Show Content condition. Therefore, when you need to specify multiple Hide Content or Show Content conditions, use only one of these conditions. Using a combination can lead to confusion.

18. Click the **0.50** data cell in the **Growth** column. In the **Conditional Formatting** task pane, click **Create**, and then click **Apply formatting**.

> **Tip** If you click to the right of a value, the Create button may not be available. Click the middle of the value so that either an xsl or an HTML tag is selected.

19. In the **Condition Criteria** dialog box, click the cell below **Field name**, click the arrow that appears, and then click **Growth**.

20. Under **Comparison**, click **Equals**, click the arrow that appears, and then click **Less Than**.

21. Click **OK** to close the **Condition Criteria** dialog box.

    The Modify Style dialog box opens.

22. Click the **color** arrow, and then click the **Red** square.

The preview section shows a sample of how the text will be displayed.

23. Click **OK** to close the **Modify Style** dialog box.

In the Growth column, negative values appear in a red font. In the Conditional Formatting task pane, an Apply Style When condition appears, displaying the criteria and a preview of the formatting.

24. Point to **Apply style when**, click the arrow that appears, and then click **Modify style**.

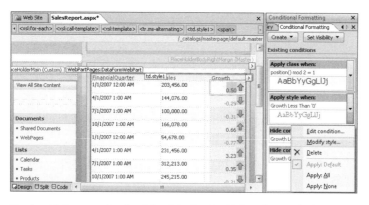

25. Under **Category** in the **Modify Style** dialog box, click **Background**, click the **background-color** arrow, and then click **Silver**.

26. Click **OK** to close the **Modify Style** dialog box.

In the Growth column, negative values appear in a red font with a silver background.

27. On the Common toolbar, click **Align Text Right**.

Align Text Right

Save

28. Click **Save**, and press F12 to review the SalesReports page in the browser. If prompted, type your user name and password, and then click **OK**.

CLOSE the browser.

Using XSLT

Data Views use XSLT to describe how to transform the XML data that SharePoint retrieves from a data source to HTML. SharePoint first converts the XML data into an XML tree, which represents the hierarchical structure of the XML elements and attributes, known as *nodes*. The Date Source Details task pane shows this hierarchical structure in a similar way to a folder structure on a file system, with the list or library represented as a Rows XML element, the list item represented as a Row XML child element, and each field represented as an XML attribute. (In XSLT, XML attributes are prefixed with the @ symbol.) The XSLT is then used to navigate the hierarchical structure, and the *XML Path Language (XPath)* is used to select one or more nodes.

The XSLT instructions themselves are also represented as XML data. The xsl:template element contains a match attribute that defines the XPath expression used to select the set of nodes to be transformed. After a node is selected, components specify how to manipulate the XML data. These components can include HTML formatting tags and other XSLT elements. For example, in the following XSLT, the xsl:template finds the Invoice XML element, and the HTML formats the xsl:value-of element. Using the XML data given as an example in the sidebar "An XML Primer" earlier in this chapter, this XSLT would render Adventure Works as a new paragraph in bold font.

```
<xsl:template match="Invoice">
  <p><strong><xsl:value-of select="Company" /></strong>
</xsl:template>
```

See Also For an excellent introduction to XSL, visit *www.w3schools.com/xsl/.*

In the Design view, SharePoint Designer automatically generates this XSLT for you. It also provides an XSLT editor to help you develop sophisticated solutions. You can directly edit the XSLT in Code view; where Microsoft IntelliSense is available to help with this task, resulting in a higher degree of flexibility and control. However, you need a deep understanding of XSLT to be able to edit it directly.

In this exercise, you will format the content of a Data View by using XSLT.

> **USE** the site you modified in the previous exercise.
>
> **OPEN** the site in SharePoint Designer, if it is not already open, and display the *SalesReport.aspx* file.

1. Under **FinancialQuarter**, click **1/1/2007 12:00 AM** to display the tag **xsl:value-of**.

Chevron

2. Click the chevron to display the **Common xsl:value-of Tasks** list.

3. Click the **DateTime formatting options** link.

   The Format Date And Time dialog box opens.

4. Click the **Date Format** arrow, and click **2007-10-14**.

   Your date may be different.

5. Clear the **Show Time** check box, and then click **OK** to close the **Format Date and Time** dialog box.

   All dates in the FinancialQuarter column are displayed in the year-month-day format.

6. Right-click **2007-01-01**, and then click **Edit Formula**.

   The Insert Formula dialog box opens.

7. In the **Edit the XPath expression** text box, delete **–dd**, and type MM.

8. Click **OK** to close the **Insert Formula** dialog box.

   All dates in the FinancialQuarter column display in the year-month format.

9. Click **Split** view.

   The document window displays both the Code and Design views.

10. Click **2007-January**.

    In the Code view, the *xsl:value-of* tag is highlighted and the DateTime formula is added as an attribute of the tag.

11. In the Design view portion of the document window, right-click **203,456.00** in the **Sales** column, point to **Format Item as**, and then click **Currency**.

    The Format Number dialog box opens.

12. Click **OK** to accept the defaults in the **Format Number** dialog box.

    The Format Number dialog box closes. A dollar sign prefixes all numbers in the Sales column.

13. Click **$203,456.00**.

In the Code view, the *xsl:value-of* tag is highlighted and the number formula is added as an attribute of the xsl:value-of tag

Allowing Insertions, Deletions, and Updates

In Chapter 5, "Working with Lists and Libraries," you created a Custom List Form for tailored data entry. The Data View provides other methods of data entry. Using the Insert Selected Field As list in the Data Source Details task pane, you can create a Data View as a single-item form, a multiple-item form, or a new item form.

> **Tip** You might want to choose a multiple-item form if users like to quickly edit the data in many list items at the same time. However, some users find this form confusing.

You can also configure an existing Data View to edit, delete, and insert data in a list item. Unlike the single-item and multiple-item forms, which can be used only in data entry mode, a configured Data View can be used to display, edit, insert, or delete list items. Whichever method you choose for data entry, you can still filter, sort, and group the data, apply conditional formatting, or create formula columns.

> **Note** The single-item and multiple-item modes are defined in the code on the SPDataSource SharePoint control, where the DataSourceMode attribute has a value of either ListItem or List. The Data View provides other modes, but SharePoint Designer does not expose them through its user interface. You would have to modify the code directly. See *blogs.msdn.com/ sharepointdesigner/archive/2007/04/24/spdatasource-and-rollups-with-the-data-view.aspx* for more information.

In this exercise, you will add editing links to an existing Data View.

> **USE** the site you modified in the previous exercise.
>
> **OPEN** the site in SharePoint Designer, if it is not already open, and display the *SalesReport.aspx* file.

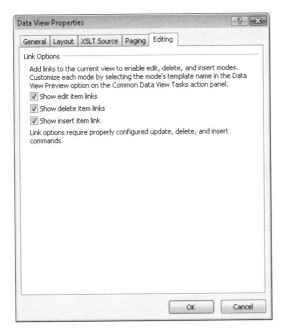

Chevron

1. Click the chevron to the right of the **DataFormWebPart** control to display the **Common Data View Tasks** list, and then click **Data View Properties**.

   The Data View Properties dialog box opens.

2. Click the **Editing** tab.

3. Select the **Show editing item links**, **Show delete item links**, and **Show insert item links** check boxes.

> **Note** If the data source is a SQL Server database, the Editing tab provides additional options.

4. Click **OK** to close the **Data View Properties** dialog box.

   The SalesReport.aspx page is redisplayed. An extra column containing edit and delete links is added to the Data View.

Save

5. Click **Save**, and then click F12 to open the page in the browser. If prompted, type your user name and password, and then click **OK**.

Edit and delete links appear to the left of each list item, and an insert link appears at the bottom of the Data View.

	FinancialQuarter	Sales	Growth
edit delete	2007-January	$203,456.00	0.50 ⬆
edit delete	2007-April	$144,076.00	-0.29 ⬇
edit delete	2007-July	$100,000.00	-0.31 ⬇
edit	2007-October	$166,078.00	⌃

6. Click **edit** to the left of **2007-January**.

The page is redisplayed, and the edit and delete links for this list item are replaced by the save and cancel links. List items whose values you can edit are shown in SharePoint form controls.

7. In the **FinancialQuarter** text box, type 4/1/2007, and in the **Growth** text box, type -10.

	FinancialQuarter	Sales	Growth
save cancel	4/1/2007 📅	203,456 -10 %	
edit	2007-April	$144,076.00	

8. Click **Save**.

The Sales report page is redisplayed, and the save and cancel links for the list item are replaced by the edit and delete links. The list item displays the new values. The green up arrow is replaced with a red down arrow.

	FinancialQuarter	Sales	Growth
edit delete	2007-April	$203,456.00	-0.10 ⬇
edit delete	2007-April	$144,076.00	-0.29 ⬇

✕ **CLOSE** the browser and any pages that are open in the document window.

Using CAML

Collaborative Application Markup Language (CAML) is a proprietary markup language specific to SharePoint technologies that the LVWP uses to dynamically find and display SharePoint items based on various criteria. Each LVWP on a Web Part starts with a *WebPartPages:ListViewWebPart* tag, followed by all the Web Part properties tags, and then the CAML statements. CAML, like XSLT, is represented as XML data. Many of the built-in site definitions use CAML, because it is easy to see in XML data format. On a page, CAML appears within the *ListViewXml* tag with the < and > characters encoded as &gt and &lt characters.

> **Tip** SharePoint Designer does not provide any IntelliSense to help you write CAML within the source code window. However, there are a number of CAML query tools that may help you write CAML, such as the one on Microsoft's open source project hosting Web site at *www.codeplex.com/SPCamlViewer/.*

The *ListViewXml* tag contains the CAML query strings used to return list items from the SQL Server databases and the CAML view elements to format the list item data. The main CAML view elements are *ViewFields*, *ViewHeader*, *ViewBody*, and *ViewFooter*. When an LVWP is first added to a Web page, it uses a default view to display the list items and does not contain the *ViewFields* element. However, if you modify the view within the browser Web Part tool pane, this element and other related elements are added, referencing the internal names of the fields.

See Also For information about the CAML View Schema in the Windows SharePoint Services Software Developer Kit, go to *http://msdn2.microsoft.com/ms439798.aspx.*

In this exercise, you will modify an LVWP and review the associated CAML.

> **USE** the site you modified in the previous exercise.
> **OPEN** the site in SharePoint Designer, if it is not already open, and display the *Products.aspx* file.

1. In the **Folder List** task pane, expand the **WebPages** library, open **LinksPage.aspx** in the document window, and then click **Links**.

   The Links LVWP is highlighted.

2. Click **Split**.

The Code view opens in the upper half of the document window, with the code for the Links LVWP highlighted.

3. In the Code view portion of the document window, scroll down, and click the **ListViewXml** tag.

4. Press Ctrl + F.

The Find And Replace dialog box opens with ListViewXml highlighted in the Find What text box.

5. Under **Find where**, select **Current page** if not selected, and under **Advanced**, select **Find in source code** if not selected.

6. In the **Find What** text box, type ViewHeader, and then click **Find Next**.

The opening CAML ViewHeader tag is found.

7. Click **Close** to close the **Find and Replace** dialog box.

8. In the Design view portion of the document window, click **Links**, click the **List View Options** smart tag arrow, and then click **Fields**.

The Displayed Fields dialog box opens.

9. Under **Available fields**, click **Notes**, and click **Add**. Then click **OK** to close the **Display Fields** dialog box.

The LinksPage.aspx page is redisplayed.

10. In the Code view, scroll down to the **ListViewXml** tag.

Field elements appear either before the ViewHeader element references the URL, URLNoMenu, and Comments fields, or further down the page.

Converting a List View Web Part to a Data View Web Part

You can use SharePoint Designer to convert an LVWP to a DVWP, so that you can use advanced tools to manipulate and format data. During the conversion process, SharePoint Designer generates the necessary XSLT to match the CAML used to render the list items data. The SharePoint SPDataSource control is added and refers to the list by a unique number called its List ID, not by its name. The value of the List ID is known as a *Globally Unique Identifier (GUID)*.

> **Warning** You cannot enable editing in a Data View that is converted from an LVWP.

In this exercise, you will convert an LVWP to a DVWP and then modify the Data View by using the extra functionality that the Data View provides.

> **USE** the site you modified in the previous exercise.
>
> **OPEN** the site in SharePoint Designer, if it is not already open, and display *LinksPage.aspx* in Split view.

1. Right-click **Links**, and then click **Convert to XSLT Data View**.

   The LinksPage.aspx page is redisplayed, and the Common Data View Tasks list opens. The WebPartPages:ListViewWebPart control is replaced by the WebPartPages:DataFormWebPart control.

2. Click the Code view, and on the **Edit** menu, click **Find** to open the **Find and Replace** dialog box.

3. Under **Find where**, select **Current page** if not selected, and under **Advanced**, select **Find in source code** if not selected.

4. In the **Find What** text box, type URLNoMenu, and then click **Find Next**.

   SharePoint Designer finds a comment with XSLT elements and HTML tags below it. This is the code that SharePoint Designer generated to replace the CAML FieldRef element.

5. Click **Close** to close the **Find and Replace** dialog box.

6. In the Design view portion of the document window, in the Links Data View, right-click **Consolidated Messenger team site**, and then click **Hyperlink Properties**.

   The Edit Hyperlink dialog box opens.

7. In the **Text to display** text box, select **{substring-after(@URL, ',')}**, right-click it, and then click **Copy**.

8. Click **Screen Tip**.

   The Set Hyperlink Screen Tip dialog box opens.

9. Right-click the **ScreenTip text** box, and click **Paste**. Then click **OK** to close the **Set Hyperlink Screen Tip** dialog box.

10. Click **Target Frame**, click **New Window**, and then click **OK**.

11. Click **OK** to close the **Edit Hyperlink** dialog box.

    The code view is redisplayed. The title and target attributes are added to the HTML <a> tag.

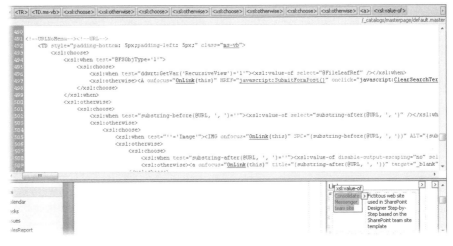

Save

12. On the Common toolbar, click the **Save** button.

Deploying Web Parts

As you develop Data Views, you may want to use the same formatted and filtered Data View on other sites within your site collection. Using the browser or SharePoint Designer, you can export the Web Part and reuse it. With both the browser and SharePoint Designer, you can save the Web Part file to the file system, and from there, you can import it into a page. SharePoint Designer allows you to export the Web Part directly to the Web Part gallery.

> **Warning** The Data View references lists by their GUID and not by their list name. An exported Web Part that references a GUID will result in a Web Part that will not render on another site. If you want to export a Data View that exposes data from a specific list type and reuse it on a different site where it points to a different list of the same list type, you will need to edit the DataFormWebPart control in the Code view. Replace all occurrences of *ListID* with *List Name* and all occurrences of the GUID value with the list name.

When you edit Web pages on team sites, every time you save your modifications, they are immediately visible to all users who view that page. By developing your solution on a "production" page, you can cause performance and rendering problems, especially if you make mistakes. You should create a test Web page, and then create and modify your Data View on that test page. When you have completed your modifications, export the Data View and add it to the production Web page, deleting the test page if necessary.

In this exercise, you will export a Data View and add it to the home page of your Web site.

> **USE** the site you modified in the previous exercise.
>
> **OPEN** the site in SharePoint Designer, if it is not already open, and display *LinksPage.aspx* in Design view.

1. Click **Links** to highlight the Data View.

2. On the **File** menu, point to **Export**, point to **Save Web Part to**, and then click **Site Gallery**.

The Save Web Part To Site Gallery dialog box opens.

3. In the **Name** text box, type *SBSLinksDataView*, and then click **OK**.

The Save Web Part To Site Gallery dialog box closes.

4. In the **Folder List** task pane, right-click **default.aspx**, and then click **Preview in Browser**.

The home page of your Web site opens in the browser.

5. Click **Site Actions**, and then click **Edit Page**.

6. In the **Left** Web Part zone, click **Add a Web Part**.

   The Add Web Parts dialog box opens.

7. Under **All Web Parts**, click **SBSLinksDataView**, and then click **Add**.

   The Add Web Parts dialog box closes, and the Data View is added as the first Web Part within the Left Web Part zone.

> **CLOSE** the browser and close the site within SharePoint Designer. If you are not continuing directly to the next chapter, exit SharePoint Designer.

Key Points

- Data Views allow you to view data and enter data into a variety of data sources.

- Data Views are also known by the names *Data Form Web Parts* (DFWPs) and *Data View Web Parts* (DVWPs).

- Data Views follow the same rules as other Web Parts.

- Data Views use XSLT to transform XML data into HTML.

- LVWPs use CAML to query and format list or library data as HTML.

- You can use SharePoint Designer to convert an LVWP to a Data View, which allows you to use advance manipulation and formatting methods.

- You can use SharePoint Designer to import and export Web Parts. When you export Web Parts, you can save them either in the Web Part Gallery or on the file system.

Chapter at a Glance

Connect to an XML Web service, **page 171**

Use linked sources, **page 173**

Display the contents of a list on another site, **page 177**

Connect Web Parts, **page 180**

7 Working with Data Sources

In this chapter, you will learn to:

- ✔ Use the Data Source Library.
- ✔ Work with XML data.
- ✔ Connect to an RSS feed XML file or server-side script.
- ✔ Connect to an XML Web service.
- ✔ Use linked sources.
- ✔ Display the contents of a list on another site.
- ✔ Connect Web Parts.

When you created a Data View in Chapter 6, "Working with Data Views," the Data Source Library task pane opened so that you could select a list or library on the current site. In the Data Source Library task pane, previously known as the Data Source Catalog task pane, you can do more than just select lists and libraries; you can also create and manage data connections for a variety of data sources. Data connections control the amount of data retrieved by Windows SharePoint Services from the data sources. After the data is retrieved, Data Views specify how to manipulate it by using XSLT and HTML tags.

In this chapter, you will use the Data Source Library task pane to create data connections to a number of data sources. You will add a Data Source Library from another site so that you can share its data connections rather than having to re-create them, and you will link data sources that contain interrelated data to one another.

Important Before you can use the practice files in this chapter, you need to install them from the book's companion CD to their default location. You will need to create a practice site for this chapter based on the site template *DataSources_Starter.stp* located in this chapter's practice file folder. Then when you perform the exercises in this chapter, remember to use your SharePoint site location in place of teams.consolidatedmessenger.com.

For more information about practice files, see "Using the Book's CD" at the beginning of this book.

Troubleshooting Graphics and operating system–related instructions in this book reflect the Windows Vista user interface. If your computer is running Windows XP and you experience trouble following the instructions as written, please refer to the "Information for Readers Running Windows XP" section at the beginning of this book.

Using the Data Source Library

The Data Source Library task pane is an easy-to-use interface for creating, managing, and modifying data connections to data sources. These data connections describe a location and provide a query that the Microsoft Windows SharePoint Services data retrieval service uses to obtain the data from the data sources. The data retrieval service provides a layer of abstraction so that both Microsoft Office SharePoint Designer 2007 and Data Views do not need to differentiate between the different methods of accessing the data sources.

When you request a page by using Office SharePoint Designer 2007, it is the responsibility of the data retrieval service on the Web server to return the data in an XML format that SharePoint Designer 2007 understands. SharePoint Designer interprets the XML data, displaying it in the Data Source Details task pane and in the Design view when the page contains any Data Views. Similarly, when you request a page by using the browser, the data retrieval service provides the XML data, which SharePoint uses together with the XSLT from the Data View to provide the page that the browser renders. In the browser, when the Data View is configured to allow the editing of data, the data retrieval service communicates any changes back to the data sources.

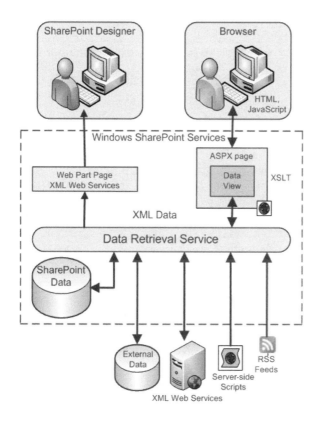

You can connect to a variety of data sources, which are grouped according to the access method they use, as described in the following table.

Data source groups	Description
SharePoint lists and libraries	Every list and library that is not hidden from the browser is listed in the Data Source Library. Using the Data Source Library task pane, you can also create new lists or libraries.
Database connections	When you first open the Data Source Library task pane, there are no connections to any databases. You can create a connection to a variety of databases that reside on Microsoft SQL Server 2000 or Microsoft SQL Server 2005, or to any data source that uses the OLE DB or ODBC protocols, such as Oracle databases, mail files, spreadsheets, and Microsoft Office Access databases. You can create multiple data sources to the same database, each using a different table, view, or query.
XML files	SharePoint Designer interrogates your current sites and lists any XML files it finds. You can also import an XML file into your site or refer to an XML file on another site by using the Add An XML File link.

(continued on next page)

Data source groups	Description
Server-side scripts	You can connect to server-side scripts that return XML data; for example, a *Really Simple Syndication (RSS)* feed may use a server-side script. Such RSS feeds have a URL ending in .aspx or .php. When an RSS feed has a URL ending in .xml or .ashx, use the XML file data connection method. You can connect to server-side scripts written in a variety of languages, including Microsoft ASP, Microsoft ASP.NET, PHP, and *Asynchronous JavaScript and XML (AJAX)*.
XML Web services	A Web service is a special site that can return XML in response to a procedural query. SharePoint itself exposes its data as a Web service, enabling you to create, for example, a list of announcements from the current site, and its child sites, known as a rollup of announcements.
Business Data Catalog	This option is available only if you are using Microsoft Office SharePoint Server 2007. Many organizations use the *Business Data Catalog (BDC)* in preference to other access methods in the Data Source Library task pane. The BDC is a shared service where you can define how to connect to data sources just once in a central location. These definitions are then available for all sites and site collections. The BDC can reference databases or XML Web services, which you can use to integrate with line-of-business applications such as SAP and Siebel. Office SharePoint Server 2007 has a number of Web Parts available for data sources defined in the BDC; it is only if those do not meet your needs that you may want to use a Data View and, therefore, need to define a reference to entries in the BDC.
Linked sources	Many data sources contain related data. You can use this data source group to combine two or more data sources into one source.
Connecting to other sites and site collections	You can access the Data Source Library of another site so that you can share its data connection definitions.

Because of the ease with which you can connect to data sources, you may unwittingly overload the Web server or create heavy network traffic while the data is retrieved from the data sources. You should decide whether you really need all the data that your connection query returns. To monitor page hits, you can use the reports provided by SharePoint Designer and the SharePoint site administration pages.

In addition, when the Data View contains a large number of rows, it may take some time for the page to render. You can use filters to limit the number of rows displayed; however, if all the data is not needed, it is better to amend the data connection query to return a smaller portion of data than to use the Data View filtering methods to limit the data.

> **Tip** Some data sources provide a mechanism to update their content. Two data source that may allow you to both view and update their content are Databases and XML services and, therefore, you will need to contact your database administrator or developer for details of the connection string, commands, query strings, and parameters you might need to use to do this. In addition, the data retrieval service is not configured to use the OLE DB protocol to update databases; however, your SharePoint administrator can use the Central Administration site or the SharePoint command-line tool, *stsadm*, to configure the data retrieval service to alter this and other settings.

When defining a data connection, you need to consider the authentication method used to connect to the data sources, because this has security and infrastructure implications. For example, when you connect to a database, the authentication method you use depends on the database location, the database access provider, and whether you use Windows SharePoint Services or SharePoint Server 2007. Consider the following:

- When you use Window SharePoint Services to connect to a SQL Server database, you need to use SQL Server authentication and specify the SQL Server user name and password in the connection query defined in the Data Source Library. The user name and password is transmitted over the network in clear text, which could have security implications.

- When you use SharePoint Server to connect to a SQL Server database, you must use single sign-on (SSO) authentication.

See Also For more information about using SSO authentication to connect to databases, see "Add a database as a data source" at *office.microsoft.com/en-us/sharepointdesigner/ HA101009081033.aspx* and "An Introduction to Single Sign-On (SSO) with Data Views" at *blogs.msdn.com/sharepointdesigner/archive/2007/08/27/an-introduction-to-single-sign-on-sso-with-data-views.aspx.*

> **Caution** Some data providers expose user permissions that affect the data displayed in the Data View. When a user does not have the right to view the data, not only might the Data View be affected, but also the page itself might not render. As you create a solution by using the Data Source Library task pane and Data Views, test your solution with users who need to access the data.

Every time you open the Data Source Library task pane, SharePoint Designer dynamically populates the task pane with references to the site's lists, libraries, and XML files. No other data sources are defined when you first create a site. These dynamically created definitions return all the available data. If you want to display only a subset of the data, you must use Data View filtering methods. Alternatively, you can create copies of the data sources for lists, libraries, and XML files and explicitly define the data to retrieve.

Each data source group in the Data Source Library task pane provides a link to create a new data source, where you specify the location and connection query to the data source. When you create the first data source for a site, SharePoint Designer creates a document library named the *fpdatasources* library in the *_catalogs* folder. This document library is visible only by using SharePoint Designer. SharePoint Designer then creates an XML file that contains the data connection information, in *Universal Data Connection (UDC)* version 1 file format, and stores it in the fpdatasources library. You can open these XML files in the SharePoint Designer document window and manually modify the data connection information, but the next time you use the Data Source Library to modify your data sources, you lose any modifications you have already manually entered.

In this exercise, you will use the Data Source Library task pane to create and modify a data connection for a SharePoint library.

> **USE** your own SharePoint site location in place of the *teams.consolidatedmessenger.com* team site.
>
> **OPEN** the site in SharePoint Designer.

1. In the **Folder List** task pane, expand **_catalogs**, and then expand **fpdatasources** if it is present.

2. If the **Data Source Library** task pane is not already open, click **Data Source Library** on the **Task Panes** menu.

3. Under **SharePoint Lists**, click **Announcements**, and then click **Copy and Modify**.

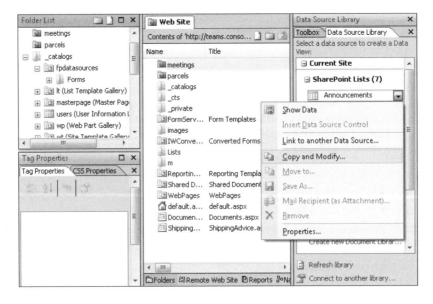

The Data Source Properties dialog box opens.

4. Under **Query**, click **Fields** to open the **Included Fields** dialog box.

5. In the **Included Fields** list, while holding down the [Shift] or [Ctrl] key, click all but the ID field. Then click **Remove** so that only ID appears in the list.

6. In the **Available Fields** list, while holding down [Ctrl], click **Title**, **Body**, and **Modified By**. Then click **Add**.

7. Click **OK** to close the **Included Fields** dialog box.

8. In the Data Source Properties dialog box, click the **General** tab, and in the **Name** text box, type AnnouncementsTitleBody.

9. Click **OK** to close the **Data Source Properties** dialog box.

In the Folder List task pane, the fpdatasources document library appears (if it didn't already exist), containing AnnouncementsTitleBody.xml. In the Data Source Library task pane, the number in brackets to the right of SharePoint Lists has increased by one, showing that this data source group now contains an extra data connection, and AnnoucementsTitleBody appears under the SharePoint Lists.

10. In the **Data Source Library** task pane, click **AnnouncementsTitleBody**, and then click **Show Data**.

The Data Source Details task pane opens and displays only these XML attributes: ID, Title, Body, Modified By, and PermMask. The other fields that the Announcements list contains are not retrieved.

11. In the **Folder List** task pane, double-click **AnnouncementsTitleBody.xml**.

The XML file opens in the document window with the data connection location and query information specified as XML data all on one line.

12. Right-click within the **AnnouncementsTitleBody.xml** document window, and then click **Reformat XML**.

The XML data is redisplayed, indented and with each XML element on a new line. The DataSourceControl contains the data connection information.

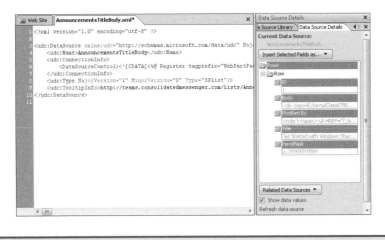

CLOSE the *AnnouncementsTitleBody.xml* file, and save it if prompted to do so.

Working with XML Data

Using the Data Source Library, you can work with XML data stored in XML files. If these files are located on your site, SharePoint Designer dynamically creates a data connection for each file under the data source XML Files access group. If you import an XML file into a site, a corresponding connection automatically appears in the Data Source Library. As you delete or add XML files to your site, the data connections dynamically appear and disappear from the Data Source Library task pane. If you do not want to retrieve all the data from the XML file, as with lists and libraries, you can copy and modify the data connection. However, if you delete the XML file, the copy of the XML file data connection remains listed in the Data Source Library task pane, and if you click *Show Data* using that copy of data connection, an error message appears in the Data Source Details task pane.

> **Note** When you work with an XML file as a data source, the XML file must contain only well-formed XML; otherwise, it may cause errors. In addition, either the XML file must contain and conform to a schema, or it must contain data from which a schema can be inferred.

In this exercise, you will add an XML file from your file system to your site.

> **USE** the site you modified in the pervious exercise, and the *Shipments.xml* file. This practice file is located in the *Documents\Microsoft Press\SPD2007_SBS\DataSources* folder.
>
> **OPEN** the site in SharePoint Designer, if it is not already open, and display the Data Source Library task pane.

1. In the **Data Source Library** task pane, expand **XML Files**, and then click **Add an XML file**.

   The Data Source Properties dialog box opens.

2. On the **Source** tab, click **Browse** to open the **File Open** dialog box.

3. Navigate to *Documents\Microsoft Press\SPD2007_SBS\DataSources*, click **Shipments.xml**, and then click **Open**.

   A Microsoft Office SharePoint Designer message box opens, asking if you'd like to import the file.

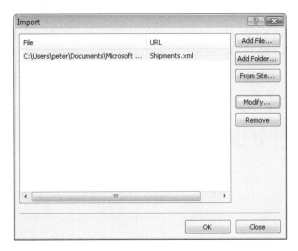

4. Click **OK** to import the file.

   The Microsoft Office SharePoint Designer message box closes, and the Import dialog box opens.

5. Click **Modify** to open the **Edit URL** dialog box.

6. In the **File location within your web** text box, type Shared Documents/
   Shipments.xml.

7. Click **OK** to close the **Edit URL** dialog box, and then click **OK** to close the **Import**
   dialog box.

   In the Data Source Library task pane, *Shipments.xml* appears, and in the Folder List
   task pane under the *Shared Documents* library, *Shipments.xml* is listed. There is no
   corresponding UDC XML file in the fpdatasources library.

8. In the **Folder List** task pane, under **Shared Documents**, right-click **Shipments.xml**,
   and then click **Delete**.

   The Confirm Delete message box opens.

9. Click **Yes** to close the **Confirm Delete** message box.

   Shipments.xml disappears from both the Shared Documents library and the Data
   Source Library task pane.

Connecting to an RSS Feed XML File

You can use the Add An XML File link in the Data Source Library task pane to connect
to an XML file located on an external server. You do not import the XML file to your site;
instead, you link the external XML file to the site by using its URL.

One popular external XML file is the one produced by an RSS feed. Servers that publish
their content as XML data that conforms to the RSS format are said to have an RSS feed.
Many Internet-facing servers produce RSS formatted XML data either as an XML file or
as a server-side script that produces RSS formatted XML data.

> **Note** Starting with Windows SharePoint Services 3.0, lists and libraries can expose their content by using RSS.

In this exercise, you will retrieve data published by an external server by linking to an XML file.

> **Important** In this exercise, you access an RSS feed over the Internet; therefore, to complete this exercise, you must have Internet access.

> **USE** the site you modified in the pervious exercise.
>
> **OPEN** the site in SharePoint Designer, if it is not already open, and display the Data Source Library task pane.

1. In the **Data Source Library** task pane, expand **XML Files**, and then click **Add an XML file**.

   The Data Source Properties dialog box opens.

2. On the **Source** tab, in the **Location** text box, type http://blogs.msdn.com/sharepointdesigner/rss.xml.

3. Click the **General** tab, and in the **Name** text box, type SharePoint Designer team blog or some other name for the RSS feed.

4. Click the **Login** tab, and verify that **Don't attempt to authenticate** is selected.

5. Click **OK** to close the **Data Source Properties** dialog box.

The SharePoint Designer Team Blog data connection appears in the Data Source Library task pane.

6. In the **Data Source Library** task pane, click **SharePoint Designer team blog**, and then click **Show Data**.

The Data Source Details task pane appears, displaying an XML root element, named *rss*, with a child element named *channel* that contains a number of *item* child elements.

Connecting to an RSS Feed Server-Side Script

With the popularity of RSS feeds, many products support this XML data format, with the result that many organizations are using the RSS *XML data schema* as a basis for exposing data not traditionally considered as RSS data. These companies use server-side scripts to produce the XML data because scripts allow more control over the XML data. The XML data produced by server-side scripts can be dependent on parameter values, where the values transmitted to the external server are either appended to the end of the URL, known as the *HTTP GET method*, or provided in the body of the request, known as the *HTTP POST method*. The HTTP GET method uses simple queries to GET (retrieve) data and is the safer method as far as the external server is concerned. The HTTP POST method is usually used to POST (send) data or instruct the external server to manipulate the data.

Whether you want to view (which in database terminology is referred to as select), insert, update, or delete data on the external server, you use the Data Source Properties dialog box to configure each command.

When you create data connections by using either XML files or server-side scripts, you may need to configure the authentication method to access the XML data. The Data Source Properties dialog box provides a choice of four options:

● **Don't Attempt To Authenticate.** Use this option for external servers that accept anonymous access or if users must supply their usernames and passwords.

- **Save This Username And Password In The Data Connection.** Use this option if the XML data is password protected and you want anyone to be able to access the data without being prompted for a user name and password. The user name and password will be transmitted over the network as clear text; so you may need to contact your IT Department to add further infrastructure security.

- **Use Windows Authentication.** Use this option when Windows SharePoint Services and the XML file are located on the same server.

- **Use Single Sign-On Authentication.** This option requires SharePoint Server. See the note earlier in this chapter about SSO.

In this exercise, you will retrieve XML data by using a server-side script.

> **Important** In this exercise, you access an RSS feed over the Internet; therefore, to complete this exercise, you must have Internet access.

USE the site you modified in the pervious exercise.

OPEN the site in SharePoint Designer, if it is not already open, and display the Data Source Library task pane.

1. Open your browser, and in the address text box, type http://search.technet. microsoft.com.

   The Microsoft TechNet site opens.

2. In the **Search** text box, type sharepoint designer, and then press [Enter] to display the search results.

   ![Microsoft TechNet Search Results page]

   Microsoft *TechNet*

   Search Results   MSDN / TechNet Search Blog ▾ | Subscribe ▾ | Feedback? | Got IE7? - Get our search.

   | sharepoint designer | 🔍 ▾ | powered by Live Search |

   Refine your search by: Results in:
   English (United
   - TechNet & MSDN Blogs   • Microsoft TechNet   • Learning   • Forefront Client Security Center   • Intelligent Application Gateway   States)
   - SharePoint Products & Technologies   • Support: Knowledge Base & Forums   • Windows Server   • Microsoft PressBooks   • Internet Explorer

   Results 1-50 of approximately 66800 for: sharepoint designer (0.2 seconds)   1   2   3   ▸

   Microsoft **SharePoint Designer** Team Blog : **SharePoint Designer** Data ...
   Would you like to help shape the future of how Microsoft Office **SharePoint Designer** works with data inside your **SharePoint** application? And be entered in a sweepstakes to win 1 of ...
   http://blogs.msdn.com/sharepointdesigner/archive/2007/09/19/sharepoint-designer-data-team-survey.aspx

RSS Icon

3. In the **Results** row, right-click the RSS icon, and then click **Copy Shortcut**.

4. In SharePoint Designer, in the **Data Source Library** task pane, expand **Server-side Scripts**, and then click **Connect to a script or RSS feed**.

The Data Source Properties dialog box opens.

5. Right-click the **Enter the URL to a server-side script** text box, and then click **Paste**.

6. Click the **Add or Modify Parameters** list box.

The parameters from the server-side script appear in the Add Or Modify Parameters list box. The *query* string has a value of *sharepoint designer*.

7. On the **General** tab, in the **Name** text box, type Microsoft TechNet Search.

8. Click **OK** to close the **Data Source Properties** dialog box.

The Microsoft TechNet Search data connection appears in the Data Source Library task pane.

9. Click **Microsoft TechNet Search**, and then click **Show Data**.

The Data Source Details task pane opens, that displays a number of item elements. Each item element displays information that was returned by the TechNet Search site as the result of searching for the terms *sharepoint designer*.

CLOSE the browser window.

Connecting to an XML Web Service

XML Web Services transport XML data between computer systems by using *Simple Object Access Protocol (SOAP)* over HTTP or HTTPS. SharePoint can act as an XML Web Services requester or client; that is, it can request XML data from an XML Web Service and present the data by using a Data View. SharePoint can also act as an XML Web Service provider, supplying XML data to other computer systems. As with server-side scripts, the requester can send XML data, instructions (known as *methods*), parameters, and values to the XML Web Service provider, depending on how the XML Web Service was written. The methods and parameters an XML Web Service supports are described in a *Web Service Description Language (WSDL)*. If supported, you will be able to select, insert, update, or delete data on the XML Web Service provider by using the Data Source Properties dialog box to configure each command.

See Also For more information about Windows SharePoint Services and SharePoint Server XML Web Services, search the Software Development Kits at *msdn2.microsoft.com/ms479390.aspx*.

In this exercise, you will add an XML Web service as a data source.

> **USE** the site you modified in the pervious exercise.
>
> **OPEN** the site in SharePoint Designer, if it is not already open, and display the Data Source Library task pane.

1. In the **Data Source Library** task pane, expand **XML Web Services**, and then click **Connect to a web service**.

    The Data Source Properties dialog box opens.

2. In the **Service description location** text box, type http://*<site>*/_vti_bin/webs. asmx?wsdl, where *<site>* is the URL of the top-level site of a site collection. For example, *<site>* might be *teams.consolidatedmessenger.com*. Then click **Connect Now**.

    > **Tip** If you cannot connect to the XML Web service or you get an error message that the server returned a non-specific error or the error message, *unable to display this Web Part when viewed using the browser*, then check the spelling of the server name *teams.consolidatedmessenger.com*, and the XML Web service *_vti_bin/webs. asmx?wsdl*. If you forget to type *?wsdl* after the name of the XML Web service, SharePoint Designer will append it to the URL. If you connect to an XML Web service on the Internet, your SharePoint Server Administrator may have to configure the *web. config* for proxy server settings. You can connect to other XML Web services at a child site level, in which case the service description location would become, for example: *http://<site>/_vit_bin/lists.asmx*, where *<site>* is the child site you created using the CD files for this chapter, such as *teams.consolidatedmessenger.com/datasources*.

SharePoint Designer connects to the server hosting the XML Web Service and populates the dialog box with the responses it received from the XML Web Service provider.

3. Click **OK** to close the **Data Source Properties** dialog box.

   The Webs On <*site*> data connection appears in the Data Source Library task pane.

4. Click **Webs On <*site*>**, and then click **Show Data**.

   The Data Source Details task pane opens, displaying an XML root element named *soap:Envelope*, which contains a number of child elements. Each *Web* element contains the title and URL of a site within the site collection.

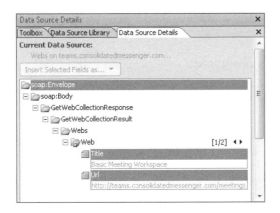

Using Linked Sources

Most organizations have data sources that contain interrelated data; for example, before customers purchase products, you may have to prepare estimates. After they place their orders, you have to prepare invoices. And, of course, you need to know where to send the products. The estimate, the invoice, and the customer contact all contain related data. In the Data Source Library, you can combine two or more related data sources so that you can expose the data in one Data View.

SharePoint Designer provides you with two options for combining related data:

● **Merge.** Use to combine data sources with the same set of fields; for example, you may store invoice data in many locations.

● **Join.** Use to combine data sources that have one field in common; for example, the customer reference number may link the customer details data source and invoice details data source.

In this exercise, you will combine two data sources into one linked data source.

USE the site you modified in the pervious exercise.

OPEN the site in SharePoint Designer, if it is not already open, and display the Data Source Library task pane.

1. In the **Data Source Library** task pane, expand **Linked sources**, and then click **Create a new linked source**.

   The Data Source Properties dialog box opens.

2. Click **Configure Linked Source** to start the **Link Data Sources Wizard**.

3. In the **Available Data Sources** list box, under **SharePoint Lists**, click **Products**, and then click **Add**.

4. Under **XML Files**, click **Consignments.xml**, and then click **Add**.

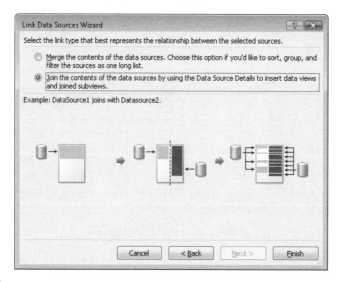

5. Click **Next** to display the next page of the Link Data Sources Wizard.

6. Click **Join the contents of the data sources by using the Data Source Details to insert data views and joined subviews**, and then click **Finish**.

The Link Data Sources Wizard closes. The Data Source Properties dialog box displays two data sources: Products and Consignments.xml.

Data Source Properties

General | **Source** | Query

Linked Data Source

Link Type: Join

[Configure Linked Source...]

Component source properties:

Data Source	Properties
Products	Edit
Consignments.xml	Edit

[OK] [Cancel]

7. On the **General** tab, in the **Name** text box, type Consignments, and then click **OK** to close the **Data Sources Properties** dialog box.

   The Consignments linked data source appears in the Data Source Library task pane.

New Document

8. On the Common toolbar, click **New Document**.

   Untitled_1.aspx opens in the document window.

9. On the **Data View** menu, click **Insert Data View**.

10. In the **Data Source Library** task pane, under **Linked sources**, click **Consignments**, and then click **Show Data**.

    The Data Source Details task pane opens displaying an XML root element named *dsQueryResponse* with two child elements: Products and Consignments. You may have to scroll down to see the Consignments child element.

11. In the **Data Source Details** task pane, under the **Products** element, click **Title**, and while holding down the Ctrl key, click **Description**; then click **Insert Selected Fields as**, and click **Multiple Item View**.

    The Untitled_1.aspx page is redisplayed, showing data from the Products list.

12. In the **DataFormWebPart** control, click **Description**, and then on the **Table** menu, point to **Insert**, and click **Column to the Right**.

13. Click a cell in the new column, and then in the **Data Source Details** task pane, under the **Shipments** child element, while holding down the ⎘Ctrl key, click **ConsignmentNumber**, **CustomerName**, and **CollectionDate**. Then click **Insert Selected Fields as** and **Joined Subview**.

The Joined Subview dialog box opens.

14. Under **Row**, click **Product_x0020_ID**, and under **Shipment**, click **ProductServicesID** to join the product list items to the consignment data.

> **Note** List items sometimes have internal names that do not match names you see in the task pane.

15. Click **OK** to close the **Joined Subview** dialog box.

The Untitled_1.aspx page is redisplayed, showing the columns from the Products list and data from the consignments XML file.

Title	Description	ConsignmentNumber	CustomerName	CollectionDate
Express 9:00	Express delivery by 09:00 next business day	123	Adventure Works	01-April-2008
		456	Blue Yonder Airlines	02-April-2008
		457	Blue Yonder Airlines	03-April-2008
Express 12:00	Express delivery by 12:00 next business day	ConsignmentNumber	CustomerName	CollectionDate
		789	Blue Yonder Airlines	01-April-2008
Express 16:00	Express delivery by 16:00 next business day	ConsignmentNumber	CustomerName	CollectionDate
		135	Contoso Pharmacueticals	01-April-2008
		124	Adventure Works	02-April-2008
Express Worldwide	Express delivery by End of next business day	ConsignmentNumber	CustomerName	CollectionDate
		Click to set the display text if no matching items are found.		

Save

16. On the Common toolbar, click **Save** to open the **Save As** dialog box.

17. Double-click **WebPages**, and in the **File name** text box, type ConsignmentsJoin.aspx. Then click **Save** to close the **Save As** dialog box.

Displaying the Contents of a List on Another Site

With the Data Source Library task pane, you can connect to another site and view data connections in its Data Source Library. This enables you to share data connection definitions across sites, which is particularly useful when many sites need to connect to the same data sources. For example, you could define all the data source connections on one central site, and then connect to the central site's Data Source Library from the other sites, using its data source connection to create your Data Views.

In this exercise, you will connect to another site and display the contents of its Data Source Library.

1. At the bottom of the **Data Source Library** task pane, click **Connect to another library**.

   The Manage Library dialog box opens.

2. Click **Add** to open the **Collection Properties** dialog box.

3. Click **Browse** to open the **Choose a Web site** dialog box.

4. In the **Web site URL** text box, type http://<*site*>, where <*site*> is the URL of another site, and then click **Open**. For example, <*site*> might be teams.consolidatedmessenger .com/parcels.

   The Choose A Web Site dialog box closes, and the URL of the parcels team site appears in the Location text box of the Collection Properties dialog box.

5. In the **Collection Properties** dialog box, in the **Display name** text box, type Parcels team site.

6. Click **OK**.

   The Collection Properties dialog box closes, and the Parcels team site appears in the Manage Library dialog box.

7. Click **OK** to close the **Manage Library** dialog box.

   The Data Source Library task pane refreshes and displays two sites: Current Site and Parcels team site.

8. Expand **Parcels team site**.

   SharePoint Designer connects with the other site, and then in the Data Source Library task pane, displays the contents of the Parcels team site Data Source Library. If the site is in the same site collection as the current site, both the SharePoint Lists and SharePoint Libraries access groups appear.

> **Tip** To modify, remove, or add new connections to other sites, click Connect To Another Library.

Connecting Web Parts

Web Parts, including Data Views, can exchange data, even when different companies produce the Web Parts, as long as they adhere to the Web Part connection interface specification. One Web Part acts as a data provider, while the other acts as a consumer of the data. A Web Part developer can choose to implement both the consumer and provider interfaces, one of the interfaces, or neither of the interfaces; for example, the List View Web Part of a Picture Library does not support Web Part connections. You can use a browser or SharePoint Designer to connect Web Parts, but SharePoint Designer provides you with additional options.

Typically, you connect Web Parts so that when you click an item in one Web Part, the contents in one or more other Web Parts change. The data sources that supply content to both provider and consumer Web Parts must share a common field that you use to link both the Web Parts. When you use a browser, you must display this common field in both Web Parts; however, this is not a requirement when you use Data Views and use SharePoint Designer to create the Web Part connection. Using SharePoint Designer, you can connect to Web Parts on the same page as well as Web Parts on other pages.

> **Note** A Web Part cannot connect to itself, either directly or through a series of Web Part connections.

In this exercise, you will create a Web Part connection to a Web Part on another page.

USE the site you modified in the pervious exercise.
OPEN the site in SharePoint Designer, if it is not already open.

1. In the **Folder List** task pane, expand **WebPages**, and double-click **Products.aspx** to open the page in the document window.
2. In **Design** view, right-click **Products**, and then click **Web Part Connections**.

   The Web Part Connections Wizard starts.

3. Click **Next** to display the second page of the **Web Part Connections Wizard**.

4. Click **Browse** to open the **Edit Hyperlink** dialog box.

5. Double-click **WebPages**, and then click **Consigments.aspx**.

   The Address text box now contains WebPages/Consignments.aspx.

6. Click **OK** to close the **Edit Hyperlink** dialog box.

   In the Web Part Connections Wizard, the Page text box contains Consignments.aspx.

7. Click **Next** to display the third page of the **Web Part Connections Wizard**.

8. Click **Next** to display the fourth page of the **Web Part Connections Wizard**.

9. Click the first cell under **Columns in Products**. Click the down arrow that appears in the cell, scroll down the list, and then click **ProductServicesID**.

10. Click **Next** to display the fifth page of the **Web Part Connections Wizard**.

11. Click **Next**, and then click **Finish** to close the **Web Part Connections Wizard**.

Save

12. On the Common toolbar, click **Save**.

    A Microsoft Office SharePoint Designer message box opens, warning you that both pages must be saved. If this warning message does not appear, save both files.

13. Click **OK** to save both pages.

14. Press [F12] to open Products.aspx in the browser.

15. Under **Express**, click **Express 9:00**.

    The Consignments.aspx page is displayed in a Multiple Item Form Data View format, showing three consignments for the Express 9:00 delivery service.

> **Tip** To remove a Web Part connection, right-click either Web Part, and then click Web Part Connections to display the Web Part Connections dialog box. Select the connection you want to remove, and then click Remove.

CLOSE SharePoint Designer if you are not continuing directly to the next chapter.

Key Points

- With the Data Source Library task pane, you can create and manage data connections to a variety of data sources, including lists, libraries, XML files, server-side scripts, XML Web services, Business Data Catalog, linked sources, and Data Sources Libraries on other sites.

- Data connections describe a location and query that the Windows SharePoint Services data retrieval service uses to obtain the data from the data sources.

- The data retrieval services on the Web server returns data in an XML format that SharePoint Designer and Data Views understand.

- SharePoint Designer dynamically creates a data connection for each list, library, and XML file for the current site.

- You can copy and modify the data connection, specifying a different set of fields, filters, or sort order for a specific data source.

- The fields and filters defined in the data connections control the amount of data that is retrieved from the data sources. Consider carefully your data connection configuration to minimize the load on the Web servers, the amount of data transmitted over the network, and the time to render a page.

- Web Parts, including Data Views, can exchange data by using Web Part connections.

Chapter at a Glance

Use standard ASP.NET controls, **page 189**

Modify controls, **page 186**

Use ASP.NET validation controls, **page 191**

Insert controls, **page 186**

Use SharePoint Data View controls, **page 195**

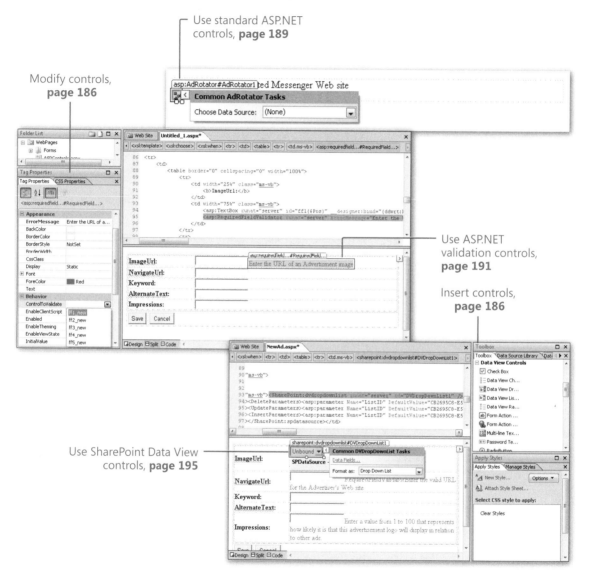

8 Using Controls in Web Pages

In this chapter, you will learn to:

✔ Insert and modify controls.

✔ Use standard ASP.NET controls.

✔ Use ASP.NET validation controls.

✔ Use SharePoint Data View controls.

✔ Use SharePoint Server controls.

Microsoft Windows SharePoint Services and Microsoft Office SharePoint Server 2007 are Microsoft ASP.NET 2.0 applications. ASP.NET is part of the Microsoft .NET Framework and enables you to separate user interface declarations from application logic. User interface declarations are typically HTML. The application logic is precompiled into *dynamic-link libraries (DLLs)* that reside on Web servers and are fast to load when a Web server needs to respond to a Web page request. These DLLs contain code for commonly used tasks, such as displaying a calendar, and are exposed in the user interface as *controls*.

Microsoft Office SharePoint Designer 2007 categorizes controls into three groups: HTML controls, ASP.NET controls, and SharePoint controls. Controls are very similar to Web Parts; you place them on a page and customize their properties to meet your needs.

See Also For more information about controls, read the article at *msdn2.microsoft.com/ 7698y1f0.aspx* and visit *www.w3schools.com/aspnet/*.

In this chapter, you will first insert ASP.NET and HTML controls on a page. You will then create pages that use standard ASP.NET controls, ASP.NET validation controls, and SharePoint Data View controls. You will also review SharePoint Server controls.

> **Important** Before you can use the practice files in this chapter, you need to install them from the book's companion CD to their default location. You will need to create a practice site for this chapter based on the site template *Controls_Starter.stp*, located in this chapter's practice file folder. Then when you perform the exercises in this chapter, remember to use your SharePoint site location in place of *teams.consolidatedmessenger.com*.
>
> For more information about practice files, see "Using the Book's CD" at the beginning of this book.

> **Troubleshooting** Graphics and operating system–related instructions in this book reflect the Windows Vista user interface. If your computer is running Windows XP and you experience trouble following the instructions as written, please refer to the "Information for Readers Running Windows XP" section at the beginning of this book.

Inserting and Modifying Controls

Many experienced users of SharePoint Designer 2007 consider the Toolbox and the Tag Properties task panes to be the most important task panes because they allow easy access to a large number of controls and their properties.

The Toolbox task pane includes the following groups of controls:

- **HTML controls.** This group is further categorized into Tags (such as <div>, <br>, and <hr>) for static display and Form Controls for user input.

- **ASP.NET controls.** SharePoint Designer 2007 includes ASP.NET controls similar to those exposed by the Microsoft Visual Studio Toolbox task pane. In both products, the controls are classified into Standard, Data, Validation, Navigation, Login, and WebParts groups. The big difference is that when you use ASP.NET controls in Visual Studio, you can write and compile code into an assembly that can be deployed on each Web server, which you cannot do with SharePoint Designer.

- **SharePoint controls.** These controls are ASP.NET controls specific to Windows SharePoint Services and SharePoint Server 2007 installations.

With SharePoint Designer, you create the presentation layer of a page. On the page, you place HTML tags, XSLT, client-side scripts, and controls that can be interpreted by SharePoint or the browser. You do not specify any server-side code that needs to be compiled, such as code written in a programming language like C# (pronounced *C sharp*), Visual Basic (commonly abbreviated as *VB*), or Visual J# (pronounced *J sharp*). However, each page does have a language associated with it.

SharePoint uses server-side controls, which execute code on the Web servers. SharePoint controls are prefixed by a set of characters that point to the DLLs, also known as *assemblies*; the entry points within an assembly are known as *namespaces*. All controls that are similar are placed in the same *namespace*. The prefix characters are used throughout the page to reference the controls in the assembly so that the full name of the namespace is not necessary. The controls contain a number of attributes (such as the *runat="server"* attribute) that identify them as server controls. They contain an *id* attribute that allows you to identify controls by name and also allows the code on the Web servers to manipulate the controls so that the correct tags and data are sent back to render a page correctly in the browser.

A control's attributes are known as *properties*. You can alter the behavior and appearance of a control by modifying its properties in the Tag Properties task pane or in Code view (in which case, SharePoint Designer provides Microsoft IntelliSense to help you).

In this exercise, you will insert controls from the Toolbox task pane and set control properties in the Tag Properties task pane.

> **USE** your own SharePoint site location in place of the *teams.consolidatedmessenger.com* team site shown in the exercise.
>
> **OPEN** the Controls child site in SharePoint Designer.

New Document

1. On the Common toolbar, click the **New Document** arrow, and then in the list, click **Page**.

   The New dialog box opens.

2. In the list of file types, click **ASPX**.

3. Under **Options**, in the **Programming Language** list, make sure **C#** is selected.

4. Click **OK** twice to close the open dialog boxes.

   The Untitled_1.aspx file opens in the document window, showing an empty form.

5. At the bottom of the **Untitled_1.aspx** document window, click **Split**.

   The Edit window divides horizontally and displays Code view in the upper pane and Design view in the lower pane. Code view reveals an *@Page* directive that sets the language for the page, and one *<form>* element containing a *runat* attribute with a value of *server*.

6. On the **Task Panes** menu, click **Toolbox**.

   The Toolbox task pane opens.

7. In the **ASP.NET Controls** section, under **Standard**, double-click **Label**.

SharePoint Designer adds the Label control inside the form element. The *asp: label#Label1* tag is active on the Quick Tag Selector. The Tag Properties task pane shows the properties of the Label control.

> **Tip** If the Tag Properties task pane is not open, click Tag Properties on the Task Pane menu.

8. In the **Misc** section of the **Tag Properties** task pane, click the cell to the right of **ID**, and type lblWelcome. Then press Enter.

   In the Design portion of the document window, the tag control is named *asp: label#lblWelcome*, where *lblWelcome* is the ID of the ASP.NET label control. This tag is active on the Quick Tag Selector. In the Code portion of the window, the ID of the label control is set to *lblWelcome*.

9. In the **Tag Properties** task pane, click the expand (+) icon next to **Appearance**, click the cell to the right of **Text**, type Welcome to the Consolidated Messenger Web site, and then press Enter.

   In Code view, the *Text* attribute is set to *Welcome to the Consolidated Messenger Web site* and in Design view, the text appears within the asp:label control.

10. In the document window, place the insertion point to the right of the word **site**. In the **HTML** section of the **Toolbox** task pane, under **Tags**, double-click **Break** to insert a line break.

11. On the Common toolbar, click **Save**.

12. In the **Save as type** list of the Save As dialog box, double-click **WebPages**. In the **File name** text box, type ASPControls.aspx. Then click **Save**.

Using Standard ASP.NET Controls

Although you can use HTML controls on all types of pages, the real power comes when you use ASP.NET controls. ASP.NET controls appear in the Toolbox task pane in the following groups:

- **Standard.** This group contains a standard set of controls, such as buttons, check boxes, drop-down lists, image maps, and calendar and wizard controls.

- **Data.** This group has two types of controls:

  - **View controls** allow you to view the content from data sources in sophisticated grids and lists, very similar to List View Web Parts (LVWPs) and Data Views.

  - **Data source controls** allow you to define a data source.

    Before you use a view control, you must insert a data source control on the page. You then bind the data source control to the view control. You can create a data source control from a data source in the Data Source Library or use one of the data source controls in the Data group.

- **Validation.** A set of controls that allows you to validate data entered on a Web form.

- **Navigation.** The Menu, SiteMapPath, and TreeView controls in this group allow you to navigate among pages in a site.

- **Login.** These controls support form authentication and allow you to create a membership system.

- **WebParts.** This group is empty if you open a SharePoint site. You manage Web Parts on SharePoint sites from the Web Parts task pane.

In this exercise, you will add one of the Standard ASP.NET controls, the AdRotator control, to a page. The AdRotator control displays a sequence of images, chosen randomly from a set of images specified in an XML file known as the *advertisement file*.

> **USE** the site you modified in the previous exercise.
>
> **OPEN** the site in SharePoint Designer, if it is not already open, and display the Toolbox task pane and the *ASPControls.aspx* page.

1. In the **Folder List** task pane, expand the **Shared Documents** section, and then double-click **AdRotator.xml**.

   The AdRotator.xml file opens in the document window, displaying the XML data needed by the AdRotator ASP.NET control.

2. Click the **Close** button, and then click the **ASPControls.aspx** page tab if the page is not the active file in the document window.

Close

3. In the document window, click the horizontal line under **Welcome to the Consolidated Messenger Web site**.

4. In the **ASP.NET Controls** section of the **Toolbox** task pane, under **Standard**, double-click **AdRotator**.

   The AdRotator control is added to the page inside the form tags and the Common AdRotator Tasks list opens.

asp:AdRotator#AdRotator1 |ted Messenger Web site
Common AdRotator Tasks
Choose Data Source: (None)   ▾

   > **Tip** ASP.NET controls must be placed inside a form. SharePoint Designer will automatically insert ASP.NET controls within form tags.

5. In the **Tag Properties** task pane, scroll to the **Behavior** section and expand it if necessary.

6. Click the cell to the right of **AdvertisementFile**, and then click the ellipsis button.

   Ellipsis

7. In the **Select XML File** dialog box, within the Controls site, navigate to the **Shared Documents** library, click **AdRotator.xml**, and then click **Open**.

   > **Tip** If the Save As dialog box does not automatically open showing the contents of the Controls child site, then under Favorite Links, click your site.

8. In the **Tag Properties** task pane, click the cell to the right of **AlternateTextField**, and type Welcome Advertisements.

9. In the **Tag Properties** task pane, click the cell to the right of **KeywordFilter**, type Shipping, and then press [Enter].

   Only advertisement images associated with that keyword are displayed.

Tag Properties	☐ ✕
Tag Properties CSS Properties	✕

   `<asp:AdRotator#AdRotator1>`

ForeColor	
⊟ **Behavior**	
AdvertisementFile	../Shared Documents/AdRo...
AlternateTextField	Welcome Advertisements
Enabled	True
EnableTheming	True
EnableViewState	True
ImageUrlField	ImageUrl
KeywordFilter	Shipping
NavigateUrlField	NavigateUrl

Save

10. On the Common toolbar, click **Save**. Then press [F12] to open **ASPControls.aspx** in your default browser.

Refresh

11. Click the **Refresh** button several times to see the advertisement image change from **Consolidated Messenger** to **Wide World Importers**.

The third image specified in the *AdRotator.xml* is not associated with the keyword *Shipping* and should not appear.

> **CLOSE** any open pages and browser windows.

Using ASP.NET Validation Controls

You can validate the data of input controls by using a validation control. The input controls can be HTML input tags or standard ASP.NET controls. However, they cannot be SharePoint controls, because they contain their own validation mechanisms based on columns settings in lists or libraries. ASP.NET includes six validation controls that solve the common validation scenarios encountered in many Web developments:

- **CompareValidator.** Compares the data entered in one field with the data entered in another field to see if the data matches.

- **CustomValidator.** Allows you to write your own validation code. This code could be server-side code or client-side code, such as code written in JavaScript or Microsoft Visual Basic Scripting Edition (VBScript). If server-side code is required, you will need to involve a developer.

- **RangeValidator.** Ensures the value entered by a user falls within a certain range.

- **RegularExpressionValidator.** Validates the data against a specific pattern.

- **RequiredFieldValidator.** Checks that a user enters data in a field.

- **ValidationSummary.** Displays a summary of validation errors for a page.

These server-side controls can be configured by using the EnableClientScript property, to complete the validation process on either the client or the server. The controls generating JavaScript will be run on a user's computer when the user browses to the page. The ASP.NET controls link to a JavaScript file, WebUIValidation.js, which is sent down to the browser when the user requests the page. By supporting client-side validation, there is no round trip to the server to validate the user's input; as the user tabs between input fields, the error message is displayed. After the page is validated, it is posted back to the server, where the validation process is repeated to guard against a security breach at the network level.

In this exercise, you will create a data entry form and use the validation controls to verify data input. You will then configure the validation controls to associate them with input controls and to define error messages.

> **USE** the site you modified in the previous exercise.
>
> **OPEN** the site in SharePoint Designer, if it is not already open.

New Document

1. On the Common toolbar, click **New Document**.

   The Untitled_1.aspx page opens in the document window.

2. On the **Data View** menu, click **Manage Data Sources** to display the **Data Source Library** task pane.

3. Expand the **XML Files** section, if necessary. Point to **AdRotator.xml**, click the arrow that appears, and then click **Show Data**.

   The Data Source Details task pane opens.

4. Click **Insert Selected Fields as**, and then click **New Item Form**.

   A DataFormWebPart control is added to the new page with the Common Data View Tasks list open.

5. Click the text box to the right of **ImageUrl**, and then click the chevron that appears.

   The Common TextBox Tasks list opens showing that the text box is bound to the *ImageUrl* data field, and the Data View XSLT will format the field as a *text box*. Similarly, all the text boxes on this page are bound to elements within the XML file.

The tag name of the ImageUrl text box is *asp:textbox#ff1_new* and, therefore, the ID of this control must be set to *ff1_new*.

> **Warning** If you change the IDs of these ASP.NET controls, the data bindings to the XML fields in the *AdRotator.xml* file will be lost, and your new form will not function correctly.

6. On the **Task Panes** menu, click **Toolbox** to open the **Toolbox** task pane.

7. In the **Toolbox** task pane, under **ASP.NET Controls**, expand the **Validation** section to display the six validation controls.

8. With the **ImageUrl** text box still selected, in the **Toolbox** task pane, double-click **RequiredFieldValidator**.

The RequiredFieldValidator control appears to the right of the ImageURL text box and the Tag Properties task pane shows the controls properties.

9. In the **Tag Properties** task pane, under **Appearance**, type Enter the URL of an Advertisement image in the cell to the right of **ErrorMessage**.

10. In the **Tag Properties** task pane, under **Behavior**, click the cell to the right of **ControlToValidate**, click the arrow that appears, and then click **ff1_new**.

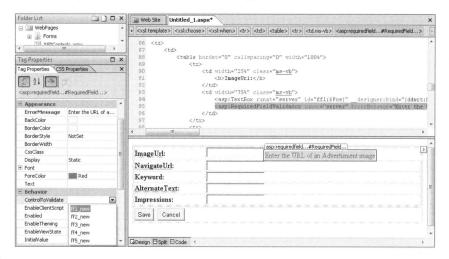

11. In the document window, click the text box to the right of **NavigateURL**.

The tag *asp:textbox#ff2_new* appears above the text box.

12. In the **Toolbox** task pane, double-click **RequiredFieldValidator**, and then double-click **RegularExpressionValidator**.

The two ASP.NET validation controls appear to the right of the NavigationUrl text box.

13. To the right of the **NavigateURL** text box, click **RequiredFieldValidator**. In the **Tag Properties** task pane, under **Behavior**, click the cell to the right of **ControlToValidate**, click the arrow that appears, and then click **ff2_new**.

14. To the right of the **NavigateURL** text box, click **RegularExpressionValidator** to show the control's properties in the **Tag Properties** task pane.

15. In the **Tag Properties** task pane, under **Appearance**, in the cell to the right of **ErrorMessage**, type Enter the valid URL for the Advertiser's Web site.

16. Under **Behavior**, click the cell to the right of **ControlToValidate**, click the arrow that appears, and then click **ff2_new**.

Ellipsis

17. Under **Behavior**, click the cell to the right of **ValidationExpression**, and then click the ellipsis button that appears.

18. In the **Regular Expression Editor** dialog box, under **Standard expressions**, click **Internet URL**.

A regular expression appears in the Validation Expression text box.

```
Regular Expression Editor                    ? ✕

Standard expressions:

German phone number                          ▲
German postal code
Internet e-mail address
Internet URL
Japanese phone number
Japanese postal code                         ▼

Validation expression:

http(s)?://([\w-]+\.)+[\w-]+(/[\w- ./?%&=]*)?

              OK            Cancel
```

19. Click **OK** to close the **Regular Expression Editor** text box.

20. In the document window, click the text box to the right of **Impressions**.

The tag *asp:textbox#ff5_new* appears above the text box.

21. In the **Toolbox** task pane, double-click **RangeValidator**.

The ASP.NET validation control appears to the right of the **Impressions** text box.

22. Click **RangeValidator** to show the control's properties in the **Tag Properties** task pane.

23. In the **Tag Properties** task pane, under **Appearance**, in the cell to the right of **ErrorMessage**, type Enter a value from 1 to 100 that represents how likely it is that this advertisement logo will display in relation to other ads.

24. Under **Behavior**, in the **ControlToValidate** list, click **ff5_new**.

25. Under **Behavior**, enter 100 in the **MaximumValue** cell, enter 1 in the **MinimumValue** cell, and then click **Integer** in the **Type** list.

26. On the Common toolbar, click **Save**.

Save

27. In the **Save As** dialog box, with the contents of the **WebPages** library displayed, type NewAd.aspx in the **File name** text box. Then click **Save**.

28. Press F12 to open **NewAd.aspx** in the browser.

29. In the **NavigateUrl** text box, type www.nosite, and then press Tab.

The insertion point moves to the Keyword text box and the message *Enter the valid URL for the Advertiser's Web site* appears.

30. In the **Impressions** text box, type none, and then click **Save**.

Three error messages appear.

ImageUrl:		Enter the URL of an Advertisment image
NavigateUrl:	www.nosite	Enter the valid URL for the Advertiser's Web site.
Keyword:		
AlternateText:		
Impressions:	none	Enter a value from 1 to 100 that represents how likely it is that this advertisement logo will display in relation to other ads.

Save   Cancel

> **Tip** The space to the left of the *Enter the valid URL error* message is for the error message associated with *NavigateURL RequiredFieldValidator* control. You can hide the space by setting the *Display* property of the *RequiredFieldValidator* control to *Dynamic*.

CLOSE the browser.

Using SharePoint Data View Controls

The Toolbox task pane categorizes SharePoint controls in four groups: Data View controls, Server Controls, Page Fields, and Content Fields. The first two control groups require only Windows SharePoint Services or SharePoint Server 2007, whereas the other two control groups will list controls only if you have a Microsoft SharePoint Publishing Page Layout page open. In this chapter, you will use the Data View controls and Server controls.

See Also For information about Page Field and Content Field controls, see Chapter 11, "Managing Web Content in a SharePoint Server Environment." SharePoint controls and their properties are described in the Windows SharePoint Services and SharePoint Server Software Development Kits.

By using SharePoint Data View controls, you can expose data from one of the data sources defined in the Data Source Library. One of the best forms of data entry validation methods is to allow users to choose from a set of options, thereby preserving data integrity. In lists and libraries, when one list contains data that you want to use in another list, you can use a lookup column. Data View controls enable you to bind to one data source, exposing the data as check boxes, radio buttons, or drop-down lists from which the user can choose. The selected input is then used in a different data source.

In this exercise, you will insert a Data View control so that a user can choose data from one data source as input to another data source.

USE the site you modified in the previous exercise.

OPEN the site in SharePoint Designer, if it is not already open, and display the Toolbox task pane and the *NewAd.aspx* page.

1. In the document window, click the text box to the right of **ImageUrl**, and then press [Del].

2. Click **Enter the URL of an Advertisement image**, and then press [Del].

   The *td.ms-vb* HTML cell should now be empty.

3. On the **Data View** menu, click **Manage Data Sources**.

   The Data Source Library task pane opens.

4. Expand the **SharePoint Libraries** section, point to **PictLib**, click the arrow that appears, and then click **Insert Data Source Control**.

   An SPDataSource control appears to the right of ImageUrl.

   > **Tip** If the *SPDataSource* control is not visible on the page, then on the View menu, point to Visual Aids, and click ASP.NET Non-visual Controls.

5. Click the **SPDataSource** control to show the control's properties in the **Tag Properties** task pane.

6. In the **Tag Properties** task pane, under **Misc**, click the cell to the right of **ID**, type SPPictLib, and then press [Enter].

   The tag above the SPDataSource control changes to *SharePoint: SPDataSource#SPPictLib*.

7. On the **Insert** menu, point to **SharePoint Controls**, and then click **More SharePoint Controls**.

   The Toolbox task pane opens with the SharePoint controls section displayed.

8. In the **Toolbox** task pane, double-click **Data View DropDownList**.

   In the document window, a drop-down list appears on the page, displaying a chevron and the tag name *sharepoint:dvdropdownlist#DVDropDownList1*above it. The text, *Unbound*, appears within the list.

Chevron

9. Click the chevron to open the **Common DVDropDownList Tasks** list.

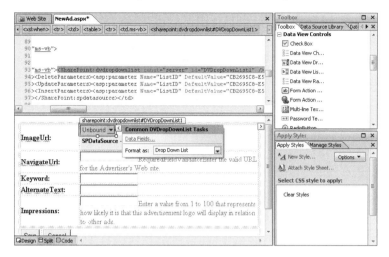

10. In the **Common DVDropDownList Tasks** list, click **Data Fields**.

The Change Data Bindings dialog box opens. In the Select A Data Source list, *SPPictLib* is already selected because there is only one data source control on the page.

11. In the **Select a data field to save values to** list, click **ImageUrl**.

12. In the **Select a data field for the display text** list, click **Title**.

13. In the **Select a data field for the value** list, click **URL Path**.

14. In the **Change Data Bindings** dialog box, click **OK**.

The *sharepoint:dvdropdownlist#DVDropDownList1* control contains the word *Databound*.

15. On the Common toolbar, click **Save**. Then press ⟨F12⟩ to open **NewAd.aspx** in the browser.

Save

16. In the **ImageUrl** list, click **Wide World Importers logo**.

17. Press [Tab] to move to the **NavigateUrl** input text box, and then type http://portal.wideworldimporters.com.

18. Press [Tab] three times to move to the **Impressions** input text box, and type 30.

19. Click **Save**.

The page refreshes and displays an empty form.

20. In the **Folder List** task pane, under **Shared Documents**, double-click **AdRotator. xml** to display the file in the document window.

The last *Ad* element in the file should contain the URL for the image file, *WideWorldImporters.png*, the Wide World Importers portal URL, and an Impressions value of *30*.

```
  </Ad>
    <Ad>
    <ImageUrl>/PictLib/worldwideimporters.png</ImageUrl>
    <NavigateUrl>http://portal.wideworldimporters.com</NavigateUrl>
    <Keyword></Keyword>
    <AlternateText></AlternateText>
    <Impressions>30</Impressions>
    </Ad>
</Advertisements>
```

CLOSE any open browser windows.

Using SharePoint Server Controls

All controls prefixed with SharePoint or WebPartPages are part of the SharePoint frame-work and can be found on the Web server in the assembly, Microsoft.SharePoint.dll. All SharePoint pages contain SharePoint Server controls, some of which are shown in the Toolbox task pane as follows:

● **CssLink.** Links to CSS files. By default this control is placed on master pages and links to a file stored on each Web server, so all pages associated with a master page have the same look and feel. When the control is used with no file specified, it defaults to core.css.

● **Theme.** Adds a reference to the site's current theme CSS file, if one is configured.

● **ScriptLink.** Links to JavaScript files. Placed on master pages and links to a file, (core.js) stored on the Web server, so all pages associated with a master page have access to the same set of JavaScript functions.

- **AspMenu.** An ASP.NET navigation control to display sites and pages within a site collection. By default, the control is placed on the master pages, so all pages associated with the master page share the same navigation.

- **RSSLink.** On lists and libraries that are enabled as RSS feeds, this control exposes the URL that RSS aggregators can use to view list items.

- **SPCalendarNavigation.** On list views, displays a calendar control that is used to navigate to specific list items. You can find examples of pages with this control in the All Items views of the Announcements and Calendar lists.

In this exercise, you will review the SharePoint controls in the Toolbox task pane and investigate their usage on pages within a site.

> **USE** the site you modified in the previous exercise.
>
> **OPEN** the site in SharePoint Designer, if it is not already open, and display the *NewAd.aspx* in Split view.

1. On the **Insert** menu, point to **SharePoint Controls**, and then click **More SharePoint Controls**.

   The Toolbox task pane opens with the SharePoint controls displayed.

2. Under **Server Controls (SharePoint)**, point to **CSSLink**.

   The tooltip that appears references the SharePoint namespace, *Microsoft.SharePoint.WebControl.CssLink*, where the code-behind logic for this control can be found.

> **Tip** The controls visible in the Toolbox will be different if your site was created on a Windows SharePoint Services installation.

3. In the **Toolbox** task pane, display the **Page Fields** and **Content Fields** control groups.

   No controls are displayed in these two groups.

4. In the code portion of the document window, scroll to the top of the page.

   Immediately after the opening form tag, there is a *WebPartPages: DataFormWebPart* control.

5. In the **Folder List** task pane, expand the **_catalogs** section and the **masterpage (Master Page Gallery)** section, and then double-click **default.master**.

   The page opens in the document window. In the *head* tag are a number of SharePoint controls, such as *CssLink*, *Theme*, *ScriptLink*, and *CustomJSUrl*.

6. In the document window, click the **newAd.spx** page tab to display the page.

7. On the **Format** menu, point to **Master Page**, and then click **Attach Master Page**.

   The Select A Master Page dialog box opens, with the Default Master Page option selected by default.

8. Click **OK** to close the **Select a Master Page** dialog box.

   The Match Content Regions dialog box opens.

9. Click **OK** to close the **Match Content Regions** dialog box.

   The NewAd.aspx page is redisplayed in the Design portion of the document window and has the same look and feel and navigation as other pages on the site. In the code portion of the document window, the *head*, *body*, and *form* tags contain no additional controls.

10. Scroll to the top of the page so that you see the @ **Page** directive, and then scroll to the right until, on the first line of the page, you see the **masterpagefile** attribute.

CLOSE any open browser windows. If you are not continuing directly to the next chapter, exit SharePoint Designer.

Key Points

- With ASP.NET, you can separate user interface declarations from application logic.

- Application logic is precompiled into DLLs that reside on the Web servers.

- There are three groups of controls: HTML controls, ASP.NET controls, and SharePoint controls.

- Controls are similar to Web Parts; you place them on a page and customize their properties to meet your needs.

- ASP.NET Data controls allow you to define data sources and view the contents of data sources. The view controls must be bound to a data source.

- ASP.NET validation controls use JavaScript, by default, to validate data entry on the client side, thereby reducing network traffic when an input form is processed. They can be configured so that only server-side logic is used to validate data entry.

- SharePoint Data View controls expose data as check boxes, radio buttons, or drop-down lists from which the user can choose. Data view controls are inserted into a data view and must be bound to a data source.

- All built-in SharePoint pages contain SharePoint Server controls.

Chapter at a Glance

Understand master pages,
page 204

Customize a
master page,
page 210

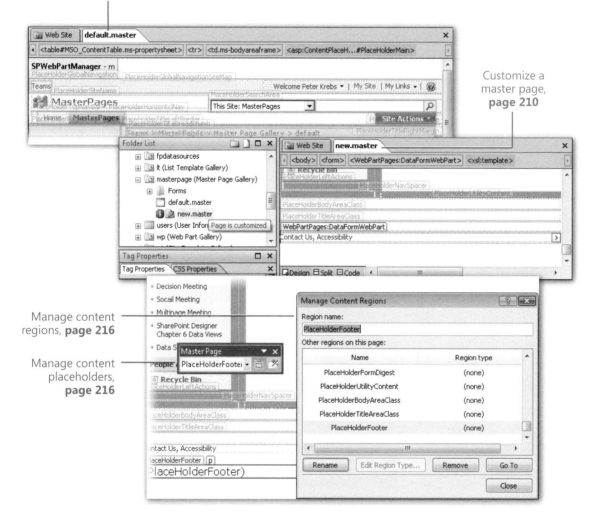

Manage content
regions, **page 216**

Manage content
placeholders,
page 216

9 Working with Master Pages

In this chapter, you will learn to:

✔ Understand master pages.

✔ Customize a master page.

✔ Change the default master page.

✔ Manage content placeholders and content regions.

✔ Reset a master page to the site definition.

You have already worked with master pages in many of the chapters in this book. For example, in Chapter 3, "Customizing a Web Page," you saw that when you use a browser to request a page from a site, the two Microsoft ASP.NET pages: a master page and a content page are combined. You also discovered that when you open a content page in Microsoft Office SharePoint Designer 2007, Design view displays the merged page (not only the content page) with the name of the master page appearing in the upper-right corner. Then in Chapter 4, "Creating and Modifying Web Pages," you attached a master page to a newly created page and you created a page from a master page. You have also seen that Microsoft Windows SharePoint Services 3.0 and Microsoft Office SharePoint Server 2007 make heavy use of master pages to control the general layout of pages within a SharePoint site.

The default master page is the page that, when you first create a site, is applied to all pages in your site. The default master page is located on the Web server. When you modify it by using SharePoint Designer 2007, the page becomes a *customized* page.

In this chapter, you will explore and modify the *default master* page, and then reset the master page back to the site definition file. You will change the default master page, and then manage the regions and controls that allow you to place content on a master page.

> **Important** Before you can use the practice files in this chapter, you need to install them from the book's companion CD to their default location. You will need to create a practice site for this chapter based on the site template *MasterPages_Starter.stp* located in this chapter's practice file folder. Then when you perform the exercises in this chapter, remember to use your SharePoint site location in place of *teams.consolidatedmessenger.com*.
>
> For more information about practice files, see "Using the Book's CD" at the beginning of this book.

> **Troubleshooting** Graphics and operating system–related instructions in this book reflect the Windows Vista user interface. If your computer is running Windows XP and you experience trouble following the instructions as written, please refer to the "Information for Readers Running Windows XP" section at the beginning of this book.

Understanding Master Pages

Master pages are a new feature included as part of ASP.NET 2.0. They were introduced to support the development of a common look and feel across entire sites. ASP.NET 2.0 merges the master page with a content page to produce one page that a browser can render. ASP.NET 2.0 also includes the concept of *nested master pages*, where a child master page inherits elements from a parent master page. A content page associated with a child master page inherits all the elements from the child master page as well as all the elements from the parent master page. Windows SharePoint Server 3.0, and, therefore, SharePoint Server 2007 are based on ASP.NET 2.0, and make heavy use of master pages, but currently do not use nested master pages.

> **Tip** Windows SharePoint Services 2.0 and Microsoft Office SharePoint Portal Server 2003 are based on ASP.NET 1.1 and therefore do not use master pages. With the release of Windows SharePoint Services 2.0 Service Pack 2 (SP2), it is possible to enable the ASP.NET 2.0 .NET runtime on these sites, so theoretically you can develop new Windows SharePoint Services 2.0 sites to use master pages and content pages. Enabling ASP.NET 2.0 functionality is a task completed by a server administrator.

> **Important** ASP.NET 2.0 functionality should never be enabled on SharePoint Portal Server sites.

Master pages have the same structure as normal pages; they contain the same tags, *<html>*, *<head>*, and *<body>*; however, their file names have an extension of *.master* in place of *.aspx*. They can also contain most of the content and functionality of normal pages, such as JavaScript, Web Parts (including Data Views), and controls; however, they cannot contain Web Part zones.

> **Tip** Although master pages can include style information, it is common practice to develop master pages to control the general layout of pages, and use cascading style sheets to apply common styles to elements on each page in a site. In Chapter 8, "Using Controls in Web Pages," you saw that master pages link to a separate file storing the cascading style sheet information. You'll discover how SharePoint Designer 2007 can help you with cascading style sheets in Chapter 10, "Changing the Look and Feel of Pages by Using Cascading Style Sheets."

Much of the functionality of a master page is provided by ASP.NET or SharePoint controls, such as *SPWebPartManager*. This control allows you to add Web Parts to master pages, and add Web Parts and Web Part zones to content pages. By adding an element to the master page, it is not necessary to add it to each content page. The controls added to a master page can be divided into three types:

- Controls for links, menus, icons, and navigation components, such as the *SiteMapPath* control that populates the global navigation breadcrumb

- Content placeholders that match areas on the content page where you can enter information, such as the *PlaceHolderMain* control

- Delegate controls, which define a region on the page where the content can be substituted with another control driven by feature activation

See Also For more information refer to Chapter 3, "Pages and Design," in the book *Inside Microsoft Windows SharePoint Services 3.0*, by Ted Pattison and Daniel Larson (Microsoft Press, 2007).

As with other pages, the site definition plays a key role with master pages. Each site definition can contain a number of master pages, one of which can be set as the default master page for the site. If a default master page is not included in a site definition, then a global default master page is used. To ensure a common look and feel, a master page is attached to each page. You can specify whether you want to use the default master page or a different master page. Therefore, theoretically, each page within a site collection could be using a different master page. Such a scenario would defeat the purposes of using master pages, which as stated earlier, were introduced to support a common look and feel across entire sites.

So how many master pages does a SharePoint installation have? In a default installation of Windows SharePoint Services 3.0, only the following master pages are provided:

- **Global default master page.** There is no master page defined in any of the team site definitions, so they use the global default master page.

- **Global meeting workspace master page.** All meeting workspaces use the global meeting workspace master page. You saw reference to this master page in Chapter 4.

- **Administration master pages.** All SharePoint sites use the *application.master* page on their *administration pages*, those pages with *_layouts* in their URL, such as the Site Settings page. This group of master pages also includes master pages for SharePoint sites that Central administrators use to manage the installation of SharePoint products.

Therefore, all your team sites will look the same, all your meeting workspace sites will look the same, and all administration pages—no matter which site—will look the same.

> **Note** In a default SharePoint Server 2007 installation, team and meeting workspace master pages work as they do in Windows SharePoint Services. Publishing sites also use a default master page, but can use alternate master pages, called *custom master pages*.

Master pages, like site definitions, are stored in the 12 hive on the Web server. As with other pages that are stored on the Web server, when you use SharePoint Designer to modify and save them, you do not alter the file on the Web server. SharePoint Designer takes a copy of the file and saves it in the Microsoft SQL Server content database; that is, the page becomes a customized page. If, subsequently, a developer changes the master page on the Web server, your site will not reflect those changes.

See Also For more information about site definitions and the 12 hive, see Chapter 1, "Introducing SharePoint Designer."

As you have seen with other SharePoint pages, SharePoint Designer provides full design-time support for master pages. In Design view, you can manipulate the elements on a master page in a WYSIWYG manner. In addition, you can modify any part of the page that is displayed; that is, you can move the pointer over the whole page, and at no point does the pointer change to the no-entry icon, unlike when working in content pages.

> **Note** In a browser, you can see only the effect of a master page merged with a content page; you cannot view a master page itself.

SharePoint Designer displays a program window for each site you open, allowing you to modify only one site at a time; there is no mechanism to push your changes from one site to another. Therefore, using SharePoint Designer, master pages are always modified at the site level.

In this exercise, you will locate the default master page and explore the ASP.NET and SharePoint controls used by a master page.

USE your own SharePoint site location in place of the *teams.consolidatedmessenger.com* team site shown in the exercise.

BE SURE TO start SharePoint Designer and close any pages that open in the document window before beginning this exercise.

OPEN the MasterPage child in SharePoint Designer.

1. In the **Folder List** task pane, expand the **_catalogs** folder and the **masterpage (Master Page Gallery)** library.

   The Masterpage (Master Page Gallery) document library expands and lists one master page, *default.master*.

   > **Tip** In a top-level team site on a SharePoint Server installation or in a publishing site, the Master Page Gallery will contain other files.

2. In the **Folder List** task pane, right-click **masterpage (Master Page Gallery)**, and then click **Properties**.

   The Document Library Properties dialog box opens.

3. Click the **Settings** tab.

   The Hide From Browsers check box is selected, major versioning is enabled, and content approval and check out is not required.

   > **Tip** If you complete the above steps on a publishing site in a SharePoint Server installation, you will notice that the Master Page Gallery has major and minor versioning enabled and content approval and check out is required. As a result, when you open default.master, you will be notified that it is under source control, and prompted to specify whether to check it out.

4. Click **OK** to close the **Document Library Properties** dialog box, and then in the **Folder List** task pane, under **masterpage (Master Page Gallery)**, double-click **default.master** to open the page in the document window.

5. Look in the status bar of the SharePoint Designer program window. If **Visual Aids** is not specified as **On**, then on the **View** menu, point to **Visual Aids**, and click **Show**.

The controls on the page are displayed, surrounded by a purple line, with the name of the control in the label above the purple box.

> **Tip** If the control names do not appear, verify that Template Region Labels is selected on the Visual Aids menu.

6. On the **View** menu, point to **Visual Aids**, and click **ASP.NET Non-visual Controls** if there is not an orange box to the right of it.

   The *default.master* page refreshes, and the hidden SPWebPartManager control appears.

> **Tip** If the Visual Aids menu remains visible, click anywhere inside the document window.

7. At the bottom of the default.master document window, click the **Split** button to display the page in both Code view and Design view.

8. On the **Edit** menu, click **Find**.

The Find And Replace dialog box opens.

9. In the **Find what** text box, type **<asp:**. Under **Find where**, click **Current page**. Under **Advanced**, select the **Find in source code** check box, and clear all other check boxes.

10. Click **Find All**.

The Find And Replace dialog box closes, and the Find 1 task pane opens, docking at the bottom of the document window. The lines returned in the results window contain ASP.NET controls.

Page	Line	Matched Text
_catalogs/masterpage/default.master (<asp:ContentPlaceHold...	14	<Title ID=onetidTitle><asp:ContentPlaceHolder id=PlaceHolderPageTitle runat=
_catalogs/masterpage/default.master (<asp:ContentPlaceHold...	20	<asp:ContentPlaceHolder id="PlaceHolderAdditionalPageHead"...
_catalogs/masterpage/default.master (<asp:ContentPlaceHold...	27	<tr><td><asp:ContentPlaceHolder id="PlaceHolderGlobalNavigation"...
_catalogs/masterpage/default.master (<asp:ContentPlaceHold...	45	<asp:ContentPlaceHolder id="PlaceHolderGlobalNavigationSiteMap"...
_catalogs/masterpage/default.master (<asp:ContentPlaceHold...	46	<asp:SiteMapPath SiteMapProvider="SPSiteMapProvider" id="GlobalNaviga...
_catalogs/masterpage/default.master (<asp:ContentPlaceHold...	88	<asp:ContentPlaceHolder id="PlaceHolderSiteName" runat="server">
_catalogs/masterpage/default.master (<asp:ContentPlaceHold...	97	<asp:ContentPlaceHolder id="PlaceHolderSearchArea" runat="server">
_catalogs/masterpage/default.master (<asp:ContentPlaceHold...	107	<asp:ContentPlaceHolder id="PlaceHolderTopNavBar" runat="server">
_catalogs/masterpage/default.master (<asp:ContentPlaceHold...	112	<asp:ContentPlaceHolder id="PlaceHolderHorizontalNav" runat="server">...
_catalogs/masterpage/default.master (<asp:ContentPlaceHold...	140	<asp:SiteMapDataSource

Found 42 occurrences of '<asp:' in 1 page.

Find and Replace

11. In the **Find 1** task pane, click the **Find and Replace** button.

The Find And Replace dialog box reopens.

12. In the **Find what** text box, type **<SharePoint:**, and then click **Find All**.

The Find And Replace dialog box closes, and the search results appear in the Find 1 task pane.

Page	L.	Matched Text
_catalogs/masterpage/default.master (<asp:ContentPlaceHold...	13	<SharePoint:RobotsMetaTag runat="server"/>
_catalogs/masterpage/default.master (<asp:ContentPlaceHold...	15	<SharePoint:CssLink runat="server"/>
_catalogs/masterpage/default.master (<asp:ContentPlaceHold...	16	<SharePoint:Theme runat="server"/>
_catalogs/masterpage/default.master (<asp:ContentPlaceHold...	17	<SharePoint:ScriptLink language="javascript" name="core.js" Defer="true"...
_catalogs/masterpage/default.master (<asp:ContentPlaceHold...	18	<SharePoint:CustomJSUrl runat="server"/>
_catalogs/masterpage/default.master (<asp:ContentPlaceHold...	19	<SharePoint:SoapDiscoveryLink runat="server"/>
_catalogs/masterpage/default.master (<asp:ContentPlaceHold...	21	<SharePoint:DelegateControl runat="server" ControlId="AdditionalPageHead"...
_catalogs/masterpage/default.master (<asp:ContentPlaceHold...	33	<SharePoint:EncodedLiteral runat="server" text="<%$Resources:wss,master_turn...
_catalogs/masterpage/default.master (<asp:ContentPlaceHold...	36	<SharePoint:EncodedLiteral runat="server" text="<%$Resources:wss,mainContent...

Found 38 occurrences of '<SharePoint:' in 1 page.

> **Note** If you completed this exercise in SharePoint Server on a publishing site, it uses the same global default.master as used on team sites, but because the Office SharePoint Server Publishing feature is activated, a second *hidden ASP.NET control*, VariationDataSource, is added.

✕ **CLOSE** the Find 1 task pane and the *default.master* page.

Customizing a Master Page

As time goes by, you may find that you want to alter all pages in your site to display a certain piece of information or image. You could modify each existing page and any new pages to include this information; however, you will then become the Web master bottleneck we described in Chapter 1.

A method that is easy to maintain is to customize a master page and then associate it with all pages in your site. This is the purpose of the default master page. Changes to the default master page cascade down to all pages that are not associated with a specific master page. Create a new master page or copy an existing one, customize it to meet your needs, and then set it as the default master page. Modifying the existing default master page is the best option if it already meets most of your needs; otherwise, create a new master page.

See Also For more information about creating a master page, see the sidebar "Creating a Master Page," later in this chapter.

In this exercise, you will copy the default.master page and add a Data View that displays links to other pages to the bottom of the page.

USE the site you modified in the previous exercise.
OPEN the site in SharePoint Designer, if it is not already open.

1. In the **Folder List** task pane, under **masterpage (Master Page Gallery)**, right-click **default.master**, and then click **Copy**.

> **Warning** When you customize the current default master page, amendments will be immediately visible on any associated content page. Therefore, as a precaution, always amend a copy of a master page. Never customize a master page associated with a "production" content page.

2. Right-click **masterpage (Master Page Gallery)**, and then click **Paste**.

    Under masterpage (Master Page Gallery), the file *default_copy(1).master* appears.

> **Tip** Although you could save your master page anywhere in your site, the best practice is to save it in the site's Master Page Gallery.

3. In the **Folder List** task pane, right-click **default_copy(1).master**, click **Rename**, type new.master, and then press Enter .

4. Double-click **new.master** to open the page in the document window.

Design

5. At the bottom of the **new.master** document window, click the **Design** button to close the Code view pane.

6. Scroll to the bottom of the page and click to position the insertion point in the document window after all the controls.

7. On the **Data View Menu**, click **Insert Data View**.

An asterisk appears on the new.master page tab, indicating that it contains unsaved content. A WebPartPages:DataFormWebPart control appears at the bottom of the page, and the Data Source Library task pane opens.

8. In the **Data Source Library** task pane, expand the SharePoint Libraries section to display all the libraries that this site contains.

9. In the **Data Source Library** task pane, point to **WebPages**, click the arrow that appears, and then click **Show Data**.

The Data Source Details task pane appears.

10. In the **Data Source Details** task pane, click **URL Path**, click **Insert Selected Fields as**, and then click **Multiple Item View**.

The page view refreshes and shows the URL for all the files stored in the WebPages document library.

> **Tip** On a master page, when you use Web Parts or a Data View, verify that users have permission to view the information they display. Test your customization by using a variety of permissions levels.

Chevron

11. Click the chevron to the right of the WebPartPages:DataFormWebPart control to display the **Common Data View Tasks** list.

12. In the **Common Data View Tasks** list, click **Filter**.

The Filter Criteria dialog box opens.

13. Click **Click here to add a new clause**, click the **Field Name** arrow that appears, and then in the list, click **PageType**.

14. Under **Value**, click **Header**, click the arrow that appears, and then click **Footer**.

15. In the **Filter Criteria** dialog box, click **OK** .

The page view refreshes and shows the URL of only two files, *Contact Us.aspx* and *Accessibility.aspx*.

16. In the **Common Data View Tasks** list, click **Change Layout**.

The Data View Properties dialog box opens.

17. Under **HTML view styles**, point to each of the styles, and click the layout that displays the tooltip *Horizontal list of titles*.

18. In the **Data View Properties** dialog box, click **OK**.

19. If a **Microsoft Office SharePoint Designer** message box appears, warning you that any custom formatting or provider Web Part connections will be removed, click **Yes**.

The page view refreshes, showing the two file names horizontally.

20. In the WebPartPages:DataFormWebPart control, right-click the URL for **Contact Us.aspx**, and then click **Edit Formula**.

The Insert Formula dialog box opens.

21. In the **Edit the XPath expression** box, delete **@FileRef**.

22. In the **Select a function category** list, click **Text / String** to display the text-related functions.

23. In the **Select a function to insert** list, double-click **substring-before**.

In the Edit The XPath Expression box, *Substring-before()* and a drop-down list appear.

24. In the list, double-click **@FileLeafRef** to insert the XML attribute in the XPath expression.

A tooltip, *Substring-before(string, Substring)*, appears, and the insertion point is placed between @FileLeafRef and the end bracket.

25. Type ,".".

26. In the **Insert Formula** dialog box, click **OK**.

The page view refreshes, showing the two files names without URLs or their file extensions.

27. On the Common toolbar, click **Save**.

Save

28. In the **Site Definition Page Warning** message box that appears, click **Yes**.

In the Folder List task pane, a blue information circle appears to the left of new.master, indicating that this page is now saved in the SQL Server content database.

CLOSE the *new.master* page.

Changing the Default Master Page

When you first create a Windows SharePoint Services or SharePoint Server site, all pages other than the administrator pages use *default.master* as their default master page. Using SharePoint Designer, you can set a new master page as the default master page.

> **Note** In a SharePoint Server installation, you can alter the master page associated with a site by using the browser. To access the master page, click Master Page in the Look And Feel list on the Site Settings page. On this page, the master page associated with team sites is referred to as the *system master page* and the master page associated with publishing sites is known as the *site master page*. You cannot change the master page associated with a Meeting Workspace by using the browser.

In this exercise, you will change the default master page.

USE the site you modified in the previous exercise.
OPEN the site in SharePoint Designer, if it is not already open.

1. In the **Folder List** task pane, right-click **new.master**, and then click **Set as Default Master Page**.

The Set As Default Master Page message box appears, warning that if you change the default or custom master page, you will break any attached pages that do not have a matching set of named content regions.

2. Click **Yes** to close the **Set as Default Master Page** dialog box.

3. In the **Folder List** task pane, double-click **default.aspx** to open the page in the document window.

> **Note** In the Folder List task pane, there is not a blue information circle to the left of default.aspx. Although the master page is a *customized* page, the content page, default.aspx is an *un-customized* page.

4. In the lower-left area of the *default.aspx* page, point to the **Contact Us** and **Accessibility** links.

> **Tip** You may need to scroll down default.aspx to see the Contact Us and Accessibility links.

A no-entry icon appears over each link.

5. Press ⌞F12⌟ to open the page in the browser.

6. At the bottom of the page, click **Contact Us**.

7. On the breadcrumb of the Contact Us page, click **WebPages**.

The All Document view of the WebPages document library is displayed. At the bottom of the page, the Contact Us and Accessibility links are displayed.

8. Point to **Terms of Use**, click the arrow that appears, and then click **Edit Properties**.

The WebPages: Terms Of Use page is displayed. At the bottom of the page, the Contact Us and Accessibility links are displayed.

9. In the **PageType** list, click **Footer**. Then click **OK** to return to the **All Documents** view of the **WebPages** document library.

There are now three links at the bottom of the page.

10. On the **Settings** menu, click **Document Library Settings**.

The Customize WebPages page appears. The page URL includes *_layouts* and the three links are not displayed at the bottom of the page.

> **Note** You cannot use SharePoint Designer to modify _layout pages or the master page they use.

CLOSE the browser.

Managing Content Placeholders and Content Regions

The *content placeholder* control is a key component of a master page. It is placed on the master page where content will eventually appear. When a user requests a page, the components from a content page are placed in content placeholders specified on the master page. A master page typically has a number of content placeholders, the most important of them being PlaceHolderMain, which usually maps to the region on the master page where the elements from the content page should be placed.

See Also For a description of the default placeholders, refer to *office.microsoft.com/en-us/ sharepointdesigner/HA101651201033.aspx*.

You might remember that back in Chapter 4, when you attached a master page to *ParcelDelivery.aspx*, SharePoint Designer opened a Match Content Region dialog box so you could match the content on *ParcelDelivery.aspx* with a content placeholder on the master page. In this case, it was easy and you accepted SharePoint Designer's suggestion of mapping the data in the *<body>* tag on *ParcelDelivery.aspx* with PlaceHolderMain control. SharePoint Designer replaced the *<body>* tag in *ParcelDelivery.aspx* with an *<asp:Content>* tag with the attribute *contentplaceholderid* set to *PlaceHolderMain*. Therefore, to plug content from a content page into a master page, there must be at least one content control on the content page that matches an ID of a content placeholder on the master page.

> **Tip** In SharePoint Designer, content placeholders are also known as *content regions*. If you developed a common look and feel in the previous version of SharePoint products by using Dynamic Web Templates (DWT), then the concept of content regions will not be new to you.

On a content page, when you see *(Master)* appended to the name of the content placeholder, content cannot be placed in these content placeholders. SharePoint Designer appends *(Custom)* to the placeholder name when a content placeholder does allow its content to be modified on the content page. You experienced this aspect of a content placeholder, when you completed an exercise in Chapter 4 to create a new page from a master page, and you found that you could not add content to the content page. All the content placeholders were marked with (Master). You enabled the PlaceHolderMain content region as editable and as a result, (Master) was replaced by (Custom) and, therefore, you were able to add content to your content page. Adding content to a content placeholder allows you to specify content on the master page that is visible on every content page associated with that master page, but allows you to customize that content on a content page by content page basis.

You can explicitly control the content that a specific content placeholders may contain. You can specify the type of content they can contain, such as text or images only. Neither Windows SharePoint Services nor SharePoint Server applies any restrictions to the content placeholders included on their master pages. These content region settings can also be linked to contributor settings, which we'll discuss in Chapter 14, "Managing SharePoint Sites."

SharePoint Designer provides the following tools to manage content placeholders and content regions:

- Master Pages toolbar
- Manage Content Regions dialog box

In this exercise, you will place the Data View you created in the previous exercise into a content placeholder on the master page. Then on a content page, you will override a content placeholder and revert back to a content placeholder on the master page.

> **USE** the site you modified in the previous exercise.
>
> **OPEN** the site in SharePoint Designer, if it is not already open, and display the *new.master* page in the document window.

1. In the document window, scroll down and place the insertion point below the Data View you inserted in the previous exercises.

2. On the **View** menu, point to **Toolbars**, and click **Master Page** to open a floating **Master Page** toolbar.

Manage
Content Regions

3. Click the **Manage Content Regions** icon to open the **Manage Content Regions** dialog box.

4. In the **Region name** text box, type PlaceHolderFooter, and then click **Add**.

> **Tip** When adding a new content region, the name must be unique.

PlaceHolderFooter appears as the last region in the Manage Content Regions dialog box. The Add button changes to a Rename button, and the *new.master* page page refreshes. At the bottom of the page, the content placeholder appears, containing the text (PlaceHolderFooter).

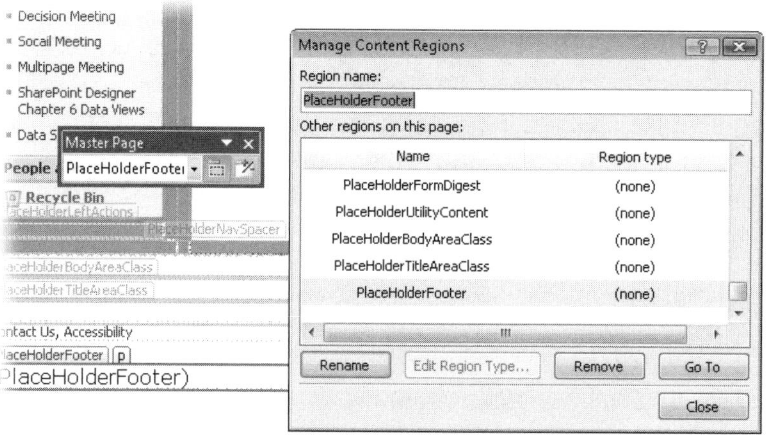

5. In the **Manage Content Regions** dialog box, click **Close**.

6. Click inside the **PlaceHolderFooter** region, and delete the text **(PlaceHolderFooter)**.

7. Click **Contact Us** so that the **WebPartPages:DataFormWebPart** label appears above the Data View.

8. Point to **WebPartPages:DataFormWebPart**. When the pointer changes to a four-way arrow, drag the Data View into the **PlaceHolderFooter** region.

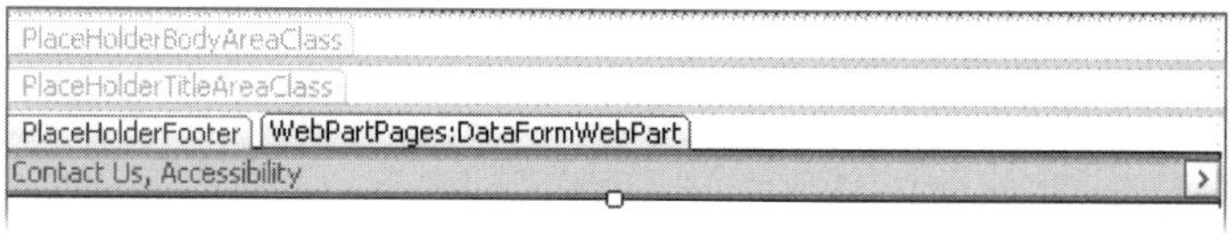

9. On the Common toolbar, click **Save**.

Save

10. In the **Folder List** task pane, expand **WebPages**, and then double-click **Contact Us.aspx** to open the page in the document window.

11. Scroll to the bottom of the page, point to **Contact Us**, and then click the chevron that appears.

The Common Content Tasks list opens.

PlaceHolderFooter (Master)		ID of the User wh
Contact Us, Accessibility	<	**Common Content Tasks**
		Create Custom Content
Design Split Code		Refresh data source

12. Click **Create Custom Content**.

    The Common Content Tasks list closes and the label above Contact Us changes from PlaceHolderFooter (Master) to PlaceHolderFooter (Custom).

13. Click **Contact Us** so that the **WebPartPages:DataFormWebPart** label appears above the Data View.

14. Click the **WebPartPages:DataFormWebPart** label, and press ⌈Del⌋ to delete the Data View.

15. If the Master Page toolbar is not already open, point to **Toolbars** on the **View** menu, and then click **Master Page**.

16. On the Master Page toolbar, click the **Regions** arrow, and then click **PlaceHolderLeftNavBar**.

    An empty PlaceHolderLeftNavBar (Custom) content region is highlighted with a chevron to the right.

> **Tip** If you cannot see the PlaceHolderLeftNav Bar (Custom) on the page, click the Template Regions Labels icon on the Master Page toolbar.

17. Click the chevron to the right of **PlaceHolderLeftNavBar (Custom)** to open the **Common Content Tasks** list, and click **Default to Master's Content**.

    The Confirm dialog box opens, stating that by defaulting to the Master Page content, everything in this region will be removed from this page.

Creating a Master Page

Depending on your requirements, creating a master page could be easy or so difficult that you need a developer. You will need to decide whether you need to change just one site or a number of sites, as this too will affect the decision on the tool to use. You must not use SharePoint Designer to open and manipulate files on the Web server.

If you would like to alter the master page for all sites on a SharePoint installation, then you will not be able to achieve this with SharePoint Designer, because you can alter master pages only at the site level. However, it is a great tool to design your master page layout and obtain business signoff, because as you have seen in this chapter, SharePoint Designer does give you a visual representation of the master page. No other tool will do this for you.

If you need to extensively customize the layout of your master page, you will need to spend time to learn the components used on a master page and their purpose. Some are obvious; for example, the *SiteActions* SharePoint control is responsible for the Site Actions menu you see on every page. Therefore, if you need this control in a different position on the page, it should be easy to move it. Others are not so obvious. If your master page does not contain all the necessary content placeholders, then any content pages based on that master page will fail to render and users will see an error message.

Do not use the *default.master* page as a basis for your new default master page. It is a very complicated master page that uses controls, such as the delegate control, whose content is decided only when the page is rendered; so it's not the easiest of pages to learn from. Microsoft has provided a number of other master pages, such as the following:

- A minimal master page for SharePoint Server publishing sites at *msdn2.microsoft.com/aa660698.aspx*

- Example master pages for Windows SharePoint Services at *www.microsoft.com/downloads/details.aspx? FamilyID=7c05ca44-869a-463b-84d7-57b053711a96*

Other people in the SharePoint community have produced minimal and example master pages that you can use as a basis for your own. When searching for these pages, use search keywords such as *SharePoint minimal master page*.

See Also For more information refer to Chapter 6, "Customizing and Branding Publishing Portals," in the book *Inside Office SharePoint Server 2007*, by Patrick Tisseghem (Microsoft Press, 2007).

18. In the **Confirm** dialog box, click **Yes**.

    The Contact Us page refreshes.

19. Close the Master Page toolbar, and scroll to the left.

    The page now has a Quick Launch bar.

20. On the Common toolbar, click **Save**, and when the **Site Definition Warning** message box appears, click **Yes**.

    In the Folder List task pane to the left of Contact Us, a blue information circle appears.

21. Press [F12] to open the Contact Us page in the browser, and then verify that the page has a Quick Launch bar and not links at the bottom of the page.

22. On the breadcrumb, click **WebPages**.

    The All Document view of the WebPages document library appears, with the links at the bottom of the page.

CLOSE the browser and all pages open in the document windows.

Resetting a Master Page to the Site Definition

In Chapter 4, you reset a content page to its site definition. Resetting a master page to its site definition is not different. You will lose any customizations you made to the page, including any static text, images, controls, or Web Parts you place on the page. SharePoint Designer will create a copy of the page before it resets it back to the site definition, so you can recover your customizations, if needed. On a content page, where you add Web Parts or Data Views to Web Part zones, resetting to the site definition, your Web Parts and Data Views will remain as long as the Web Part zones were defined in the site definition file and had the same Web Part zone label as the customized content page.

In this exercise, you will reset a customized master page to the site definition, and you will see that your modifications are lost.

> **USE** the site you modified in the previous exercise.
> **OPEN** the site in SharePoint Designer, if it is not already open.

1. In the **Folder List** task pane, right-click **new.master**, and then click **Reset to Site Definition**. When the **Site Definition Page Warning** dialog box opens, click **Yes**.

   In the Folder List task pane, the blue information icon to the left of *new.master* disappears and *new_copy(1).master* appears, with a blue information icon.

2. In the **Folder List** task pane, double-click **new.master** to open it in the document window.

3. Scroll to the bottom of the page, and notice that the Data View you added earlier has disappeared.

4. In the **Folder List** task pane, double-click **Contact Us**.

   A Master Page Error message appears, because we customized the PlaceHolderFooter content placeholder, which no longer exists on the master page.

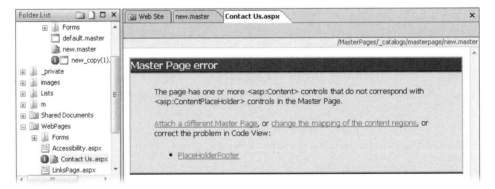

> **CLOSE** all pages open in the document windows, and exit SharePoint Designer if you are not continuing directly to the next exercise.

Key Points

- Master pages are an ASP.NET 2.0 feature that both Windows SharePoint Services 3.0 and SharePoint Server use extensively.

- Master pages have the same structure as normal pages; however, their file names have an extension of .*master* instead of .*aspx*.

- Use master pages to control the general layout of pages, and use cascading style sheets to apply common styles to elements on each page in a site.

- Windows SharePoint Services 3.0 provides a global default master page, a global meeting workspace master page, and a number of administration master pages. Administration master pages are applied to pages that include _*layouts* in their URL.

- SharePoint Server provides the same master pages as Windows SharePoint Services 3.0, plus a number of custom master pages for publishing sites.

- When you save any of the provided master pages by using SharePoint Designer, you will create customized pages.

- Much of the functionality of a master page is provided by ASP.NET or SharePoint controls.

- Content placeholder controls, also known in SharePoint Designer as content regions, specify on the master page when content from content pages should be placed. They also define content on the master page that can be customized on content pages.

- Modify the default master page, if it already meets most of your needs.

- Learn how to create a new master page by using a minimal master page.

Chapter at a Glance

Identify styles in cascading style sheets, **page 230**

Use the Style Application toolbar, **page 239**

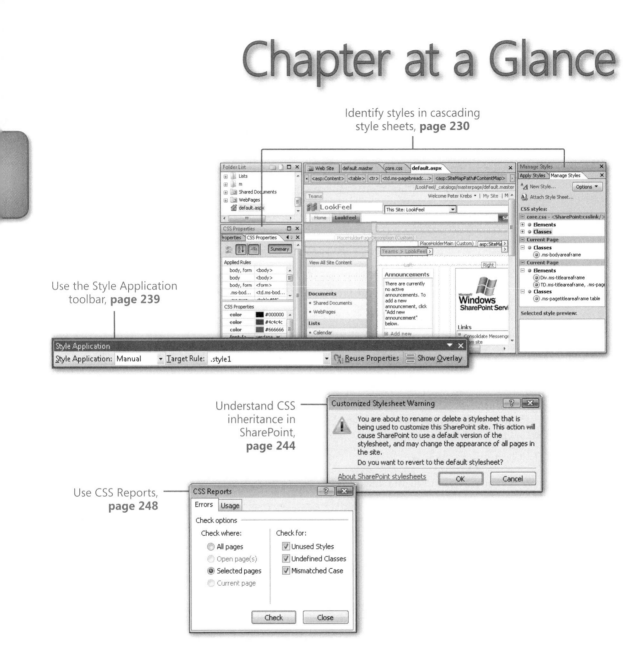

Understand CSS inheritance in SharePoint, **page 244**

Use CSS Reports, **page 248**

10 Changing the Look and Feel of Pages by Using Cascading Style Sheets

In this chapter, you will learn to:

✔ Understand the CSS and color-coding options.

✔ Identify styles in cascading style sheets.

✔ Create, modify, and delete styles.

✔ Use the Style Application toolbar.

✔ Create and attach CSS files.

✔ Understand CSS inheritance in SharePoint.

✔ Use CSS Reports.

When you create a site by using Microsoft Windows SharePoint Services 3.0 or Microsoft Office SharePoint Server 2007, your site will contain more than information. As we saw in Chapter 1, "Introducing SharePoint Designer," both SharePoint products contain a considerable amount of functionality you can use to create rich sites that facilitate collaboration and social networking.

All sites need to interact with their users, and a SharePoint site is no different. Of course, there are some design best practices you should follow, such as *never* create pages that require a user to scroll to the right to see all the information—users never will; they are used to scrolling down but not across, so make sure you preview your page in the screen size that most visitors to your site will use. For internal sites, your Information Technology (IT) department should be able to provide you with details of the typical screen size your company uses. Currently, for sites that are accessible from the Internet (Internet-facing sites), if you design your page for a screen size of 1024×768 pixels, then more than 80 percent of users will be able to read your page without needing to scroll to the right. On SharePoint sites, a common cause for creating a right-scrolling bar is too many tabs on the top horizontal navigation bar. In Microsoft Office SharePoint Designer 2007, you can preview pages in multiple screen sizes and browsers, if you have more than one browser installed on your computer.

See Also For more information about browser statistics, visit *www.w3schools.com/browsers/.*

Most sites include more than text; they all are designed to try to be interactive with their users and convey information in an engaging manner, especially Internet facing sites. Your company may require a certain look and feel for all its sites. Therefore, the visual representation of your site is one of the areas you may have to invest some time in. Like most industry-standard sites, SharePoint sites use cascading style sheets (CSS). SharePoint Designer and Microsoft Expression Web contain one of the best cascading style sheet editors available. SharePoint Designer provides you with three task panes and two toolbars, together with several menu links to help you manipulate cascading style sheet styles and files. This method of manipulating cascading style sheets has proved so useful, that, the next version of Microsoft Visual Studio 2005, Visual Web Developer 2008, will have similar cascading style sheet editing tools.

In this chapter, you will explore the cascading style sheet editing options for SharePoint Designer. Then, through the cascading style sheet task panes and toolbars, you will iden-tify, modify, and create styles. Next, you will create a style sheet and attach it to a page. You will also look at style inheritance on SharePoint sites. Finally, you will use CSS reports.

Important Before you can use the practice files in this chapter, you need to install them from the book's companion CD to their default location. You will need to create a practice site for this chapter based on the site template *LookFeel_Starter.stp* located in this chapter's practice file folder. Then when you perform the exercises in this chapter, remember to use your SharePoint site location in place of *teams.consolidatedmessenger.com.*

For more information about practice files, see "Using the Book's CD" at the beginning of this book.

Troubleshooting Graphics and operating system–related instructions in this book reflect the Windows Vista user interface. If your computer is running Windows XP and you experience trouble following the instructions as written, please refer to the "Information for Readers Running Windows XP" section at the beginning of this book.

Understanding the CSS and Color-Coding Options

When you use format elements in a page, SharePoint Designer uses a set of configura-tion options to decide how it should add the cascading style sheet tags to your page. You can change these default settings from within the Page Editor Options dialog box.

This dialog box has 12 tabs, some of which we looked at in Chapter 3, "Customizing a Web Page." Here, we'll explore the tabs that are related to cascading style sheets.

You can choose from many options; for example, you can configure SharePoint Designer to generate styles automatically or you can chose to create the styles yourself. You can also limit SharePoint Designer so that it can modify only those styles that it automatically created and no others. Usually, the default settings of these options work well, so you may not need to change them. However, it is important to know what SharePoint Designer is doing on your behalf, because it may not be quite what you want.

CSS Primer

Cascading style sheets were first unveiled to the world in 1994. You can consider cascading style sheets to be a smart language that browsers interpret to format the font color or size of elements, and which you can use to position elements on the page. Each style consists of a rule that has a selector and one or more properties, where each property has a value. Cascading style sheets are not case sensitive.

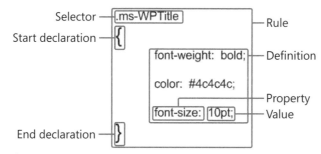

SharePoint Designer includes a number of style types, which can be identified by a different color icon. Refer to the table at the end of this sidebar for examples.

All but the *inline style* must be defined with a tag; all other styles can reside in a page or in a separate file that can be attached to a page. Files that contain styles usually have an extension of *.css*.

If you do define styles within a page, to reduce your time in searching for them, place them all in the same location, for example, in the <head> tag of the file. To define a style in a page, you must surround the style attributes with a open and close <style> tag, referred to as a *style block*.

Styles can be defined multiple times on a page, and in many files, attached to a page; each style could apply a difference property value to an element; for example, a <div> tag could have multiple class styles assigned to it, each defining a different color. Styles go by a number of rules, which browsers use to determine which style to apply: inheritance rules, cascade order, and *CSS specificity*.

For example, a tag will take on the style of its parent, so if the property, *color*, is specified for the <body> tag but not the <p> tag, then text within the <p> tag will use the style defined on the <body> tag. Cascade order specifies the order that styles are applied. Cascading style sheet files are applied in a specific order and read sequentially, and then the styles on the page are applied in sequential order. Therefore, in general terms, the style used by the browser to render an element's font color is the style that last defined the color property. CSS specificity adds a few more rules to this equation, such that each selector is given a value where an ID selector has more power than the element or class selectors. In a group of nested selectors, these values are used to decide which style attributes to apply.

See Also Other resources for learning to use cascading style sheets can be found at *w3schools.com/css/ and csszengarden.com*. For more information about the order in which styles are applied, search on the keywords *CSS specificity* in any search engine.

> **Tip** The quickest way to learn more about cascading style sheets is to work in Split view as much as you can.

Icon	Style type	Description and examples
● (Yellow)	Inline	This is the simplest of styles and affects only the tag where it is defined. Use this style type if you do not plan to use this styling elsewhere. `<p style="text-align: center;">`
● (Blue)	Elements	This style affects all instances of the specified element (tag) on the page. `body { font-family: "Trebuchet MS",arial; }`

● (Green)	Classes	This style is applied to those elements that reference it.
		`.ms-quicklaunch { background-color: #d6e8ff; }`
		
		The tag that references the style looks similar to:
		`<div class="ms-quickLaunch">`

● (Red)	IDs	This style can be used only once per page, and is usually reserved for structural elements.
		`#page_content { font-weight: 700; }`
		
		The tag that references the style looks similar to:
		`<div id="page_content">`

◉	Style in use	SharePoint Designer places a grey circle around the style icon if the style is used on the page.

In this exercise, you will explore the different tabs of the Page Editor Options dialog box that relate to cascading style sheets.

USE your own SharePoint site location in place of the *teams.consolidatedmessenger.com* team site shown in this exercise.

OPEN the LookFeel child site in SharePoint Designer, and close any pages that may open in the document window.

1. On the **Tools** menu, click **Page Editor Options**.

   The Page Editor Options dialog box opens.

2. Click the **CSS** tab to display the options that SharePoint Designer uses when creating and modifying styles on your pages.

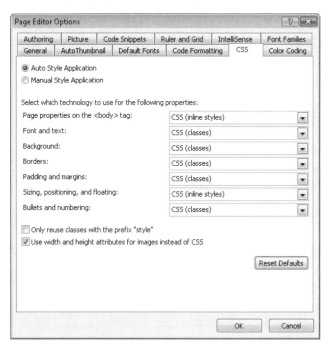

3. Click the **Color Coding** tab to display the code coloring options that SharePoint Designer uses in the Code and Design views of the document window.

4. Click the **Authoring** tab.

   In the CSS Schema section, the CSS 2.1 option is selected by default, therefore, SharePoint Designer uses CSS 2.1 when you type style-related text in the Code view of the document window.

5. Click **OK**.

   The Page Editor Options dialog box closes.

Identifying Styles in Cascading Style Sheets

As you have seen earlier, both Windows SharePoint Services and Office SharePoint Server 2007 use a number of master pages. In Chapter 8, "Using Controls in Web Pages," you saw that the default.master page links to a cascading style sheet named *core.css*. SharePoint Server includes many more style sheets. At the top-level site of a site collection created from the Collaboration or Internet portal site templates is a library named *Style Library*, which contains some of these SharePoint Server specific style sheets. However, for both products, core.css is the main cascading style sheet file that defines most of the styles you will need to customize your site.

See Also   For more information about core.css and the style definition it contains, refer to *msdn2.microsoft.com/ms438349.aspx*, or search on the keywords *sharepoint core.css* in any search engine.

By the very fact that you are reading this book, and not one on Expression Web, for example, you are interested in customizing sites based on Windows SharePoint Services and SharePoint Server; hence, you need to get to know the cascading style sheets and their definitions that Microsoft created.

> **Tip** Not all styles are exposed in SharePoint Designer, specifically those dynamically created by controls. It is only when the page is rendered in the browser that you can see the styles and the elements to which they are applied. Therefore, you may find it useful to use other tools that complement those that SharePoint Designer provides. One such tool is the Internet Explorer Developer toolbar that is available from the Microsoft download center.

In this exercise, you will identify styles used on a site based on the team site template.

> **USE** the site you modified in the previous exercise.
> **BE SURE TO** have only one SharePoint Designer window open.
> **OPEN** the site in SharePoint Designer, if it is not already open.

1. On the **Task Panes** menu, click **Reset Workspace Layout**.

   SharePoint Designer displays the default task panes in their original position. The Tag Properties and CSS Properties task panes appear in the lower-left area, and the Apply Styles and Manage Styles task panes appear in the lower-right area.

2. In the lower-left area, click the **CSS Properties** tab to bring it to the front, and in the lower-right area, click the **Manage Styles** tab to bring that tab to the front.

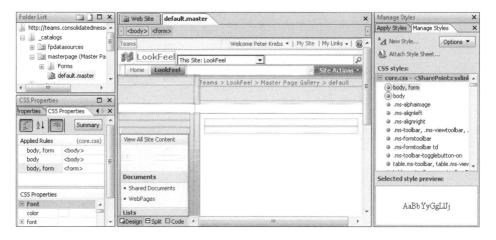
Close

3. In the upper-right area, close the **Toolbox** task pane so that the Manage Styles area expands across the length of the window.

4. In the **Folder List** task pane, expand the **_catalogs** folder, and then the **masterpage (Master Page Gallery)** folder. Then double-click **default.master** to display the page in the document window.

In the Quick Tag Selector, the <form> tag is highlighted. In the CSS Properties task pane, (core.css) is displayed, indicating that this is a linked style sheet. Three rules applied to the <form> tag, in the order they were applied, appear under Applied Rules. The first rule applied at the top of the list. In the Manage Styles task pane, core.css also appears; below which, two CSS elements are listed and surrounded by a grey circle, indicating that the CSS elements are used within the current document.

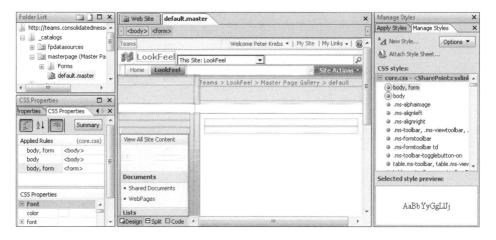

Tip By default, the Manage Styles task pane lists the styles in the order in which they appear in their style sheet. When you have multiple style sheets, each style sheet is listed separately. When viewing style by order, you can move them by dragging the style up or down the list or from a style that was on the page to a style in a file, and vice-versa. If the current page does not appear in the Manage Styles task pane, then it currently contains no styles; therefore, to make the page appear in the list, add a script block (<script>...</script>) to the head tags of the page.

5. In the **Manage Styles** task pane, click **Options**, and then click **Show Styles Used In Current Page**.

The Manage Styles task pane refreshes. All CSS elements and classes are surrounded by a grey circle.

6. In the **Manage Styles** task pane, click **Options**, and then click **Categorize By Type**.

The style types are listed in a tree-link structure, with group headings of Elements and Classes.

7. In the **Manage Styles** task pane, scroll down, and then click **.ms-globalbreadcrumb**.

The Selected Style Preview, at the bottom of the Manage Styles task pane, displays right-aligned text with a background of light blue. The CSS Properties task pane displays the CSS Properties associated with the .ms-globalbreadcrumb style. No style was applied to default.master.

8. In the **Manage Styles** task pane, right-click **.ms-globalbreadcrumb**, and then click **Select All 1 Instance(s).**

On the Quick Tag Selector, the tag <td.ms-globalbrea..> is highlighted in orange. A purple rectangle appears around the top area of the page that contains the global navigation breadcrumb and the links such as Welcome, My Site, and the Help icon.

9. In the **Manage Styles** task pane, scroll down, and point to the **.ms-globalbreadcrumb**, so that a tooltip appears with the rule styles.

10. In the **CSS Properties** task pane, under **Current Rule**, point to **.ms-globalbreadcrumb**, so that a tooltip appears.

The text in this tooltip should match the text in the tooltip shown in the Manage Styles task pane.

Show alphabetized list

11. In the **CSS Properties** task pane, click the **Show alphabetized list** icon (if it is not already selected), and then click the **Show set properties on top** icon.

The CSS properties defined for the .ms-globalbreadcrumb rule appears in bold blue text.

Show set
properties on top

12. In the document window, click the content breadcrumb (the one under the site tabs and Site Actions button).

In the Manage Styles task pane, the style starting with the text *.ms-titleareaframe table td.ms.titlearea*, is highlighted, showing that multiple styles are applied to this object. In the CSS Properties task pane, under Applied Rules, multiple rules are listed with the Padding property in bold blue text with a red line through it, showing that this property is overridden.

13 In the **CSS Properties** task pane, click the **Summary** button.

A summarized list of all properties appears. The properties are listed in the order in which they were applied; for example, two occurrences of the color property are listed. The first color property has a red line thought it, showing it was over ridden. The second color property, immediately under the first color property, does not have a red line through it. This property overrode the first property.

14. In the **CSS Properties** task pane, click the **color** property that has a red line through it.

Under Applied Rules, the body rule has a blue rectangle drawn around it. This is the rule where the overridden color property was defined.

15. In the **CSS Properties** task pane, point to the **color** property that has a red line through it, so that a tooltip appears with the name of the rule overriding this property: .ms-titlearea, ms-mwstitlearea.

> **Tip** On a content page, the SharePoint Designer style task panes and toolbars display information for text, images, controls and other elements that you place on the content page. To use the style task panes and tool bars for tags placed on the master page, you must display the master page.

16. In the **Folder List** task pane, double-click **default.aspx** to open in the document window.

The CSS Properties task pane contains no rules or properties and the Manage Styles task pane contains Elements and Classes style types from core.css plus Elements and Classes style types from the current page.

17. In the document window, click **Welcome**.

A purple rectangle surrounds the global navigation breadcrumb, but no control label is visible, nor is the Quick Tag Selector, and no rules are listed in the CSS Properties task pane.

18. To the right of **Welcome**, click the **chevron** to open the **Common Content Tasks** list.

Chevron

The Common Content Tasks list displays a link named Create Custom Content. This indicates that the area surrounded by the purple rectangle is a control from the master page.

19. Click the content navigation breadcrumb (the one under the site tabs and Site Actions button).

The Quick Tag Selector appears and the PlaceHolderMain (Custom) label appears above the breadcrumb. The CSS Properties task pane lists a number of rules and properties.

CLOSE all open pages in the SharePoint Designer program window.

Creating, Modifying, and Deleting Styles

In the previous section, you learned that by highlighting elements in the Design view of a page and using the information in a combination of task panes, you could identify the styles you need to modify, and so the next task is to modify them. With SharePoint Designer, you do not need to be a cascading style sheet expert. Just as it provided you with visual methods of creating, modifying, and deleting other elements, so it provides you with tools to manipulate styles, such as the Quick Tag Selector, the information in the Apply Styles task pane, and the Style and Style Application toolbars. If you are famil-iar with the Style pane in Microsoft Word, then you will find that the Apply Styles task pane works in a similar manner. However, if you are new to cascading style sheets, don't start using SharePoint Designer with a very complicated page; start with a simple example so you understand the tools first.

As when you do other modifications, by using the Preview In Multiple Browsers option, keep checking your design in a variety of different browsers and screen sizes to ensure it will display correctly for users, and simply hit the Undo button if the latest edit is not to your liking.

In this exercise, you will create, modify, and delete styles.

> **USE** the site you modified in the previous exercise.
> **OPEN** the site in SharePoint Designer, if it is not already open.

New Document

1. On the Common toolbar, click the **New Document** arrow, and then click **Page** to open the **New** dialog box.

2. In the **New** dialog box, click **CSS Layouts**, click **Two columns, right fixed**, and then click **OK**.

   Two new files, *untitled_1.css* and *untitled_1.htm*, open. In the Manage Styles task pane, under untitled_1.css, three ID-based styles appear. On the untitled_1.htm page, the <div#page_content tag> is selected and the CSS Properties task pane shows the rules and properties that affect this tag.

3. On the Common toolbar, click the **Save** button.

Save

4. In the **Save As** dialog box that opens, double-click **WebPages**. In the **File name** text box, type ApplyStyles.aspx, and then click **Save**.

   The Save As dialog box redisplays with untitled_1 in the File Name text box.

5. In the **File name** text box, type ApplyStyles.css, and then click **Save**.

   The Save As dialog box closes. The untitled_1.css and untitled_1.htm tab are renamed as *ApplysStyles.css* and *ApplyStyles.aspx*.

Split

6. At the bottom of the document window, click **Split** to display both the Code and Design views.

Show set
properties on top

7. In the **CSS Properties** task pane click the **Show set properties on top** button if it is not already selected, and click the **Summary** button to deselect it to show all properties.

   The CSS Properties task pane shows that the margin-right property is set.

8. In the right task pane area, click the **Apply Styles** tab.

   In the Apply Styles task pane, the three ID styles are listed.

9. In the Design portion of the document window, place the insertion point under the **div#page_content** label, and then type Consolidated Messenger.

B
Bold

10. Select **Consolidated Messenger**, and then on the Common toolbar, click **Bold**.

    In the CSS Properties task pane, the font-weight property appears at the top of the list with a value of 700, and in the Apply Styles task pane, #page-content is bold.

> **Tip** To format objects such as text and images in Design view, use the visual editing capabilities in the CSS Properties task pane and the Apply Styles task pane, and the formatting icons on the Common toolbar. In Code view, type the first few characters of the style attribute, and then choose the complete style attribute from the IntelliSense list. In Code view, if you mistype a style attribute or tag, a squiggly red line appears under the attribute or tag, in the same way that a misspelled word is identified in Microsoft Office Word.

11. In the **CSS Properties** task pane, click the cell to the right of **background-color**, and then click the arrow that appears.

12. In the list, click **silver**.

In the CSS Properties task pane, the background-color property is set to hex code #C0C0C0, in the document window the text *Consolidated Messenger* has a background color of silver, and in the Apply Styles task pane, the #page-content style has a background color of silver.

13. Place the insertion point on the line after **Consolidated Messenger** (outside the **<div>** tag), and then type Parcels and Boxes.

The text is placed inside a <p> tag.

14. Select **Parcels and Boxes**, and then on the Common toolbar, click **Center**.

SharePoint Designer creates a new class-based style in the current page, named *.style1*, and associates it with the <p> tag. This new tag appears in the Apply Styles and CSS Properties task panes. The Current Page heading is lower in the Apply Styles task pane, indicating that styles defined on the current page are applied after styles in the *ApplyStyle.css* file.

> **Tip** If a class style was not created, verify that the CSS tab of the Page Editor Options dialog box is set to Auto Style Application.

15. Place the insertion point on the line after **Parcels and Boxes** (outside the **<p>** tag), and then type Air and Ocean.

The text is placed inside a <p> tag and the tag is associated with the style1 class.

> **Tip** You can remove styles from an element by selecting the element, and then on the Apply Styles task pane, clicking Clear Styles.

16. Select **Air and Ocean**, and then on the Common toolbar, click **Align Text Right**.

SharePoint Designer creates a new class-based style, *.style 2*.

> **Tip** You can create a new style by using an existing style as a basis. In the Apply Styles task pane, right-click the style you want to use as a basis, and then click New Style Copy.

17. Click **Air and Ocean**, and then in the **Apply Styles** task pane, click **.style1** to revert the <p> tag to .style 1.

The class-based style, style 2, is deleted from the current page.

> **Tip** If you had clicked Align Text Right again, this would also have reverted the <p> tag back to .style 1.

18. In the **Apply Styles** task pane, point to **.style 1**, click the arrow that appears, and then click **Modify Style**.

The Modify Style dialog box opens.

19. Under **Category**, click **Border**. Under **border-style**, in the **top** list, click **double**.

20. Click **OK** to apply the style and to close the **Modify Style** dialog box.

The two <p> tags are surrounded by a double-line border.

21. In the **Code** view, while holding down Ctrl, click **style 1**.

The Code view displays the .style 1 rule enclosed in a <style> tagin the <head> portion of the page.

22. Right-click the **ApplyStyle.aspx** tab, and then click **Save**.

The Save Embedded Files dialog box opens.

23. Click **OK**.

Both *ApplyStyle.aspx* and *ApplyStyle.css* files are saved and the Save Embedded Files dialog box closes.

Using the Style Application Toolbar

The purpose of the Style Application toolbar is like any other toolbar. Its main function is so you can quickly access components you use often. In the first topic of this chapter, you saw that by using the Page Editor Options dialog box, you could configure SharePoint Designer to automatically create styles on your behalf or you can configure SharePoint Designer so you can manually create the styles. If you work a great deal with cascading style sheets, you might find that staying in one of these modes all the time does not suit you. This is where the Style Application toolbar can help, because you can use it to switch easily between these two modes, thereby providing you with the control over how styles are generated. You can also use the Target Rule list on the Style Application toolbar to quickly apply styles you have already created.

In this exercise, you will use the Style Application toolbar.

USE the site you modified in the previous exercise.

OPEN the site in SharePoint Designer, if it is not already open, and display the *ApplyStyle* page.

1. On the **View** menu, point to **Toolbars**, and then click **Style Application** to display a floating Style Application toolbar.

> **Tip** You can also display the Style Application toolbar by clicking Format on the CSS Styles menu or by double-clicking Style Application in the status bar of SharePoint Designer.

2. In the **Style Application** list, click **Manual**.

In the SharePoint status bar, the type of style application changes to Manual.

3. Click **Parcels and Boxes**.

The Target Rule list of the Style Application toolbar is populated with the style(s) of the currently selected style. Both the Reuse Properties and Show Overlay buttons are highlighted in orange, indicating that they are both selected.

Style Application	
Style Application: Manual ▼ Target Rule: .style1 ▼ ⌖ Reuse Properties ≣ Sho

4. On the Style Application toolbar, click the **Target Rule** arrow, and then in the list, click **< New Inline Style >**.

Align Text Right

5. On the Common toolbar, click **Align Text Right**.

The *.style 1* class-based style is modified and the text in the two <p> tags are aligned to the right.

Center

6. On the Style Application toolbar, click **Reuse Properties** to deselect the button, and then on the Common toolbar, click **Center**.

SharePoint Designer creates an inline style. In the Apply Styles task pane, the Inline Style heading is below the Current Page heading. Therefore, the styles in the *ApplyStyle.css* file are applied first, followed by those styles in <script> tags on the current page, followed by the inline styles.

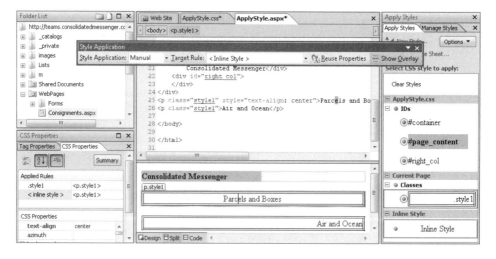

7. On the Style Application toolbar, in the **Target Rule** list, click **(New Auto Class)**.

8. On the Common toolbar, click **Align Text Right**.

   SharePoint Designer creates a new class-based style, *.style 2*, that appears in the Target Rule list box on the Style Application toolbar, in the Code view, and in the Apply Styles and CSS Properties task panes.

Save

9. On the Style Application toolbar, in the **Target Rule** list, click **Apply New Style**.

   The New Style dialog box opens.

10. In the **Selector** text box, type .spd-text1. Under **Category**, click **Font**, if not already selected, and click **font-family**. Then scroll down the list, and click **Trebuchet MS**.

11. Under **Category**, click **Block**, click the **text-align** arrow, and click **left**. Then click **OK** to close the **New Style** dialog box.

    In the Apply Styles task pane, both the .spd-text1 and inline styles are displayed with a surrounding blue box, indicating that both styles are applied to the text. The <p> tag is displayed without a double-line border. The text remains centered and in the new font.

12. Right-click the **ApplyStyle.aspx** tab, and then click **Save**.

> **CLOSE** all open pages in the SharePoint Designer program window.

Creating and Attaching CSS Files

By placing styles in a file, you can centrally manage those styles and apply the same styles to a number of pages. Both Windows SharePoint Services and SharePoint Server make heavy use of styles that reside in files. Earlier in this chapter, when you chose a CSS layout, SharePoint Designer created both a page and a style sheet. You can also create a new style sheet from the New Document list or from the New Style dialog box, which you can open from the Format menu, the Manage Styles and Apply Styles task panes, and the Style Application and Style toolbars.

When you create styles in a cascading style sheet file, for those styles to apply to a page, the file needs to be attached to that page. Again, SharePoint Designer provides you with many interfaces to complete this task; for example, you can use links in both the Apply Style and Manage Styles task panes. When you attach a file, <link> tags are placed in the <head> tags.

In this exercise, you will attach a cascading style sheet file to a page.

> **USE** the site you modified in the previous exercise.
> **OPEN** the site in SharePoint Designer, if it isn't already open.

Design

1. In the **Folder List** task pane, under **WebPages**, double-click **LookFeel.aspx** to open the page in the document window. Then click **Design**.

   The page contains some text and one Web Part zone named *Main* and a List View Web Part (LVWP) of the Products list, which is not formatted because no styles are associated with this page.

2. On the **Format** menu, click **New Style** to open the **New Style** dialog box.

3. In the **Selector** text box, type **.ms-pagetitle**. Then in the **Define in** list, click **New style sheet**.

4. With **Font** selected under **Category**, in the **color** list, click **Teal**. Then click **OK**.

5. In the dialog box that opens asking if you want to attach the style sheet, click **Yes**.

   Both the New Style dialog box and the confirmation box close, and *untitled_1.css* appears as a tab.

6. In the **Apply Styles** task pane, click the **Options** button, and then click **Show All Styles**.

   The class style, *.ms-pagetitle*, appears in the Apply Styles task pane.

7. On the **View** menu, point to **Toolbars**, and then click **Style**.

   A floating toolbar named Style opens.

8. In the document window, click **Consolidated Messenger**. Then on the **Style** toolbar, in the **Class** list, click **.ms-pagetitle**.

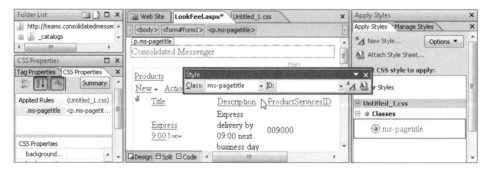

9. In the **Folder List** task pane, expand **_catalogs**. Then expand **masterpage (Master Page Gallery)**, and drag **default.master** on to the page in the document window.

10. When the **Match Content Regions** dialog box opens, click **OK**.

    The Match Content Regions dialog box closes, and in the Apply Styles task pane, core.css appears. The text *Consolidated Messenger* appears in bold in a larger font size. The LVWP toolbar is now formatted.

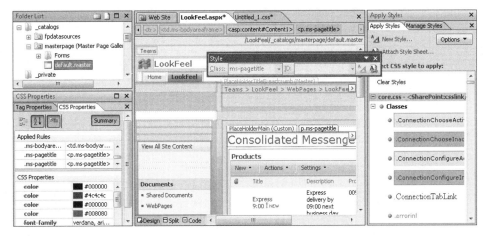

Attach
Style Sheet

11. On the right of the floating Style toolbar, click **Attach Style Sheet**.

    The Attach Style Sheet dialog box opens.

12. Click the **Current Page** option if it is not already selected. Then click **Browse** to open the **Select Style Sheet** dialog box.

13. Double-click WebPages, click **WPTitle.css**, and then click **Open** to close the **Select Style Sheet** dialog box.

    The Attach Style Sheet dialog box now contains the URL of the *WPTitle.css* file.

14. Click **OK** to close the **Attach Style Sheet** dialog box.

    The Web Part title background for the Products LVWP is dark teal.

15. In the **Folder List** task pane, under **WebPages** pages, drag **HideQuickLaunch.css** to the **PlaceHolderMain (Custom)** control in **LookFeel.aspx**.

    The HideQuickLaunch style sheet is attached to the page, and the Quick Launch bar disappears.

16. Right-click the **LookFeel.aspx** tab, and click **Save**. Save **Untitled_1.css** as LookFeel.css.

CLOSE all open pages in the SharePoint Designer program window.

Understanding CSS Inheritance in SharePoint

As with many other files, you have worked with in this book, core.css and the other style sheets lives in the 12 hive on each Web server; therefore, if you modify and save them with SharePoint Designer, you will create *customized* pages. Child sites do not inherit from a customized core.css; they will still point to the un-customized page in the 12 hive. If you repeat this on a number of sites, each site will have its own copy of core.css. Then if the core.css in the 12 hive is changed and distributed to the Web server(s), those changes will not affect your sites.

See Also For more information about the 12 hive, see, Chapter 1, "Introducing SharePoint Designer."

When you need all sites in a site collection to have the same branding, then breaking the link with the *un-customized* core.css file can be a major problem. Therefore, a best practice is not to change core.css or any of the other built-in style sheets by using SharePoint Designer or any other product.

Warning If the built-in style sheets on the Web servers are changed, you could potentially lose your modifications if a service pack is installed.

Using SharePoint Designer to customize one site, you should take a copy of the styles you want to amend, and then place those styles in the master page surrounded by <script> tags.

To brand more than one site, you need to involve a developer, investigate the use of a separate style sheet, and obtain a greater understanding of the inheritance structure of the different methods that both Windows SharePoint Services and SharePoint Server have to offer. For example, master pages link to core.css by using a control; therefore, the styles in core.css are applied after styles in files you have attached to the master page. However, if you customize core.css, then the styles in the attached files are applied after the styles in core.css. In addition, using SharePoint Designer to attach a new style sheet to a master page also results in a *customized* master page, which is something you may not want.

SharePoint Server has a mechanism for attaching an alternative style sheet. Styles defined in this file are always applied after the styles in core.css, whether or not you customize core.css. Add to this discussion themes and the ability to define additional cascading style sheets in site definitions and features, you can understand why you need the skills of a developer.

> **Note** Windows SharePoint Services comes with a number of themes you can apply to your site. These contain a number of cascading style sheets and images and are also stored in the 12 hive, but are not exposed to SharePoint Designer over HTTP. For more information about themes, search on the keywords *SharePoint 2007 themes*.

In this exercise, you will review the relationship that core.css has with the default master page. You will also edit a style within core.css, resulting in a customized page that you will then revert back to a file on the Web server.

> **USE** the site you modified in the previous exercise.
> **OPEN** the site in SharePoint Designer, if it isn't already open.

1. In the **Folder List** task pane, expand **_catalogs**. Then expand **masterpage (Master Page Gallery)**, and double-click **default.master** to open the page in the document window.

   In the Quick Tag Selector, the <form> tag is highlighted.

2. In the **Manage Styles** task pane, click **core.css**, then continue to point to it until a tooltip appears.

The tooltip points to a location in the _layouts directory, which is a folder in the 12 hive on the Web servers.

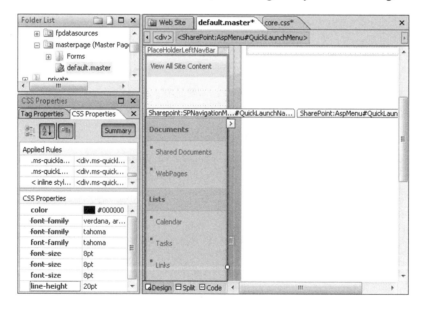

3. On default.master on the Quick Launch bar, click **Documents**. Then in the **CSS Properties** task pane, click **Summary**.

The Quick Launch Navigation control is selected and only styles that are applied to that control are listed in the CSS Properties task pane.

4. In the **CSS Properties** task pane, click the cell to the right of **line-height**, and type **20pt**. Then press [Enter].

The core.css file opens in the document window; both default.master and core.css have an asterisk on their tab labels, indicating that you have changed both files.

> **Tip** If the core.css file does not open in the document window, you may have another SharePoint Designer program window open, which is where you will find the core.css file open. When working with styles, open only one SharePoint Designer program window.

5. Right-click the **core.css** tab, and then click **Save**.

A Stylesheet Customization Warning dialog box opens.

6. Click **Yes** to close the warning dialog box.

A folder named _styles is created in the Folder List task pane a folder is created named _styles. You may need to scroll down to see this folder.

7. In the **Folder List** task pane, expand **_styles**.

The file core.css is listed with a blue information circle to its left.

8. In the document window, click the **default.master** tab. Then in the **Manage Styles** task pane, click **core.css**, leaving your pointer over it so that a tooltip appears.

The tooltip indicates that core.css is now stored in _/LookFeel/_styles_.

9. In the **Folder List** task pane, right-click **core.css**, and then click **Reset to Site Definition**. When the **Site Definition Page Warning** dialog box opens, click **Yes**.

The _styles folder contains core.css and _core_copy(1).css_.

10. In the **Manage Styles** task pane, click **core.css**, leaving your pointer over it so that a tooltip appears.

The tooltip states that core.css is still located in _/LookFeel/_styles_.

11. In the **Folder List** task pane, right-click **core.css**, and click **Delete**.

A Customized Stylesheet Warning dialog box opens, stating that this action will cause you to use a default version of the stylesheet.

12. Click **OK** to close the **Customized Stylesheet Warning** dialog box.

13. In the **Confirm Delete** dialog box that opens, click **Yes**.

The _style folder now contains only the _core_copy(1).css_ file.

CLOSE the default.master page without saving your changes.

Using CSS Reports

As with any other customization technique, you can make mistakes easily or produce a solution that is hard to maintain. This is where the SharePoint Designer CSS reports can help you. The CSS reports check one or more pages within your site, as well as produce a Usage report showing you where class, ID, and tag selectors are used and on what lines. These reports can help you find errors and identify styles that are defined but not used.

In this exercise, you will use the CSS Reports to validate the default.master page.

> **USE** the site you modified in the previous exercise.
>
> **OPEN** the site in SharePoint Designer, if it isn't already open.

1. In the **Folder List** task pane, under **masterpage (Master Pages)**, click **default.master**.

2. On the **Tools** menu, click **CSS Reports** to open the **CSS Reports** dialog box.

3. Verify that **Selected pages** is selected, as well as the three check boxes under **Check for**, and then click **Check**.

   The Check Reports task pane opens in the lower area of the document window, and lists a number of errors.

4. In the **CSS Reports** task pane, double-click the first line to open **default.master** at the line where the style error occurred.

> **CLOSE** the SharePoint site and the CSS Reports task pane. If you're not continuing directly to the next chapter, exit SharePoint Designer.

Key Points

- SharePoint Designer provides you with three task panes and two toolbars, together with several menu links, to help you manipulate cascading style sheet styles and files.

- SharePoint Designer uses a set of configuration options to decide how it should add the cascading style sheet tags to your page.

- The main cascading style sheet for both Windows SharePoint Services and SharePoint Service is core.css.

- The Manage Styles and CSS Properties task panes provide useful tools to identify where styles are used and the cascade order of those styles. With the Style Application toolbar, you can switch between automatic and manual CSS modes and quickly apply styles.

- You can save your styles in files that you can attach to pages; however, if you attach a file to a master page, the styles in core.css will override them.

- Use the CSS reports to check your styles and to produce CSS Usage reports.

Chapter at a Glance

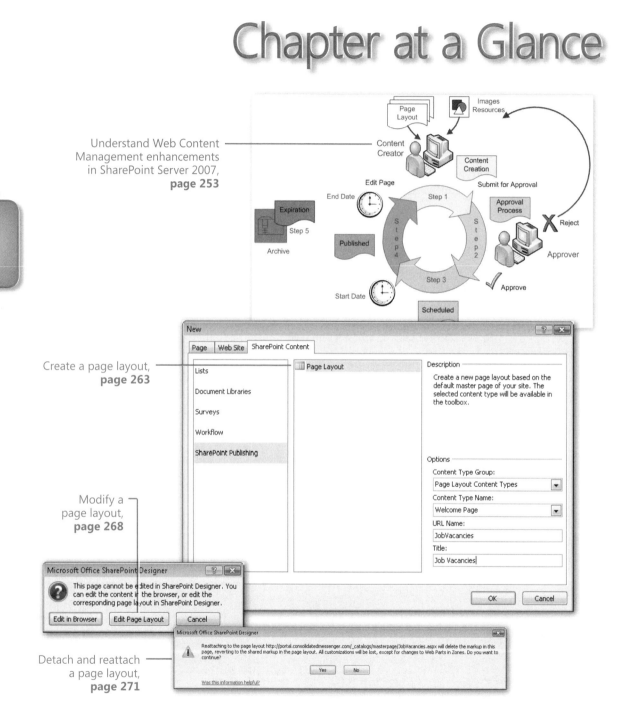

Understand Web Content
Management enhancements
in SharePoint Server 2007,
page 253

Create a page layout,
page 263

Modify a
page layout,
page 268

Detach and reattach
a page layout,
page 271

11 Managing Web Content in a SharePoint Server Environment

In this chapter, you will learn to:

- ✔ Understand Web Content Management enhancements in SharePoint Server 2007.
- ✔ Understand the page model.
- ✔ Create a page layout.
- ✔ Modify a page layout.
- ✔ Restore an earlier version of a page layout.
- ✔ Detach and reattach a page layout.

Web Content Management is just one of the features included in the Enterprise Content Management (ECM) feature area of Microsoft Office SharePoint Server 2007. This feature has its origins in Microsoft Content Management Server (CMS), but it is not just an upgrade; it has been totally revised and recoded for Office SharePoint Server 2007, and uses other features with SharePoint Server to provide a total solution.

Web Content Management uses the document management features to manage pages. This places the content pages in a source control system so that you can check pages in and out, as well as use the Approval workflow. SharePoint Server provides a number of publishing templates, see the sidebar "Publishing Site Templates" in Chapter 2,"Working in SharePoint Designer." With the *Publishing Site with Workflow* site template, many of these features are automatically enabled, so that you can build the kind of strict content management process that is needed by many commercial Internet sites.

See Also For more information about workflows, see Chapter 12, "Understanding Workflows."

The Web Content Management features are available to you when you create sites based on the Publishing Site and the Publishing Site With Workflow site definitions. The Collaboration Portal and Internet Portal site definitions use these publishing site definitions to build intranet, extranet, and Internet sites. Both of these publishing site definitions use Microsoft Windows SharePoint Services as a basis, to provide the Web content management solution. Such a solution can be customized by using a browser, Microsoft Office SharePoint Designer 2007, and Microsoft Visual Studio 2005, and this solution integrates with the Microsoft Office client applications.

Both the Publishing Site and the Publishing Site With Workflow site definitions enable the Office SharePoint Server Publishing feature. This feature provides a number of additional features not available on team sites, such as an extended Site Actions menu, and the ability to produce reports that you can use to manage not only pages that you own, but any document in any library, across more than one site. It also provides additional Web Parts—such as the Content Query Web Part (CQWP)—that you can use to aggregate data from multiple data sources, and provides the ability to use *variations* to support the creation and management of multilingual sites.

However, one of the key constructs of publishing sites is the ability to control the strict layout of content on a page, known as *page layout*. So each Web content management page, also known as a publishing page, is based on a page layout. Each page layout is associated with a master page, so the branding and navigation is the same on Web Content Management pages, as it is on ordinary content pages. However, on a publishing page, you are not modifying a live page, where your changes are immediately visible to visitors. You can restrict the content shown in different areas of the page to be just text or not to include images. These features are available because the publishing page is associated with a page control, and it is the page control that dictates the content rules and the look and feel in the content portion of the page.

> **Important** In this chapter, we concentrate on how to use SharePoint Designer with the Web Content Management feature of SharePoint Server, in particular the page layouts; therefore, if you do not have SharePoint Server installed on your computer, you will not be able to complete the exercises in this chapter.

In this chapter, you will explore the Web Content Management features of SharePoint Server and the publishing page model. You will create a new page layout, which you will modify and then restore to a previous version. Finally, you will detach a page from its page layout and then reattach the page layout with the page.

> **Important** No practice files are required to complete the exercises in this chapter. Nor is there a solution file, because the browser does not provide a supported mechanism for saving publishing sites as site templates. For more information about practice files, see "Using the Book's CD" at the beginning of this book.

> **Troubleshooting** Graphics and operating system–related instructions in this book reflect the Windows Vista user interface. If your computer is running Windows XP and you experience trouble following the instructions as written, please refer to the "Information for Readers Running Windows XP" section at the beginning of this book.

Understanding Web Content Management Enhancements in SharePoint Server 2007

As with any other Web content management program, with SharePoint Server, you can create and manage Web content from its creation to live publication. The process is iterative due to periodic modifications. Using the Web Content Management functionality of SharePoint Server, a content approval process could look similar to the following process:

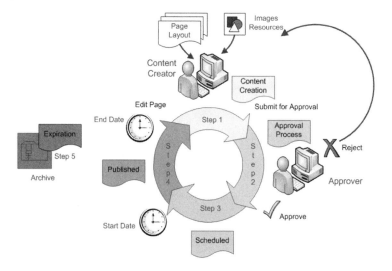

● **Step 1: Content Creation.** The content creator creates a page from a page layout, which is the blueprint of how a page looks without any content. Pages created from page layouts are known as *publishing pages*. In a live Internet site, each page layout would have dozens or hundreds of publishing pages associated with it. Each page layout contains a number of *field controls* that the content creator can use to enter data, and the page layout can optionally contain one or more Web Part zones. Each field control can provide a number of tools that the content creator can use to choose fonts, links, images, and other resources to make content creation as simple as possible, such as a spelling checker. Each site collection contains a Site Collection Images library that the content creator can use to store images that are used through the site collection. Page layouts are stored in the Master Page Gallery.

- **Step 2: Approval Process.** After a publishing page is formatted, including any scheduling properties, the content creator submits it for approval. The approver can edit, reject, or approve the page.

- **Step 3: Scheduled.** After approval, the publishing page is either published or scheduled for publication.

- **Step 4: Published.** The publishing page is visible to all visitors to the site.

- **Step 5: Expiration.** When the publishing page reaches the end of its life, the content is no longer visible on the site and can be archived.

Within a site based on the Collaboration Portal site template, most sites use the Publishing Site template, in which case, the default content approval process contains only steps 1 and 4. The Publishing Site template does not have content approval enabled but is enabled for major and minor versions. Therefore, as the content creator amends the page, draft copies of the page are stored as a minor version, and only when a content creator has completed the page to his or her liking and clicked Publish will the page move from step 1 to step 4. The page is then converted into a major version. The page moves from step 4 to step 1 whenever a content creator decides to amend it.

On a site based on the Publishing Site With Workflow template, both content approval and the approval workflow are enabled so that a page will move from step 1 to step 2, before moving on to either step 3 or step 4. Also, by configuring the page's schedule settings, the content creator can place the page in a scheduled state (step 3), whereby the page will not be visible until that date is reached. The content creator can also configure an end date with the option to automatically send the page's contact an e-mail message when the page expires.

To maintain a large Internet site, you will need a number of people who have the following roles:

- **Site Owners.** For a large site that contains many child sites, this may be a team of people who decide the site structure and governance, as well as managing centrally stored resources such as images. Within each child site, another person or team may decide on the list and libraries the site contains, or the pages required. Such a team would produce wire diagrams that represent how each component on the page should be laid out.

- **Page Layout designer.** This person uses SharePoint Designer to create and maintain page layouts. You might need a developer, depending on the complexity of the requirements.

- **Content creator.** These users create and modify publishing pages based on page layouts. Users who are placed in the Members SharePoint Groups on a Collaboration Portal or Internet Portal can amend items, documents and publishing pages. Therefore, most installations will create an additional SharePoint Group, so they can differentiate between users who can edit and modify publishing pages and those, for example, who can upload and approve files in other document libraries.

- **Approver.** These users moderate, edit and approve publishing pages. On a Collaboration Portal or Internet Portal, a special SharePoint Group is created that is automatically linked to the Approval workflow, if enabled. Users in this group can approve any item or document in any list or library that has Content Approval enabled.

- **Visitor.** These users have read-only access to pages.

> **Important** For the exercises in this chapter, you will need to create a practice child site for this chapter based on the Publishing Site template. In the exercises, the child site will be referred to as *PageLayouts* and should be created under a Collaboration Portal site.

In this exercise, you will explore a publishing page.

> **USE** your own SharePoint site location in place of the *portal.consolidatedmessenger.com* publishing site shown in the exercise.
> **OPEN** the *PageLayouts* child site in the browser.

1. Click **Site Actions**, and then click **Create Page**.

   The Create Page page opens.

2. In the **Title** text box, type **Welcome**. Then press [Tab].

   The URL name text box is automatically populated with the text *Welcome*.

   See Also For details about good naming conventions, see the sidebar "Best Practices for Naming URLs" in Chapter 2, "Working in SharePoint Designer."

3. In the **Page Layout** section, scroll down the list, and click **(Welcome Page) Welcome page with summary links**.

   In the Page Layout section, a preview of the page is displayed.

4. Click **Create**.

   The page is displayed in edit mode with the page-editing toolbar visible and a status message saying Only You Can See And Modify This Page. Within the content portion of the page, four field controls are displayed: Page Image, Page Content, Summary Links, and Summary Links 2; as well as three Web Part zones: Top, Left Column, and Right Column.

5. In the **Page Content** field control, click **Edit Content**.

   A floating content-editing toolbar appears. The insertion point is placed inside the field control.

6. In the **Page Content** field control, type Welcome to the Consolidated Messenger Human Resources site.

7. In the **Summary Links** field control, click **New Link**.

The New Link – Webpage Dialog dialog box opens.

8. In the **Title** text box, type Consolidated Messenger Internet site, and in the **Link URL** text box, type http://www.consolidatedmessenger.com. Then click **OK**.

The New Link – Webpage Dialog dialog box closes, and *Consolidated Messenger Internet site* appears in the Summary Links field control.

9. In the **Top** Web Part zone, click **Add a Web Part** to open the **Add Web Parts to Top** dialog box.

10. Under **Lists and Libraries**, select the **Pages** check box, and then click **Add**.

The Add Web Parts To Top dialog box closes, and the Pages LVWP appears in the Top Web Part zone.

Page ▾
11. On the page-editing toolbar, click the **Page** arrow, and then click **Save and Stop Editing**.

The page is taken out of editing mode, but is still checked out to you. The field controls and Web Part zones that do not contain information are not displayed.

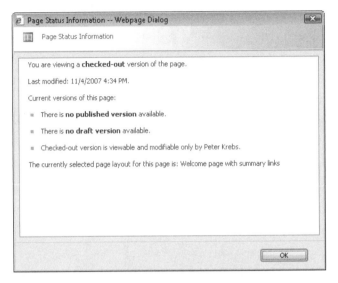

12. On the page-editing toolbar, click the **Tools** arrow, and then click **View Page status**.

The Page Status Information – Webpage Dialog dialog box opens.

> **Page Status Information -- Webpage Dialog**
>
> Page Status Information
>
> You are viewing a **checked-out** version of the page.
>
> Last modified: 11/4/2007 4:34 PM.
>
> Current versions of this page:
> - There is **no published version** available.
> - There is **no draft version** available.
> - Checked-out version is viewable and modifiable only by Peter Krebs.
>
> The currently selected page layout for this page is: Welcome page with summary links
>
> OK

13. Click **OK** to close the **Page Status Information – Webpage Dialog** dialog box.

BE SURE TO leave the browser open if continuing to the next exercise.

Understanding the Page Model

When you click Create Page on the Site Actions menu of a publishing site, a Microsoft ASP.NET page is created in the Pages document library. On a publishing site, even the home page, default.aspx, is stored in this library. If you look at the Address box of a browser, you will see that it ends with *Pages/default.aspx*.

The field controls on a page map to columns within the Pages library. When a content creator enters data into a field control, for example, into the Page Content field control on the Welcome.aspx page, the creator is actually entering data into the Page Content column in the Pages library. Using terminology used previously in this book, by entering data into field controls, you're associating metadata with the Welcome.aspx file.

When you look at the column types used within the Pages library, they do not look different from the column types you use to create columns on a team site. However, there is a difference; the Pages library is associated with a Pages content type, which uses column types that are associated with field controls. Only if a column is associated with a field control can the column data be displayed on publishing pages. When you delete a column within the Page library, you delete the data held in that column for *all* publishing pages; therefore, if a page layout references that column, no pages display that data. When you remove a field control from a page layout, then any pages based on that page layout do not display information from that column; however, you have not deleted any information by removing field controls. If you place the field control back on the page layout, the data is redisplayed.

The benefit of this method is that you have all the power of saving information in a library and yet you can display the data as you would on a traditional site. You can create pages to display, and edit a subset of column values; therefore, content creators know that by creating a page based on a specific page layout, the page will contain all the fields needed and that it's laid out for a particular purpose. Say, for example, that you need to create a solution for maintaining job vacancy details in one location, so you create one content type for job vacancies, from which you create multiple page layouts. Job vacancies that need to specify security levels have one job page layout, and those that have no security clearance have another page layout; yet both page layouts have job title, job description, and date posted fields. Similarly, a vehicle manufacture can store all of its publishing pages in one Pages library, but have different layout for cars than for trucks; yet both have the same field controls to display information, such as the model name, picture, top speed, fuel consumption, and CO_2 emissions.

Each page layout is based on a content type, which in turn specifies the field controls (columns) it can use. Field controls have not only the responsibility of displaying the contents of a column, but when used for data entry purposes, they have the responsibility of writing content back to the column. Because field controls represent the data that is held in columns in the Pages library, if you place the same field control twice on a page, you will be showing the same data twice. If a user then uses both field controls to enter data, the data is saved to the same column, and the field control that saved its data last overrides the data of the previous field control. Therefore, placing multiple copies of a field control on a page layout is *not* similar to placing multiple copies of an LVWP or the Content Editor Web Part on a page. The Web Parts in the Web Part task pane are templates that you can use repeatedly, whereas field controls in the Toolbox task pane represent a specific column in the Pages library and should be placed only once on the page layout.

See Also For details about content types, see the sidebar "Content Types and Site Columns" in Chapter 5, "Working with Lists and Libraries."

In Chapter 3, "Customizing a Web Page," we detailed what happens when a user requests the home page of a team site. When you request a publishing page, such as Welcome.aspx, the following things happen:

- The master page, the Welcome.aspx page, and the site properties are retrieved, such as the site title, permissions, and what should be shown on the Quick Launch bar.

- The Welcome.aspx page properties are retrieved, such as its title, *plus* the page layout it is using.

- The page layout file and its properties are retrieved, such as the field controls and Web Part zones it contains.

- The Welcome.aspx properties associated with the page layout are retrieved, such as the values from the columns that map to the field controls and if the Web Part zones contain any Web Parts.

- The Web Parts data that populate the Web Part zones are retrieved.

- The master page, page layout, the Welcome.aspx page, the information from the field control as to how the column data should be displayed, and all the data retrieved—taking into account the security settings of the user—are merged to form one HTML page that is sent to the user.

In this exercise, you will explore page layouts and the Pages library.

> **OPEN** the Welcome.aspx page in the browser, if it is not already open.

`Page ▼`

1. On the page-editing toolbar, click the **Page** arrow, and then click **Page Settings**.

2. On the **Page Settings** page, in the **Page Layout** section, click the **(Welcome Page) Welcome page with summary links** arrow, and then click **(Welcome Page) Welcome page with Web Part zones**. Then click **OK**.

   The Welcome page is displayed, with the Pages LVWP to the right of the Welcome To The Consolidated Messenger text you entered in the previous exercise.

   > **Tip** On the Page Settings page, page layouts are referred to by both their content type name and their page layout name. The content type's name is in brackets, and the names of the page layouts are to the right of the bracket.

`Edit Page`

3. On the page-editing toolbar, click **Edit Page** to display the page in edit mode.

   Within the content portion of the page, two field controls are displayed: Page Image, Page Content. Also displayed are five Web Part zones: Top Zone, Middle Left Zone, Middle Right Zone, Bottom Zone, and Right Zone.

> **Tip** Web Parts use the Web Part zone name to determine which Web Part zone they should appear in. When a page layout does not contain a Web Part zone with that name, then it is placed in the Web Part zone last added to the page layout. If there are no Web Part zones on a page layout, the Web Part is not displayed; therefore, when you design your page layouts, use consistent Web Part zone names.

4. On the page-editing toolbar, click the **Page** arrow, and then click **Page Settings**.

5. On the **Page Settings** page, in the **Page Layout** section, click the **Welcome page with Web Part zones** arrow, and in the list, click **Welcome page with summary links**. Then click **OK**.

The Welcome page is displayed, showing the Consolidated Messenger Internet site link and the Pages LVWP in the Right Column Web Part.

6. On the Quick Launch bar, click **View All Site Content**.

7. On the **All Site Content** page, under **Document Libraries**, click **Pages**.

8. In the **Pages** library, click **Settings**, and then click **Document Library Settings**.

9. On the **Customize Pages** page, under **Content Types**, click **Page**.

The List Content Type: Page page is displayed, and under Columns, the following columns are listed: Name, Title, Description, Contact, Contact E-mail Address, Contact Name, Contact Picture, Rollup Image, and Target Audiences.

10. On the breadcrumb, click **Settings** to display the Customize Pages page.

11. Under **Content Types**, click **Welcome Page**.

The List Content Type: Welcome Page is displayed, and under Columns, the same columns from the Page content type are listed, in addition to the following columns: Page Image, Page Content, Summary Links, and Summary Links 2.

12. On the breadcrumb, click **Pages**.

13. In the **Pages** library, point to **Welcome**, click the arrow that appears, and then click **Edit Properties**.

The Pages: Welcome page is displayed. Toward the bottom of the page, the Page Content field and Summary Links field are displayed.

14. In the **Page Content** section, click **Edit Content**.

A floating content-editing toolbar appears.

15. Click to place the insertion point at the end of the sentence, after *site*, and type On this site, you will find information on job vacancies, benefits, and polices such as annual leave and expense claims.

Tip You can't modify all of the page content column types from the Pages: [Page Name] page. The Summary Links column is an example: You can only enter data. The Summary Links field control offers similar features to the Summary Links Web Part and allows content creators to create a list of hyperlinks grouped as required.

---

16. Click **OK**, and then in the Pages library, click **Welcome** to view the page.

Version: Checked Out   Status: Only you can see and modify this page.

Page ▾ | Workflow ▾ | Tools ▾ | 🖥 Edit Page | 🗐 Check In to Share Draft | 🗐 Publish

ℹ Remember to check in so other people can see your changes. (Do not show this message again)

View All Site Content
Document Center
News
PageLayouts
Reports
Search
Sites
🗑 Recycle Bin

Portal > PageLayouts > Welcome
Welcome to the Consolidated Messenger Human Resources site. On this site, you will find information on job vacancies, benefits, and polices such as annual leave and expense claims.

Consolidated Messenger Internet site

Pages

Type	Name	○ Modified By
📄	Welcome ⁞ NEW	Peter Krebs
📄	default	Peter Krebs

⊞ Add new document

BE SURE TO close the browser.

Creating a Page Layout

You can create a page layout by using a browser and SharePoint Designer. To create a page layout, you need to specify a page layout content type, which in turn, specifies which field controls (columns) you can place on your page layout.

SharePoint comes with a set of default content types, which SharePoint installs when you create a site collection (Collaboration Portal). Root level content types are used to create all the default lists, libraries, and page layouts. SharePoint Server comes with the following built-in page-layout content types:

- **Page Layout.** Use this content type when you want to create your own page layout.

- **Article Page.** This content type is based on the Page content type and is used to create the Article page layouts. SharePoint Server provides four Article Page page layouts; for example, the Article Page With Image On The Right is used for presenting an article (as in a magazine article) on a Web site. It contains a Page Image field control and a Page Content field control to capture data as well as a few other simple field controls.

- **Welcome Page.** This content type is based on the Page content type and is used to create Welcome Page page layouts. A site created from the Collaboration Portal site template contains 13 Welcome Page page layouts, and these page layouts are used extensively throughout the Collaboration Portal site to create pages.

- **Redirect Page.** This content type is used to create a variations page layout, to direct users to the variations home page when the variations settings are configured.

All page layouts are stored in the Master Page Gallery of the top-level site of a site collection, which is a document library. Although it has all the features of a normal document library because of its importance for the whole site collection, it is secured to limit the rights of most users. As a page layout designer, you must have at least design permission levels or higher to work with the files in this library. Such permission levels are automatically assigned to you if you are a member of the Designers SharePoint Group. To protect the contents of the Master Page Gallery further, content approval and minor and major versioning is enabled by default; therefore, for users to see pages based on your page layouts, the page layouts must be published as a major version and approved. To facilitate this process, you might consider enabling the approval workflow for the Master Page Gallery.

Using a browser, you can configure each site within a site collection to display all or some of the page layouts. Therefore, if you create page layouts that are specific to the Human Resources department, you can limit the Human Resources site to use only the Human Resources page layouts, and any child site of the Human Resources site can be configured to inherit the preferred layouts from its parent site.

To display new data on a page layout, you must first add a new column to the content type used to create the page layout. The new column then exposes a new field control for you to use on your page layout. Microsoft has provided a number of new column types specifically for publishing sites—that is, those that have *Formatting And Constraints For Publishing* features and the *Summary Links* data field controls. To create new columns for a content type, you need to create a site column. You can only create site columns and content types by using a browser.

See Also   For more information about creating content types and site columns, refer to Chapter 4, "Working with Lists," in *Microsoft Windows SharePoint Services 3.0 Step by Step* by Olga Londer, Bill English, Todd Bleeker, and Penelope Coventry (Microsoft Press, 2007).

In this exercise, you will create a new page layout.

> **USE** your own SharePoint site in place of the *portal.consolidatedmessenger.com* publishing site shown in this exercise.
>
> **OPEN** the *PageLayouts* child site that you used in the previous exercise in SharePoint Designer.

New Document

1. On the Common toolbar, click the **New Document** arrow, and then click **SharePoint Content** to open the **New** dialog box.

2. Click **SharePoint Publishing**, and then click **Page Layout**.

3. Under **Options**, in the **Content Type Name** list, click **Welcome Page**. Then in the **URL Name** text box, type JobVacancies, and in the **Title** text box, type Job Vacancies.

4. Click **OK** to close the **New** dialog box.

JobVacancies.aspx opens in a new SharePoint Designer window.

5. On the **Task Panes** menu, click **Toolbox** if it is not already open.

6. Close the **Apply Styles** task pane, so that the **Toolbox** task pane expands to the length of the window.

7. In the **Toolbox** task pane, scroll down to view the **SharePoint Controls**.

The Page Fields control section lists field types (columns) from the Page content type, and the Content Fields section lists field types from the Welcome Page content type.

8. Place the insertion point inside the **PlaceHolderMain (Custom)** control. Then on the **Table** menu, click **Insert Table**.

The Insert Table dialog box opens.

9. In the **Rows** text box, type **5**, and then click **OK** to close the **Insert Table** dialog box.

10. Place the insertion point inside the first cell of the second row.

> **Tip** To see the outline of the table, turn Visual Aids on by clicking Visual Aids either in the Status bar, or on the View menu, point to Visual Aids, and click Show. If they still do not appear, verify that Visual Aids, Visible Borders is selected.

11. In the **Toolbox** task pane, under **Page Fields**, double-click **Title**.

In the document window, the text *Job Vacancies* appears with a *Title* label above it.

12. Place the insertion point inside the first cell of the fourth row. Then in the **Toolbox** task pane, under **Page Fields**, double-click **Description**.

In the document window, the text Description Field Value appears with a *Description* label above it.

13. On the Common toolbar, click **Save**.

Save

14. In the **Folder List** task pane, expand the **_catalogs** folder, and the **masterpage (Master Page Gallery)** folder. Then scroll down until you can see *JobVacancies.aspx*.

A green check mark icon is displayed to the left of *JobVacancies.aspx*.

15. In the **Folder List** task pane, right-click **JobVacancies.aspx**, and then click **Check In**.

16. When the **Check In** dialog box opens, click **OK**.

The file *JobVacancies.aspx* is checked in as a minor (draft) version and will be visible only to other page layout designers.

17. Open *portal.consolidatedmessenger.com/pagelayouts* in the browser. On the Quick Launch bar, click **View All Site Content**, and under **Document Libraries**, click **Pages**.

18. When the All Documents view of the Pages library is displayed, click **New**.

The Create Page page is displayed.

19. In the **Title** text box, type HR Manager EMEA, and in the **URL Name** text box, type HRMgrEMEA.

20. In the **Page Layout** section, scroll down the list, and click **(Welcome Page) Job Vacancies**. Then click **Create** to display the All Documents view of the Pages library.

21. Click **HR Manager EMEA**, and then click **Edit Page**.

The two field controls are listed: Title and Description. Neither provides you with the ability to edit the text by using the floating HTML editor toolbar.

CLOSE both SharePoint Designer windows.

Modifying a Page Layout

As with any other component you use to develop your solution, you will need to modify the page layout, adding, removing and configuring field controls, Web Part zones, and Web Parts. Field controls, like Web Parts, can have a number of properties. Field controls that are created from some of the basic column types might not have any properties. Others like the *Full HTML Content With Formatting And Constraint For Publishing* column type, has nearly 50 properties, as well as its own cascading style sheet. Because a field control is an ASP.NET control, its properties can be configured by using the Tag Properties task pane. Your developer can also create additional field controls.

In this exercise, you will add and delete field controls in a page layout and configure the properties of a field control.

> **USE** your own SharePoint site location in place of the *portal.consolidatedmessenger.com* publishing site shown in this exercise.
>
> **OPEN** the *PageLayouts* child site that you used in the previous exercise.

1. Click **Site Actions**, point to **Site Settings**, and then click **Modify All Site Settings**.

2. When the Site Setting page is displayed, under **Galleries**, click **Master pages and page layouts**.

   The Master Page Gallery page is displayed. Notice that you are at the top-level site of the site collection.

3. Scroll down the page and point to **JobVacancies.aspx**, click the arrow that appears, and then click **Edit in Microsoft Office SharePoint Designer**.

   A Windows Internet Explorer message box appears, asking if you want to check out the item.

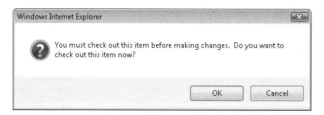

4. In the **Windows Internet Explorer** message box, click **OK**.

   SharePoint Designer opens, with *JobVacancies.aspx* open in the document window.

5. In **Design** view, click the **Description** label. Then press [Del].

   The Description field control is deleted from *JobVacancies.aspx*.

6. In the **Toolbox** task pane scroll down, in the **SharePoint Controls** header section, under **Content Fields**, double-click **Page Content**.

   The Page Content field control is added to the *JobVacancies.aspx* page.

7. In the **Tag Properties** task pane, click in the cell to the right of **AllowImages**, click the arrow that appears, and then click **False**.

Save

8. On the Common toolbar, click **Save**.

9. In the browser, open the *PageLayouts* child site, click **View All Site Content**, and then under **Document Libraries**, click **Pages**.

   The All Documents view of the Pages library is displayed.

10. Click **HRMgrEMEA**, and then click **Edit Page**.

11. In the **Page Content field** control, click **Edit Content**.

   The floating HTML editor toolbar appears, but the Insert Image icon is unavailable.

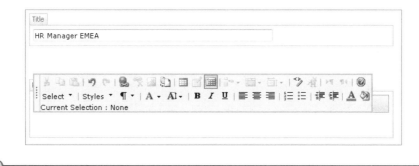

CLOSE the browser.

Restoring an Earlier Version of a Page Layout

All page layouts are stored in the Master Page Gallery for the top-level site of a site collection. This library has versioning enabled, and, therefore, you can restore previous versions of page layouts, if you decide that your current modifications do not now meet your business needs or want to start modifying your page layout from a previous basis.

In this exercise, you will restore an earlier version of a page layout.

OPEN the *PageLayouts* child site that you used in the previous exercise.

1. In the **Folder List** task pane, expand **Pages**, and then double-click **HRMgrEMEA.aspx**.

   A Microsoft Office SharePoint Designer dialog box opens, stating that you cannot edit the page in SharePoint Designer, and would you like to edit the corresponding page layout.

   Microsoft Office SharePoint Designer

   This page cannot be edited in SharePoint Designer. You can edit the content in the browser, or edit the corresponding page layout in SharePoint Designer.

   [Edit in Browser]   [Edit Page Layout]   [Cancel]

2. Click **Edit Page Layout**.

   The Microsoft Office SharePoint Designer dialog box closes.

   The *JobVacancies.aspx* page opens in a separate SharePoint Designer window.

3. In the **Folder List** task pane, expand **_catalogs**, and then expand **masterpage (Master Page Gallery)**. Scroll down to *JobVacancies.aspx*, right-click it, and then click **Version History**.

   The Versions Save For JobVacancies.aspx dialog box opens.

   Versions saved for JobVacancies.aspx

   Versions saved to: http://portal.consolidatedmessenger.com/_catalogs/masterpage/

No.	Modified	Modified By	Size	Comments
0.3	11/20/2007 11:40 PM	CONSOLIDATED\peterk	1.8 KB	
0.2	11/20/2007 11:33 PM	CONSOLIDATED\peterk	1.8 KB	
0.1	11/20/2007 11:29 PM	CONSOLIDATED\peterk	1.2 KB	

   [Open]   [Restore]   [Delete]   [Close]

4. Click **0.2**, and then click **Restore**.

   A Microsoft Office SharePoint Designer dialog box opens, asking if you are sure you want to replace the current version with the selected version.

5. Click **Yes** to close the **Microsoft Office SharePoint Designer** dialog box and the **Versions Save For JobVacancies.aspx** dialog box.

   The *JobVacancies.aspx* page is redisplayed and contains the Title and Description field controls.

   > **Tip** If you restore version 0.1, you have not gained anything more than you would have done by re-creating a page layout, that is restoring version 0.1 results in page layout with no field controls.

Detaching and Reattaching a Page Layout

If you do want to edit a page associated with a page layout, you can use SharePoint Designer to detach the page from the page layout. This turns the page into an ordinary content page, similar to the default.aspx page of a team site. The page is associated with a master page and contains a PlaceHolderMain (Custom) control. With SharePoint Designer, you can reattach the page with its original page layouts; however, when reattaching to the original page layout, you lose any customizations you may have completed on the page.

> **Tip** You cannot attach a page layout to a page that was not originally associated with the page layout.

The detach and reattach methods for page layouts are the reverse of one another, unlike the detaching and attaching of master pages. When you detach a page from its master page, all the controls and tags are copied from the master page to the content page. When you then attach a master page back to the content page, the original controls from the master page remain on the content page with the effect that controls are applied twice, once from the original master page that was detached and the second set from the attaching of the master page. With the effect that you have two Site Actions menus, two navigation bars, two Quick Launch bars, and other duplicates. And although detaching and reattaching page layouts does not suffer from this effect, you should think carefully what you are trying to achieve, because an "undo" mechanism might not readily be available to you.

In this exercise, you will detach and reattach a page layout.

OPEN the *PageLayouts* child site that you used in the previous exercise.

1. In the **Folder List** task pane, expand **Pages**. Then right-click **HRMgrEMEA.aspx**, and click **Detach from Page Layout**.

   A Microsoft Office SharePoint Designer dialog box opens, warning you that detaching from the page layout will copy the page layout's markup to the page, and any changes to the page layout will not affect the page.

2. Click **Yes** to close the Microsoft Office SharePoint Designer dialog box.

   Another Microsoft Office SharePoint Designer dialog box opens, stating that the detachment was successful.

3. Click **OK** to close the Microsoft Office SharePoint Designer dialog box.

4. In the **Folder List** task pane, double-click **HRMgrEMEA.aspx**.

   The page opens in the document window.

5. In the **Folder List** task pane, right-click **HRMgrEMEA.aspx**, and then click **Reattach to Page Layout**.

   A Microsoft Office SharePoint Designer dialog box opens, warning you that by reattaching the page, any customizations will be lost, except for changes to Web Parts in Web Part zones.

6. Click **Yes** to close the dialog box.

   The dialog box closes, and a Microsoft Office SharePoint Designer dialog box opens stating that the reattachment was successful.

7. Click **OK** to close the dialog box.

CLOSE all browser windows and close any of the sites open within SharePoint Designer. If you are not continuing directly to the next chapter, exit SharePoint Designer.

Key Points

- Web Content Management is just one of the functions included in the ECM feature of SharePoint Server.

- Both the publishing and the publishing with workflows site definitions enable the SharePoint Server Publishing feature, which provides a number of additional features not available on team sites.

- The key concept of publishing sites is page layouts. A master page controls the look and feel of the branding and navigation, whereas the page layout controls the look and feel of the content portion of the page.

- Page layouts are stored in the Master Page Gallery library in the top-level site of a site collection. Content approval, minor versioning, and major versioning are enabled on this library; therefore, you must publish a page layout as a major version and approve it before pages based on it can be viewed by visitors to your site.

- Page layouts are created from page layout content types and publishing pages are created from a page layout.

- Page layouts control where content can be placed on a publishing page by using field controls and Web Part zones.

- Content creators using a browser manage publishing pages, which are stored at a site level in the Pages library.

- Field controls map to columns in the Pages library and are responsible for displaying and modifying column values.

- Microsoft has provided a number of new column types specifically for publishing sites, such as those that have *Formatting And Constraints For Publishing* features.

Chapter at a Glance

Create a workflow, **page 282**

Workflow Designer - StartersWorkflow

Define your new workflow

Choose the type of workflow and the conditions under which this new workflow should run.

Give a name to this workflow:

StartersWorkflow

What SharePoint list should this workflow be attached to?

Planning Proposals

Select workflow start options for items in Planning Proposals:
- ☑ Allow this workflow to be manually started from an item
- ☐ Automatically start this workflow when a new item is created
- ☐ Automatically start this workflow whenever an item is changed

Help
- The workflow name given here will be used to identify the workflow to end users.
- By attaching this workflow to a List, it makes it possible to initiate the workflow for Items in that List.
- The start options reflect when the workflow will be run for Items in the attached List.

Click here for more help...

Workflow Designer - StartersWorkflow

Step Name: TeamManager

Specify details for 'TeamManager'

Choose the conditions and actions that define this step of the workflow.

Conditions ▼   If Status equals Draft

Actions ▼   Assign a to-do item to these users

Add 'Else If' Conditional Branch

Workflow Steps

TeamManager

Add workflow step

Create a multi-step workflow, **page 295**

Use conditions and actions, **page 285**

Step Name: TeamManager

Specify details for 'TeamManager'

Choose the conditions and actions that define this step of the workflow.

Conditions ▼   If Status equals Draft

Actions ▼   Assign ReviewPlanningProposal to paula@consolidatedmessenger.com

then Update item in Planning Proposals

then Email peter@consolidatedmessenger.com

Add 'Else If' Conditional Branch

Workflow Steps

TeamManager

Add workflow step

Move Action Up

Move Action Down

✕ Delete Action

Modify a workflow, **page 292**

12 Understanding Workflows

In this chapter, you will learn to:

✔ Work with workflows.

✔ Create a workflow.

✔ Use conditions and actions.

✔ Verify and deploy a workflow.

✔ Modify a workflow.

✔ Create a multi-step workflow.

✔ Delete a workflow.

The workflow technology included in Microsoft Windows SharePoint Services 3.0 and Microsoft Office SharePoint Server 2007 can help you automate new and existing business processes. In the past, creating a workflow was typically a task for developers. Most companies have many different types of workflows, and hiring a developer to create workflows can be time consuming and expensive. Microsoft Office SharePoint Designer 2007 offers a better alternative; you can create your own ad hoc workflows in a visual way. Mastering the creation of workflows by using SharePoint Designer 2007 may take some time, but it is well worth the effort.

In this chapter, you will learn the fundamentals of the workflow architecture and what workflows are provided by default when you install Windows SharePoint Services and Office SharePoint Server 2007. You will learn how to create, delete, and modify workflows by using SharePoint Designer 2007, and how to track the status of workflows that are currently running or have run in the past.

> **Important** Before you can use the practice files in this chapter, you need to install them from the book's companion CD to their default location. You will need to create a practice site for this chapter based on the site template *Workflows_Starter.stp* located in this chapter's practice file folder. Then when you perform the exercises in this chapter, remember to use your SharePoint site location in place of the *teams.consolidatedmessenger.com* site shown in the exercises.
>
> For more information about practice files, see "Using the Book's CD" at the beginning of this book.

> **Troubleshooting** Graphics and operating system–related instructions in this book reflect the Windows Vista user interface. If your computer is running Windows XP and you experience trouble following the instructions as written, please refer to the "Information for Readers Running Windows XP" section at the beginning of this book.

Working with Workflows

All workflow functionality provided by either Windows SharePoint Services or SharePoint Server 2007 is built using *Windows Workflow Foundation (WF)*, which is part of the *Microsoft .NET Framework 3.0*. SharePoint products cannot be installed on a server without first installing the .NET Framework 3.0.

> **Warning** To use SharePoint Designer to create workflows, you must have the .NET Framework 3.0 installed on your computer. Windows Vista includes the .NET Framework 3.0, but if you are using Windows XP or Windows Server 2003, you may need to install this before you can work with workflows in SharePoint Designer. The .NET Framework 3.0 is available from the Microsoft Download Center (*www.microsoft.com/downloads/*).

WF offers all kinds of functionality required for building enterprise-level workflows, such as built-in support for transactions, tracking, and notifications. Windows Workflow Foundation does not act as a stand-alone application but always works with a program, which in this instance is Windows SharePoint Services 3.0. Because SharePoint Server is built on top of Windows SharePoint Services, it, too, has workflow capabilities.

In the same way that you base a new site, list, or library on a template, you base a new workflow on a workflow template. These templates are implemented as features that can be activated or deactivated by using the browser or programmatically. A workflow template is available only when a workflow feature is activated.

You can think of a workflow as a series of tasks that produce an outcome. Windows SharePoint Services and SharePoint Server provide a number of built-in workflow templates that define those tasks and outcomes.

Each of the built-in workflow templates can be customized in a limited fashion to define the exact process necessary to meet your business needs. An instance of a workflow uses the configured workflow template as a blueprint, which defines the conditions that should be tested to decide which tasks to complete to produce the outcome. In SharePoint technologies, an instance of a workflow can apply those tests and actions only in association with a list item or document. Workflow templates are associated with lists, libraries, or content types.

Windows SharePoint Services ships with only one generic workflow, the Three-state workflow that can be used across multiple scenarios; whereas SharePoint Server contains the following additional document-centric workflows:

- **Approval.** Provides an approval mechanism for documents.
- **Collect Feedback.** Provides a feedback mechanism for documents.
- **Collect Signatures.** Provides a mechanism for collecting digital signatures for completing a document.
- **Disposition Approval.** Provides an expiration and retention mechanism that allows you to decide whether to retain or delete expired documents. This workflow can be started only by using the browser.
- **Group Approval.** Similar to the Approval workflow, however, it is available only for East Asian versions of SharePoint Server.
- **Translation Management.** Provides a mechanism for document translation by creating copies of documents to be translated, and assigns tasks to translators. This workflow is available only when you create a Translation Management library.

See Also For more information about the built-in workflows, visit *office.microsoft.com/en-us/sharepointserver/HA101544241033.aspx.*

Tip When you create a site, you may find that a workflow is not available; for example, the Three-state workflow is not immediately available in a SharePoint Server installation. A site collection administrator can activate the Three-state workflow feature from the Site Collection Features page, which you can access from the Site Settings page on the top-level site of a site collection.

The workflow process always has a start and an end. An instance of workflow is created when a workflow event is triggered. The workflow instance then enters the workflow process at its start point and progresses through the workflow process as defined by the workflow template until it reaches the end point, at which time the workflow instance is set to Completed. The workflow process then does no other work until a new workflow instance is created.

Depending on the workflow template and its configuration, the event that triggers the start of a workflow can occur in the following ways:

- Manually from Microsoft Office Word 2007, Microsoft Office Excel 2007, Microsoft Office PowerPoint 2007, Microsoft Office InfoPath 2007, Microsoft Office Access 2007, or a browser.

- Automatically when you save a major version of a document. This method of starting a workflow is not available on lists. It is available only for libraries that have major and minor versioning enabled.

- Automatically when you create a list item or document.

- Automatically when you change a list item or document.

Not all workflow templates support all the workflow start methods listed above. The following table lists the workflow templates and the workflow start methods they can use.

Workflow start method	Three-state	Approval	Collect Feedback	Collect Signatures	Disposition Approval
Manually	Yes	Yes	Yes	Yes	Yes
Publish major version*	No	Yes	No	No	No
New item	Yes	Yes	Yes	No	Yes
Change item	No	Yes	Yes	No	Yes

* This option is not available in lists; it is available only for libraries that have major and minor versioning enabled.

Some kind of event must occur to create an instance of a workflow. The built-in workflow templates use a limited number of events, such as the following:

- Create a new task for an end user participating in the workflow.

- Send an e-mail message.

- Change the workflow status of the item the workflow operates on.

The browser, SharePoint Designer, and Microsoft *Visual Studio 2005* use the term *workflow* for a workflow template, a workflow process, and an instance of a workflow, which can be confusing. Therefore, you must infer what you are working with according to the context. For example, you associate a workflow (template) with a list, library, or content type. You configure a workflow (process) by using a built-in workflow (template), a SharePoint Designer workflow, or a custom workflow created by a developer using Visual Studio 2005. An instance of workflow is created when the workflow process is started either automatically or manually for a list item or document that you associated with a workflow (template).

Although it is not strictly required, most workflows use both a Task and History list while the workflow process executes. Workflows add tasks to a Task list so that users can keep track of all the work that needs to be finished to complete the workflow process for a particular workflow instance.

The History list keeps track of the workflow instances that are running or have been completed for a given list item or document. Based on the contents of the history list, you can create Activity Duration reports that you can use to analyze the duration of workflow instances and the activities within the workflow process. You can also create Cancellation and Error reports that show which workflow's processes are being cancelled, or which workflow instances have encountered errors during execution.

In the following exercise, you will use the browser to configure a built-in workflow. You will then manually start the workflow, monitor its progress, and view the task item it produces.

> **USE** your SharePoint site location in place of the *teams.consolidatedmessenger.com* site shown in the exercise.
> **BE SURE TO** start SharePoint Designer before beginning this exercise.
> **OPEN** the Workflow child site in the browser.

1. On the Quick Launch bar, click **PlanningProposals**.

2. On the **Settings** menu, click **Document Library Settings** to display the **Customize Planning Proposals** page.

3. Under **Permissions and Management**, click **Workflow settings**.

   The Add A Workflow: PlanningProposals page appears.

4. In the **Workflow** section, under **Select a workflow template**, click **Three-state**.

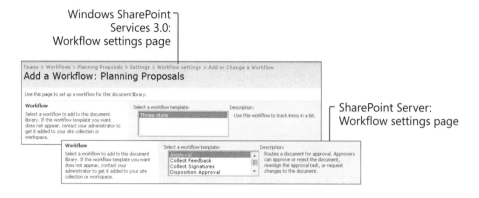

Windows SharePoint Services 3.0: Workflow settings page

SharePoint Server: Workflow settings page

> **Tip** In a SharePoint Server installation, you might have to scroll the list to find the Three-state workflow. If it is not listed, navigate to the Site Settings page at the top-level site of the site collection. Under Site Collection Administration, click Site Collection Features, and from that page, activate the Three-state workflow.

5. In the **Name** section, type: Three-state test workflow. Retain the default settings in the other sections, and click **Next**.

The Customize The Three-state Workflow page opens. The Workflow States section displays the Choice column: Status, and its three states: Draft, ReviewedByTeamManager, and Final.

> **Tip** For most lists and libraries, you would have to create this choice column before configuring the Three-state workflow.

6. Clear the **Send e-mail message** check boxes in each of the two **Specify what you want to happen** sections, and then click **OK**.

The All Documents view of the PlanningProposals library appears.

7. Point to **Consignments**, click the arrow that appears, and then click **Workflows**.

The Workflows: Consignments page is displayed.

> **Tip** In a Windows SharePoint Services installation, the Approval and Collect Feedback workflows will not be listed on the Workflows: Consignments page.

Teams > Workflows > PlanningProposals > Consignments > Workflows

Workflows: Consignments

Use this page to start a new workflow on the current item or to view the status of a running or completed workflow.

Start a New Workflow

Approval
Routes a document for approval. Approvers can approve or reject the document, reassign the approval task, or request changes to the document.

Collect Feedback
Routes a document for review. Reviewers can provide feedback, which is compiled and sent to the document owner when the workflow has completed.

Three state test workflow
Use this workflow to track items in a list.

Workflows

Select a workflow for more details on the current status or history.

Name	Started	Ended	Status
Running Workflows			
There are no currently running workflows on this item.			
Completed Workflows			
There are no completed workflows on this item.			

8. In the **Start a New Workflow** section, click **Three-state test workflow**.

The Operation In Progress page appears, followed by the All Documents view of the PlanningProposals library. An extra column, labeled Three-State Test Workflow, has been added to the view, with a status of In Progress for the Consignments document.

> **Tip** Starting a new workflow from within an Office client looks much the same, and the process for starting a workflow is identical for Word, Excel, and PowerPoint.

9. Click **In Progress**.

The Workflow Status page appears, displaying one task and one Workflow History event.

10. In the **Tasks** section, click **Workflow initiated** to display the **Tasks: Workflow initiated: Consignments.xml** task list item. The task item contains a hyperlink to the document, consignments.xml. If you were to continue with this workflow you would review the document, and then you would alter the task list status to completed. This would complete the first state (Draft) of the workflow. A second task item would be created for the second state (ReviewedByTeamManager), and so on.

CLOSE the browser.

Creating a Workflow

When you create a workflow by using SharePoint Designer, you are creating a workflow template. You use a Workflow Designer Wizard to create the workflow template and configure how workflows associated with the workflow template can start. You can use the SharePoint Designer workflow templates, with a few restrictions, like the built-in workflow templates. For example, your workflow can be configured to start manually or automatically, and users can interface with it by using either the browser or the 2007 Office clients programs.

Using SharePoint Designer, you must define the workflow process, the interaction with the users, and what you want the computer to do. Do not assume that because most of the built-in workflow templates work in a certain way, yours will too. They won't—unless you tell them to, so your workflow will not automatically create task list items or write to the history list. Therefore, the same reporting facilities that users expect when they use the default templates will not be there for your workflows if you do not include those aspects.

SharePoint Designer provides you with a Workflow Designer wizard to create and configure SharePoint Designer workflow templates; it does not provide you with any interface to configure any of the built-in workflow templates. In addition, you cannot start a workflow on a document or list item from SharePoint Designer.

Whether you can create workflows in SharePoint Designer depends on your contributor settings and whether the SharePoint server administrator has enabled user-defined workflows by using the Application Management tab on the SharePoint Central Administration site.

See Also For more information about contributor settings, see Chapter 14, "Managing SharePoint Sites."

In this exercise, you will create a workflow in SharePoint Designer and associate it with a specific library.

> **USE** your SharePoint site location in place of the *teams.consolidatedmessenger.com* site shown in this exercise.
>
> **OPEN** your LookFeel child site in SharePoint Designer.

New Document

1. On the Common toolbar, click the **New Document** arrow, and then click **Workflow** to start the **Workflow Designer** wizard.

   The Define Your New Workflow page of the wizard appears.

   > **Tip** If you are unable to launch the Workflow Designer wizard in SharePoint Designer 2007, contact the site and/or SharePoint administrator.

Comparing Workflows by Using SharePoint Designer and Visual Studio 2005

The built-in workflow templates may help you to solve some of your immediate needs, but eventually you will need to create new types of workflows. Microsoft offers two tools that can help you create workflow templates, SharePoint Designer and Visual Studio 2005 using the Visual Studio 2005 Extensions for the .NET Framework 3.0. The following table compares the two tools.

SharePoint Designer	Visual Studio 2005
There is a learning curve but in general, easy to use.	Requires the skills of a developer.
Limited to the conditions and actions exposed via a workflow designer wizard; for example, cannot create folders, update lists on other site, even in the same site collection, and cannot initiate another workflow.	Can create advanced workflows and custom activities.
Can create only workflows that execute steps in a sequential order.	Creates workflows that move through states in a sequential order or in no fixed order (a ,machine state workflow).
Workflows are bound to one list or library.	Workflows can be associated with multiple lists or libraries, a content type, or to a site.
Can use only Microsoft ASP.NET forms for data entry.	Supports the use of both ASP.NET forms and InfoPath forms for data entry.
Creates workflows in a visual way by using a visual workflow wizard that does not require code; workflows are automatically deployed.	Uses a combination of a visual workflow wizard and server-side code to produce an assembly that must be deployed on each Web server.
No debugging capabilities.	Offers step-by-step debugging capabilities.

Use SharePoint Designer to create ad-hoc workflows on a per-list or per-library basis, or to prototype a workflow that will subsequently be created by using Visual Studio 2005.

See Also For information about porting a SharePoint Designer workflow to Visual Studio 2005, visit *blogs.msdn.com/sharepointdesigner/archive/2007/07/06/porting-sharepoint-designer-workflows-to-visual-studio.aspx.*

2. In the **Give a name to this workflow** text box, type: StartersWorkflow.

3. In the **What SharePoint list should this workflow be attached to?** list, click **PlanningProposals**.

4. Verify that the **Allow this workflow to be manually started from an item** check box is selected.

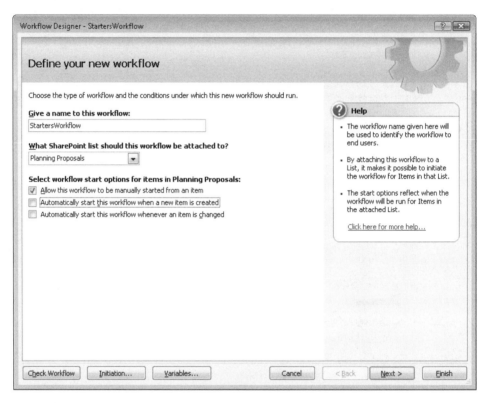

> **Tip** The three workflow start options can be configured only by using SharePoint Designer unless you provide a page for the user.

5. Click **Next** to display the second page of the Workflow Designer wizard.

> **Tip** To collect information from a user when he or she manually starts a workflow, you need to specify a set of initiation parameters by clicking the Initiation button at the bottom of the Workflow Designer wizard. These initiation values must have default values if the workflow is to be configured to start automatically. You can design the data entry form that users will see when they start the process. You can customize this form by using SharePoint Designer as you can any other page. If the site is created on an installation where the Enterprise edition of SharePoint Server is installed and Office Forms Server is configured, you can use an InfoPath form.

Using Conditions and Actions

When you create a workflow, you define one or more *workflow steps*. In each step, you have to define the set of *workflow actions* that need to be performed and a *workflow condition* that triggers those workflow actions. The combination of a condition and the associated actions is known as a *workflow rule*. Also, in workflow terminology, both conditions and actions are *workflow activities*, where an activity is something that needs to be done, for example, a test for a certain value in a list item's column or setting an e-mail address.

SharePoint Designer provides you with a set of 9 conditions and 23 actions that you can use to create your workflows. A condition is a kind of filter; for example, if the condition is true, the associated action or actions are executed. The conditions available to your workflow are dependent on the list or library you associate a workflow with; for example, the condition that checks the size of a file is available only on libraries and lists that allow attachments.

An action defines a set of tasks that needs to be completed. Actions can be configured to execute in serial or parallel. When you run actions in serial, an action will start only when the preceding one completes. When you run actions in parallel, all actions start at the same time. SharePoint Designer provides you with 23 workflow actions that can be divided into of the following groups:

- **Core actions.** This group contains 14 actions that allow you to manipulate dates and times, build a form to collect information from users, and write information in the history list.

- **List actions.** This group contains 7 actions that allow you to manipulate list items, including creating, copying, and deleting list items. These actions can be applied to documents within libraries, because libraries are only special lists. This category also includes specific document-related actions, such as undoing a check out.

- **Task actions.** This group contains 2 actions that allow you to assign a task to either one specific user or a group.

See Also An overview of the default workflow conditions and actions can be found in the Appendix at the end of this book.

If the set of available conditions and actions does not meet your business needs, then you can extend this collection; such new conditions or actions are called *custom activities*. Custom activities can be created only by using Visual Studio 2005 or a third-party tool.

See Also For more information about building custom activities for use in SharePoint Designer, visit *msdn2.microsoft.com/bb629922.aspx*.

In this exercise, you will build the first step of a workflow that includes one condition and two actions.

> **USE** the workflow you began creating in the previous exercise.
> **BE SURE TO** continue directly from the previous exercise.

1. In the **Step Name** text box, type TeamManager.

2. In the **Conditions** list, click **Compare PlanningProposals field**.

   The text If Field Equals Value appears to the right of the Conditions button.

   Workflow Designer - StartersWorkflow

   Step Name: TeamManager

   Workflow Steps

   TeamManager
   Add workflow step

   Specify details for 'TeamManager'

   Choose the conditions and actions that define this step of the workflow.

   Conditions ▼   If field equals value

   Actions ▼

   Add 'Else IF' Conditional Branch

3. Click **field** to display a list of columns in the PlanningProposals library.

4. Scroll down and click **Status**.

5. Click **value**, and then in the list, click **Draft**.

   > **Tip** You do not have to specify a condition for a workflow. There may be circumstances when you require an action to always occur; for example, you may want to create a new list item in the History list when a workflow starts and when it finishes.

6. Click the **Actions** button, and then click **Assign a To-do Item**.

   > **Tip** The actions in your list might not be in the same order as those in the graphics. If you do not see the action you want, at the bottom of the list, click More Actions to open the Workflow Actions dialog box, which lists all available actions.

The text Assign A To-do Item To These Users appears to the right of the Actions button.

7. Click **a to-do item** to start the Custom Task wizard.

8. Click **Next**, type ReviewPlanningProposal in the **Name** text box, and then click **Finish** .

9. On the Workflow Designer wizard page, click **these users** to open the **Select Users** dialog box.

10. Click the user or type the e-mail address of the user you want to assign the task to, and then click **Add**.

11. In the **Select Users** dialog box, click **OK**.

   On the Workflow Designer wizard page, the text These Users is replaced by the specified e-mail address.

12. On the **Actions** menu, click **Update List Item**.

   > **Tip** The word *Then* before the *Update item* action indicates that this action is dependent on the previous action completing successfully; that is, this is a serial action. To change this action to execute in parallel with the first action, click the arrow to the far right of the Conditions button, and click Run All Actions in Parallel.

13. Click the **this list** link to open the **Update List Item** dialog box.

14. Verify that **Current Item** appears in the **List** list, and then click **Add**.

   The Value Assignment dialog box opens.

15. In the **Set this field** list, click **Status**, and in the **To this value** list, click
ReviewedByTeamManager.

16. Click **OK** twice to close the **Value Assignment** and the **Update List Item** dialog boxes.

This step contains one condition and two actions.

Verifying and Deploying a Workflow

As you develop your workflow, and definitely before using a workflow in production, you
should test your solution. The Workflow Designer wizard provides you with a method to
check the validity of your workflow. When you click the Check Workflow button, either
a dialog box appears to inform you that the workflow contains no errors, or a warning
sign is positioned next to any faulty workflow step, with asterisks (*) before and after the
incorrect value.

After completing the Workflow Designer wizard validity check, you can deploy the
workflow to the SharePoint library you associated with it on the first page of the
Workflow Designer wizard. To deploy a workflow, you click the Finish button and wait

until SharePoint Designer has processed, validated, and associated the workflow with a SharePoint list on the SharePoint site.

For each workflow, the Workflow Wizard creates a folder in a Workflows document library. The *Workflows* folder is hidden from the browser. Each *Workflows* folder contains at least one file with each of the following file extensions:

- **.aspx.** These represent forms used for data entry by the users. You can configure these as you can any other page in SharePoint Designer.

- **.xoml.** This is the main workflow markup file, which contains the *Extensible Application Markup Language (XAML)* that Windows Workflow Foundation uses.

- **.xoml.rules.** This file contains details of the workflow rules.

- **.xoml.wfconfig.xml.** This file includes the site and list or library details, as well as the workflow start configuration settings.

> **Caution** If you delete any of these files, then the workflow may fail to deploy; for example, if you delete the .xoml.wfconfig.xml file, then the workflow loses its association with the list or library. You may think that this is a method of associating the workflow with a different list or library than the one you originally associated it with. However, to reassociate the workflow with a list or library, you will need to revisit all the conditions and actions, and reassociate them with columns and the values held within those columns. This is a large task if you have many conditions and actions, and you will then have to retest the workflow thoroughly to ensure you have not missed anything.

In this exercise, you will validate, deploy, and test a workflow.

> **USE** the workflow you created in the previous exercise.
> **BE SURE TO** continue directly from the previous exercise.

1. In the lower-left corner of the Workflow Designer wizard, click **Check Workflow**.

   A message box informs you that the workflow is valid.

2. Click **OK** to close the message box, and then in the lower-right corner of the Workflow Designer wizard, click **Finish**.

A progress window opens, displaying the progress of the deployment process.

Microsoft Office SharePoint Designer

Processing StartersWorkflow

Validating the workflow

Cancel

When the deployment process is complete, the progress window and the Workflow Designer wizard close.

In the Folder List task pane, an extra folder labeled *Workflows* appears.

3. In the **Folder List** task pane, expand **Workflows**, and then expand **StartersWorkflow**.

The folder contains the files produced by the deployment process. There are two .aspx files; one will be used to start the workflow and the other to change the status of the task item.

4. In the **Folder List** task pane, click **PlanningProposals**, and then press F12 to display the All Documents view of the library in the browser.

5. Point to **Consignments**, click the arrow that appears, and then click **Workflows**.

The Workflows: Consignments page is displayed with StartersWorkflow listed under the Start A New Workflow heading.

6. Click **StartersWorkflow** to display the **StartersWorkflow** page. Then click **Start**.

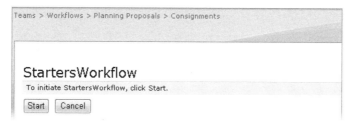

The All Documents view of the Planning Proposals library is displayed with an extra column labeled *StartersWorkflow*.

7. In the **StartersWorkflow** column, click **In Progress** to display the **Workflow Status: StartersWorkflow** page.

One task and no Workflow History events are displayed.

8. In the **Tasks** section, point to **ReviewPlanningProposal**, click the arrow that appears, and then click **Edit Item**.

The ReviewPlanningProposal page is displayed.

9. Click **Complete Task**.

The Workflow Status: StartersWorkflow page is displayed

10. In the breadcrumb, click **Planning Proposals**, and then on the Quick Launch bar, under **Lists**, click **Tasks**.

The All Tasks view of the Tasks list is displayed. One ReviewPlanningProposal task is listed.

Teams > Workflows > Tasks

Tasks

Use the Tasks list to keep track of work that you or your team needs to complete.

New ▾	Actions ▾	Settings ▾					View:	**All Tasks** ▾
⬤	Title	Assigned To	Status	Priority	Due Date	% Complete	Link	Outcome
	Workflow initiated: Consignments.xml ⚠ NEW	Peter Krebs	Completed	(2) Normal	11/14/2007	100%	Consignments	The task has been completed.
	ReviewPlanningProposal ⚠ NEW		Completed	(2) Normal		100%	Consignments	Completed
	Review task Consignments.xml ⚠ NEW	Peter Krebs	Not Started	(2) Normal	11/14/2007		Consignments	

> **Tip** If you want to retest the workflow at any time, edit the properties of the consignments.xml and set the status to Draft.

CLOSE the browser window.

Modifying a Workflow

Any business process is likely to change; therefore, you will need to modify any associated workflows. If you modify an existing workflow that is already in use, it is possible that you will break instances of the workflow that are already running. Therefore, before modifying a workflow, you should make the workflow unavailable to users. (Do not delete it.)

When all the workflow instances have completed, then you can remove the workflow from the list or library to which it is associated. Using the browser, you can allow users to use your workflow template, prevent any new workflow instances, and remove it from the list or library. Removing a workflow from a list or library does not delete it. You can still access it by using SharePoint Designer. When you next deploy the workflow in SharePoint Designer, it reattaches itself to the list or library.

See Also For information about removing a workflow from a list or library to prevent users from creating new instances of that workflow, see "Deleting a Workflow" later in this chapter.

Like any other list or library, you can make a copy of the Workflow document library and the workflow's folders. Therefore, before modifying a workflow, you should make it unavailable to users and create a copy of the workflow folder. This copy of a workflow will not appear in the browser or the Office clients applications unless you open and deploy it in the Workflow Designer wizard by clicking the Finish button. Technically, the Workflows document library does have Major versioning enabled, so theoretically, you could restore a previous version of a file, but because libraries do not have any view pages, there is no mechanism available that allows you to do this.

In this exercise, you will modify an existing workflow.

> **USE** the workflow you created in the previous exercise.
> **BE SURE TO** continue directly from the previous exercise.

1. On the **File** menu, click **Open Workflow**.

    The Open Workflow dialog box opens, listing all the SharePoint Designer workflows created for the site.

Open Workflow		? ✕
Name	Modified	
StartersWorkflow	10/31/2007 15:28	
		OK Cancel

    > **Tip** You can reopen the Workflow Designer wizard for a workflow by double-clicking the relevant .xoml file in the Folder List task pane.

2. Click **StartersWorkflow**, and then click **OK**.

    The Workflow Designer wizard starts.

3. Click the **Actions** button, and then click **Send an Email**.

    The text Then Email This Message appears to the right of the Actions button.

4. Click **this message** to open the **Define E-mail Message** dialog box.

Address Book

5. To the right of the **To** text box, click the **Address Book** icon to display the **Select Users** dialog box.

6. Double-click the name of the person you want to send the e-mail message to.

7. Click **OK** to close the **Select Users** dialog box.

Function

8. Next to the **Subject** text box, click the **function** button to open the **Define Workflow Lookup** dialog box.

9. In the **Source** list, verify that **Current Item** is selected, and in the **Field** list, click **Name**.

10. Click **OK** to close the **Define Workflow Lookup** dialog box.

   The Subject text box is grayed out (unavailable), and contains the document library name, PlanningProposals, and the column name.

11. In the **Subject** text box, type Please review the work preferences of our new employee. Click the following link to open his/her work preferences document:

12. At the bottom of the **Define E-mail Message** dialog box, click the **Add Lookup to Body** button.

   The Define Workflow Lookup dialog box opens.

13. In the **Source** list, verify **Current Item** is selected, and in the **Field** list, scroll down, and click **Encoded Absolute URL**.

14. In the **Define Workflow Lookup** dialog box, click **OK**.

15. In the **Define E-mail message** dialog box, place the insertion point at the end of the line after the square bracket, press Enter twice, and then type After you review the schedule, mark the relevant task in the Tasks list as complete, press Enter twice, and type Kind regards.

![Define E-mail Message dialog box. To: peter@consolidatedmessenger.com. CC: (blank). Subject: PlanningProposals:Name. Body: Please review the work preferences of our new employee. Click the following link to open his/her work preferences document:[%PlanningProposals:Encoded Absolute URL%] After you review the schedule, mark the relevant task in the Tasks list as complete. Kind regards. Buttons: Add Lookup to Body, OK, Cancel.]

16. Click **OK** to close the **Define E-mail Message** dialog box.

In the Workflow Designer wizard, the Actions text is replaced with *Email* and an e-mail address.

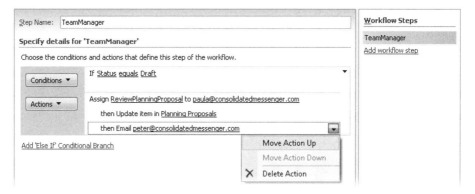

17. Point to **Email**, click the arrow that appears, and click **Move Action Up**. Then repeat this step once more.

The Email action is now the first action for the TeamManager step.

Creating a Multi-Step Workflow

Most business processes will need more than one step; that is, the rules defined in one step must be completed before the rules in the second step can be started. For example, a bank has to complete several financial and security checks before creating a bank account for a person.

We have seen that each step has one or more conditions, and each condition has one or more actions. A step can also consist of multiple branches, such that if condition A is true, one set of actions is executed, and if condition B is true, another set of actions is executed. However, a branch cannot extend from one step to another. To create multiple conditions, you click Add 'Else If' Condition Branch in the Workflow Designer wizard.

In this exercise, you will add a second step, which contains one condition and one action.

> **USE** the workflow you created in the previous exercise.
> **BE SURE TO** continue directly from the previous exercise.

1. In the upper-right corner of the Workflow Designer wizard, under **Workflow Steps**, click **Add workflow step**.

   The Step Name text box containing Step 2, and a Step 2 list, appear in the Workflow Steps section.

2. In the **Step Name** text box, type ProjectCoordinator.

3. In the **Conditions** list, click **Compare PlanningProposals field**.

   The text If Field Equals Value appears to the right of the Conditions button.

4. Click **field**, then in the list, click **Status**.

5. Click the **value** link, and then in the list, click **ReviewedByTeamManager**.

6. In the **Actions** list, click **Assign a To-do Item**.

   The text Assign A To-do Item To These Users appears to the right of the Actions button.

7. Click **a to-do item** to open the **Custom Task Wizard** dialog box.

8. Click **Next**, type UpdateProjectSchedule in the **Name** text box, and then click **Finish**.

9. Click **these users** to open the **Select Users** dialog box.

10. Select the user to which you want to assign the to-do task, or type his or her e-mail address. Click **Add**, and then click **OK** to close.

Step Name: ProjectCoordinator

Specify details for 'ProjectCoordinator'

Choose the conditions and actions that define this step of the workflow.

Conditions ▼   If Status equals ReviewedByTeamManager

Actions ▼   Assign UpdateProjectSchedule to bruce@consolidatedmessenger.com

Add 'Else If' Conditional Branch

Workflow Steps

TeamManager

ProjectCoordinator

Add workflow step

11. In the **Workflow Designer** wizard, click **Finish** to deploy the workflow.

Deleting a Workflow

Business processes do not last forever and neither will your workflows. Deleting a work-flow will disrupt the execution of any running workflow instance, so before you delete a workflow template using SharePoint Designer, you must first prevent the creation of any new workflow instances, and then wait for workflow instances that are still in progress to complete. SharePoint Designer does not provide a mechanism to manage workflow in-stances; you must use the browser. Similarly, you cannot delete a SharePoint workflow through the browser; you must use SharePoint Designer.

In this exercise, you will prevent the creation of new instances of a workflow, and then delete the workflow.

USE the workflow you created in the previous exercise.
BE SURE TO continue directly from the previous exercise.
OPEN your SharePoint site in the browser.

1. In the browser, on the Quick Launch bar, under **Documents,** click **PlanningProposals**.

2. In the **Settings** list, click **Document Library Settings** to display the Customize PlanningProposals page.

3. Under **Permissions and Management**, click **Workflow settings** to display the **Change Workflow Settings: PlanningProposals** page listing the workflows associated with this library and their status.

4. Click **Remove a workflow** to display the **Remove Workflow: PlanningProposals** page.

5. To the right of **StartersWorkflow**, click **No New Instances**.

> **Tip** By clicking No New Instances, you prevent the creation of any new workflow instances.

Teams > Workflows > Planning Proposals > Settings > Workflow settings > Remove Workflows

Remove Workflows: Planning Proposals

Use this page to remove workflow associations from the current list or library. Note that removing a workflow association cancels all running instances of the workflow. To allow current instances of a workflow to complete before removing the association, select No New Instances and allow the current instances to complete, and then return to this page and select Remove to remove the workflow association.

Workflows	**Workflow**	**Instances**	**Allow**	**No New Instances**	**Remove**
Specify workflows to remove from this document library. You can optionally let currently running workflows finish.	StartersWorkflow	0	⦾	⦿	⦾
	Three-state test workflow	0	⦿	⦾	⦾

OK   Cancel

6. Click **OK**.

   The Change Workflow Settings: PlanningProposals page is displayed.

7. In SharePoint Designer, in the **Folder List** task pane, right-click **StartersWorkflow**, and then click **Delete**.

   The Confirm Delete dialog box opens.

8. Click **Yes** to delete the workflow.

> **Tip** Just like any other list or library, when you delete the Workflow library, it will be moved to the Recycle Bin from where you can restore it. Similarly, if you delete any files from the Workflow library, they, too, will be moved to the Recycle Bin.

CLOSE the browser. If you are not continuing directly to the next chapter, exit SharePoint Designer.

Key Points

- Windows SharePoint Services and SharePoint Server use the Windows Workflow Foundation to provide document-centric workflows.

- Windows SharePoint Services and SharePoint Server provide a set of built-in workflow templates usually associated with a Tasks list and a History list.

- Workflows created in SharePoint Designer are associated with a specific list or library.

- Workflows consist of steps containing conditions and actions (activities). The default installation of SharePoint Designer provides an extensive set of built-in activities.

- You can interact with SharePoint workflows via the browser and most 2007 Microsoft Office system applications.

- With SharePoint Designer, you can create workflows in an easy and visual manner. Developers can use Visual Studio 2005 to access advanced workflow features.

- You cannot change or delete a workflow without running the risk of disrupting existing instances of a workflow. Use the browser to configure the workflow to allow the current instances of the workflow to complete and prevent the creation of new instances.

Chapter at a Glance

Customize a
site, **page 302**

Form Actions

Set the form actions for the "Form Action" control.

Actions List:

Refresh
Cancel
Navigate to source
Navigate to page

Add >>

<< Remove

Current Actions (run in order shown):

Commit
[Custom action]

Settings...

Move Up

Move Down

Perform a custom form action.

Web Site | manifest.xml

```
 1 <?xml version="1.0" encoding="UTF-8" ?>
 2 <Web Url="http://wss/BuildApps" ID="{7A6F9335-DE6F-451D-8566-248D83D8E604}">
 3 <MetaInfo><MetaKey Name="vti_defaultlanguage" Value="SW|en-us" /><MetaKey Name="vti_toolpaneurl
 4 <Details>
 5 <TemplateDescription></TemplateDescription>
 6 <TemplateTitle>Build Application Solution</TemplateTitle>
 7 <ProductVersion>3</ProductVersion>
 8 <Language>1033</Language>
 9 <TemplateID>1</TemplateID>
10 <Configuration>0</Configuration>
11 <Title>BuildApps</Title>
12 <Description></Description>
13 <CalendarType>1</CalendarType>
14 <AlternateCSS></AlternateCSS>
15 <CustomJSUrl></CustomJSUrl>
16 <AlternateHeader></AlternateHeader>
17 <Subweb>1</Subweb>
18 <Locale>1033</Locale>
19 <Collation>25</Collation>
20 <TimeZone>2</TimeZone>
21 <EnableTreeView>0</EnableTreeView>
22 <EnableQuickLaunch>1</EnableQuickLaunch>
23 </Details>
24 <WebFeatures>
25 <Feature ID="00bfea71-c796-4402-9f2f-0eb9a6e71b18" />
```

Explore a site
template,
page 311

Test a site
template
solution,
page 313

Workflow History

History list for workflow.

New ▾ | Actions ▾ | Settings ▾   View: **All History** ▾

Workflow History Parent Instance	Workflow Association ID	Workflow Template ID	List ID	Primary Item ID	User ID	Date Occurred	Event Type	Group Type	Outcome	Duration	Description	Data
{467ba7bc-2db9-4921-b56a-cae1761206b5}	{75b25e35-d70f-4862-829e-7858dc620388}	{5f884bc9-dfe1-4d2b-bc38-39fa670298af}	{f9edcc6c-2b1a-44a1-b417-7571baf0f26f}	2		11/7/2007 6:38 AM	Comment	0		0	Adventure Works	

13 Building a Windows SharePoint Services Application

In this chapter, you will learn to:

✔ Customize a site.

✔ Create a site template.

✔ Explore a site template.

✔ Test a site template solution.

As we described in Chapter 1, "Introducing SharePoint Designer," when you first install Microsoft Windows SharePoint Services or Microsoft Office SharePoint Server 2007, you are provided with a number of site definitions. In Chapter 2, "Working in SharePoint Designer," we listed those site definitions. When the SharePoint products are first installed, the team site definition is frequently used as a basis for many of the sites, because it is the closest to the needs for collaborating at a team level. However, before long, these sites will need to be customized to meet your business needs. After reading this book and customizing your own site, other users will soon come to you for similar modification on their sites. You will find that your colleagues will request similar lists, libraries, forms, branding, and workflows. Therefore, you need a method of packaging your solutions so that you can quickly re-create them.

Site definitions and Features provide a method of packaging and deploying solutions, but do require the skills of a developer and access to the Web servers. There are alternatives, some of which are detailed in Chapter 14, "Managing SharePoint Sites," to the methods of packaging solutions, which we will concentrate on in this chapter, for example, lists and site templates—in particular, site templates.

A site template is a site you create from a site definition, and then save as a template from which you can create other sites. A list template is similar: You create a list, which points to a list definition. List definitions, like site definitions, are files within the 12 hive, which you customize and save as a list template, from which you can create other lists.

Much of the details in this chapter concerning site templates are true of list templates; for example, both have an extension of .stp and are stored in the Microsoft SQL Server database. Of course, you cannot produce all your solutions in this manner, but they may be the answer to deploying some of your solutions.

See Also For more information on the 12 hive see Chapter 1, "Introducing SharePoint Designer."

In this chapter, you will use some of the skills you have learned in previous chapters to create a solution, which you will then package as a site template. You will save and explore a site template, create a site from that site template, and then test your solution. You will also look at the limitations of this approach and how, by using the skills of a developer, you can deploy solutions that are more complex.

Important Before you can use the practice files in this chapter, you need to install them from the book's companion CD to their default location. You will need to create a practice site for this chapter based on the site template *BuildApps_Starter.stp* located in this chapter's practice file folder. Then when you perform the exercises in this chapter, remember to use your SharePoint site location in place of *teams.consolidatedmessenger.com*.

For more information about practice files, see "Using the Book's CD" at the beginning of this book.

Troubleshooting Graphics and operating system–related instructions in this book reflect the Windows Vista user interface. If your computer is running Windows XP and you experience trouble following the instructions as written, please refer to the "Information for Readers Running Windows XP" section at the beginning of this book.

Customizing a Site

Similar to any other application development, you need to do some thinking before your start. You need to decide what business process you want to build, how soon you want it, who is going to use it, the resources available to help build the solution, where the data is located, the relationship between the data, and of course what tools you are going to use to build your solution. Always involve the people who are going to use your solution, because they are key to the success of your application. By listening to them and understanding the business process, you will be able to decide, for example, the number of forms you need to create for a particular library, and the workflows you need to develop.

During this required gathering phase, you should build prototypes to discover what you can easily do with a browser and Microsoft Office SharePoint Designer 2007. After you have built these prototypes, you may find that all you need to do is transfer to other users the skills you have learned. If you do find you need to build a solution, you may find that you need to invest more time building prototypes before building, testing, and deploying a Windows SharePoint Services or Office SharePoint Server application.

Assuming that the application you are building is based on Windows SharePoint Services or SharePoint Server; you need to decide whether to use a site definition or a site template for your application. When creating sites, there is no visible difference between using site templates and using site definitions. The following tables compare the two.

Advantages of Site Definitions	Advantages of Site Templates
• Data is stored directly on the Web servers, so performance is typically better. • A higher level of list customization is possible through the creation and editing of files on the Web servers. • Certain kinds of customization to sites or lists require use of site definitions or Features, such as introducing new file types, defining view styles, or modifying the Edit menu. • Site Definitions can be listed under different tabs on the site creation page.	• Data is stored in the SQL Server content database, and, therefore, you don't need to synchronize files on each Web server. • Custom templates are easy to create. • Most customizations can be achieved by using a browser or SharePoint Designer and can be preserved in the template. • Custom templates are easy to deploy. • Using either the browser or SharePoint Designer you can easily incorporate certain functionality like contributor settings

Disadvantages of Site Definitions	Disadvantages of Site Templates
• Site definitions require more work than site templates, especially if you're required to manipulate components not readily available using the SharePoint object model (SOM), such as contributor settings—and they require the skills of a developer. • Editing a site definition after it has been deployed is difficult. • Doing anything other than adding code can break existing sites. • Users cannot apply a SharePoint theme through a site definition. • Users cannot create two lists of the same type with different default content. • Site definitions must be deployed to each Web server and require IT department involvement and possibly a facilities management company if your company has outsourced its IT infrastructure.	• Custom templates are not created in a development environment, and, therefore, may lack in formal source control. • Custom templates are less efficient in large-scale environments. • If the site definition on which the custom template is based does not exist on the front-end server or servers, the custom template does not work. • All site templates appear under the same tab, *Custom*, on the New SharePoint Site page.

As part of your planning process, you should devise some standards, and encourage other users who develop solutions to maintain the same standards. This will help when you need to alter your own, or maintain other, solutions. You could include standards such as the following:

- Devise a naming standard for components, such as URLs, pages, placeholders, cascading style sheet styles, and Web Part zones, incorporating whenever possible the names used by Windows SharePoint Services and SharePoint Server. Some functions, such as Edit In Datasheet, require that specific Web Part zone names are present on the page.

- Develop branding, including fonts, colors, the use of images, and cascading style sheet standards. Keep similar styles together in logical groupings. Copy existing styles from core.css, and override the defaults, maintaining accessibility and standards compatibility.

- Comment your code. When you revisit your solution many months later, these comments will help you understand why you built your solution in a specific manner.

- Comment before deleting components. When creating pages based on the default pages, such as master pages, comment out the controls before you delete them. Some pages must have certain elements in place—even if they're hidden—or they won't render properly. You'll save yourself a great deal of frustration by working backward through commented code than trying to add it back in later.

- Test frequently. Never assume that the modifications you make in one page or site will work in another; for example, one page may be a publishing page and the other may be a content page from a team site. Similarly, some sites may have a Feature activated, which is not on another site.

- Base site templates on one of the default site templates, such as the Blank Site template.

- Modulate and reuse your customizations. For example, do not create an excess number of site definitions or site templates, because these increase your company's maintenance burden and can confuse users.

- Developers should create their standards that complement your standards and vice-versa, especially where there is an overlap, for example, cascading style sheets and master pages. Such standards could include standards for creating Web Parts, server controls, code access security, Features, client-side scripts, packaging of solutions, and, of course, coding and testing standards. This is particularly important if you outsource your development or acquire developer skills only when needed from the contracting market.

See Also For more information about site definitions, see the sidebar "Site Definitions, Features, and Solution Files Primer," later in this chapter.

In this exercise, you will build an application—using a combination of XML data, Data Views, Microsoft ASP.NET and SharePoint controls, and workflows—by using a browser and SharePoint Designer.

> **USE** your own SharePoint site location in place of the *teams.consolidatedmessenger.com* team site.
>
> **BE SURE TO** start SharePoint Designer and close any pages that are open in the document window before beginning this exercise.
>
> **OPEN** your BuildApps child site in SharePoint Designer.

1. In the **Folder List** task pane, expand **WebPages**, and then double-click **SalesReport.aspx** to open the page in the document window.

   A Data View displays XML data from the Consignments.xml file in the Shared Documents library.

2. Under **Consignment Number**, right-click **123**, point to **Format Item as**, and then click **Text Box**.

   The Consignment Number column is formatted as an input text box.

3. Under **Customer Name**, right-click **Adventure Works**, point to **Format Item as**, and then click **Label**.

   The Customer Name field is converted into an ASP.NET label so that you can reference it in other controls.

4. On the **Insert** menu, point to **SharePoint Controls**, and then click **More SharePoint Controls**.

   The Toolbox task pane opens, with the Data View Controls section expanded.

5. In the document window, right-click **Delivery Location**, point to **Insert**, and then click **Column to the Right**.

   A column is added to the table.

6. Click in the new column to the right of **UK**, and on the **Toolbox** task pane, under **Data View Controls**, double-click **Form Action Button**.

   A Form Action button is added to the cell to the right of UK. The Form Actions dialog box opens.

7. Under **Actions List**, click **Commit**, and click **Add**. Then click **[Custom Action]**, and click **Add**.

The two actions, Commit and [Custom Action], are listed under Current Actions (Run In Order Shown).

8. In the **Form Actions** dialog box, click **Settings**.

The Workflow Designer – Custom Form Action 2 dialog box opens.

9. In the **Step Name** text box, type Consignment Number Update.

10. Under **Specify details for Step 1**, click **Actions**, click **More Actions**, click **Log to History List**, and then click **Add**.

The text *Log This Message To The Workflow History List* appears to the right of Actions.

11. Click **this message**, and then click the **Function** button to open the **Define Workflow Lookup** dialog box.

12. Verify that **Form Fields** is selected in the **Source** list. Then in the **Field** list, click **Form Fields: ff2 (CustomerName)**.

This will write the customer name to the hidden Workflow History list every time the workflow runs.

13. Click **OK** to close the **Define Workflow Lookup** dialog box.

The text *Log Form Fields: ff2 To The Workflow History List* appears to the right of Actions.

Workflow Designer - Custom Form Action 2   ? ✕

Step Name: Consignment Number Update   Workflow Steps

Specify details for 'Consignment Number Update'   Consignment Number Update

Choose the conditions and actions that define this step of the workflow.   Add workflow step

┌─────────────┐   ▼
│ Conditions ▼ │
└─────────────┘
┌─────────────┐   Log Form Fields: ff2 to the workflow history list
│ Actions ▼ │
└─────────────┘

Add 'Else If' Conditional Branch

Check Workflow   Variables...   Cancel   Finish

14. Click **Finish** to deploy the workflow.

The Workflow Designer – Custom Form Action 2 dialog box closes.

15. Click **OK** to close the **Forms Actions** dialog box.

The Form Action button appears in all the cells in the new column.

16. In the **Tag Properties** task pane, click in the cell to the right of **value**, and type
Save. Then press Enter.

The buttons in the new column are re-labeled to *Save*.

Save

17. Click **Save**.

On the CD Further examples of creating solutions based on Windows SharePoint Services
3.0 are provided in the *Application Templates Under the Hood* document on the book's
companion CD.

Site Definitions, Features, and Solution Files Primer

Site definitions are packaged business solutions and can contain everything from Web Parts and master pages to workflows and navigation settings. They are stored in the 12 hive, in the *TEMPLATE\SiteTemplate* folder, and can contain one or more site configurations. For example, the STS site definition contains the Blank Site, Team Site, and Document Workspaces configurations.

Two new components introduced with Windows SharePoint Services 3.0 increase the power of site definitions:

- **The Global site definition.** This folder, located in the 12 hive in the *TEMPLATE\Global* folder, contains components that are necessary for every site, such as the files that define galleries, base lists, libraries, and column types. Every site definition references the Global site definitions; therefore, there is no longer the need to have redundant files and code in each site definition.

- *Features*. These define a specific set of functionality. Features are stored in the *TEMPLATE\Features* folder in the 12 hive. Using Features, you could create a site based on the team site definition, and, over time, install and activate all the Features that enable that same site to function like a publishing site. With the use of this new component, new site definitions are needed less often, because new functionality is created by using Features.

A powerful technique that combines both the site definitions and Features is Feature Stapling. When you staple a Feature to a site configuration, that Feature is automatically activated when you create a site. And when you staple a Feature to the Global site definition, every new site has that Feature. Features can also be stapled to existing sites and activated as necessary.

Site definitions and Features can be deployed manually to each Web server, but such a method is prone to error. Therefore, Microsoft introduced a new form of deployment that developers can use to package them into a SharePoint solution. Central administrators using the stsadm tool and the Central administration site can install solutions, which are saved in the SQL Server database. It is then the responsibility of Windows SharePoint Services to ensure that each Web server contains the same files.

A solution file is a cabinet file with a .wsp extension, which stands for Windows SharePoint Services Solution Package. This file is similar to a compressed file and, therefore, you can rename the file's extension to .cab to see its content.

To help in the development of developer-based solutions, you can use Microsoft Visual Studio Extension for WSS (VSeWSS), an add-in for Visual Studio 2005. It is available from the Microsoft Download Center and adds the necessary references, creates the folder structure needed for Features, and adds configuration and deployment files. Like any tool, it does have its limitation; for example, it does not support Microsoft Visual Basic .NET and does not allow you to edit solution files. Therefore, you still need an experienced SharePoint developer.

See Also For more information about site definitions, Features, and solution files, refer to Chapter 9, "Solutions and Deployment," in *Inside Microsoft Windows SharePoint Services 3.0*, by Ted Pattison and Daniel Larson (Microsoft Press, 2007).

Creating a Site Template

After customizing your site by adding or removing lists, libraries, pages, and even subsites you can package everything for further reuse by making your own site template. A site template is represented by one .stp file.

When you create a site template, you can choose to save its content, which includes lists, libraries, pages, custom pages, master pages and configurations; however, a number of components are not saved, such as permissions. Site templates have a size limit of 10 megabytes (MB), but your SharePoint server administrator can change the size limit for .stp files by using the stsadm command-line tool with the setproperty operation; for example:

```
stsadm -o setproperty -propertyname max-template-document-size -propertyvalue
50000000
```

Because site templates are based on site definitions, if you copy the site template to another server, that server must have those site definitions installed. For this reason, many companies use the team site or the blank site as their basis for creating site template solutions. Similarly, if your lists or libraries use any custom content types, those content types must be re-created in the destinations site collection's Site Content Type Gallery.

Microsoft has released two additional sets of application templates. These templates are an excellent example that you can use as a basis for learning more about building applications with Windows SharePoint Services and SharePoint Server, most of which can be achieved by using the browser or SharePoint Designer. The two sets of templates are:

- Application Templates for Windows SharePoint Service 3.0, also known as the *Fabulous 40*, which contains 20 site templates and 20 site definitions. Many of the site templates are based on the blank site definition.

● Splendid 7, which is a set of role-based templates for My Site.

See Also To obtain the additional site templates, refer to the Web site *www.microsoft. com/sharepoint/templates.mspx*.

Site templates are stored in a site template gallery, of which there are two types:

● **Central Site Template Gallery.** Only a server administrator can install site templates into this gallery. Site templates stored in the Central site template can be used to create top-level sites of a site collection and are available to all site collections within a Windows SharePoint Services or SharePoint Server installation.

● **Site Collection Template Gallery.** Using either a browser or SharePoint Designer, you can store site templates in the top-level site of a site collection.

> **Note** A third gallery, the List Template Gallery, contains list templates. List templates are used in a similar way to site templates. That is, you can take a default list such as the Links list, customize it by adding columns and list items, and then save the list as a list template, with or without its contents. You can then create other lists from your list template.

In SharePoint Server, you can limit the site templates that are visible by using the Site Master Page Settings page, which you can navigate to from the Site Settings page; under Look And Feel, click Page Layouts And Site Templates.

In this exercise, you will use SharePoint Designer to create a site template.

> **USE** the site you modified in the previous exercise.
> **OPEN** the site in SharePoint Designer, if it is not already open.

1. On the **File** menu, point to **Export**, and then click **SharePoint Site Template**.

   The browser opens and the Save Site As Template page is displayed.

2. In the **File name** text box, type SPDBuildSol, and in the **Template name** text box, type Build Application Solution.

3. In the **Include Content** section, select the **Include Content** check box.

4. Click **OK**.

   The Operation Completed Successfully page is displayed, stating that the newly created template is stored in the Site Template Gallery.

> **CLOSE** SharePoint Designer.

Exploring a Site Template

Site templates contain the differences between the customized site and the original site definition. The .stp file is actually a cabinet file that contains a manifest.xml that lists all the other files that the cabinet file contains.

Each site definition is given a number; so is each site configuration within a site definition. You can use this information to identify the site definition a site template was created from. The template and configuration number for team and Meeting Workspace site definitions are listed in the following table.

Template	Configuration
1. STS	0 Team Site
	1 Blank Site
	2 Document Workspace
2. MPS	0 Basic Meeting Workspace
	1 Blank Meeting Workspace
	2 Decision Meeting Workspace
	3 Social Meeting Workspace
	4 Multipage Meeting Workspace

In this exercise, you will save a site template and review its contents.

USE the site you modified in the previous exercise.
OPEN the site in the browser, if it is not already open.

1. On the **Operation Completed Successfully** page, click **site template gallery**.

   > **Tip** If the Operation Completed Successfully page is not displayed, click Site Actions, and then click Site Settings. If you are at a child site, click Go To Top Level Site Settings. On the Site Settings page, under Galleries, click Site Templates.

2. Right-click **SPDBuildSol**, and then click **Save Target As** to open the **Save As** dialog box.

3. Navigate to *Documents\Microsoft Press\SPD2007_SBS\BuildSoln*, and then click **Save**.

   The Save As dialog box closes.

4. Use Windows Explorer to navigate to *Documents\Microsoft Press\SPD2007_SBS*, and rename **SPDBuildSol.stp** as SPDBuildSol.cab.

   A Rename warning box opens, stating that the file may become unstable.

5. Click **Yes** to close the **Rename** warning box.

6. Double-click **SPDBuildSol.cab** to open the cabinet file, locate **manifest.xml**, and drag it to your desktop.

7. Right-click **manifest.xml** and click **Edit with Microsoft Office SharePoint Designer**.

   SharePoint Designer opens and displays manifest.xml in the document window.

```
Web Site | manifest.xml                                                            X
 1 <?xml version="1.0" encoding="UTF-8" ?>
 2 <Web Url="http://wss/BuildApps" ID="{7A6F9335-DE6F-451D-8566-248D83D8E604}">
 3 <MetaInfo><MetaKey Name="vti_defaultlanguage" Value="SW|en-us" /><MetaKey Name="vti_toolpaneurl
 4 <Details>
 5 <TemplateDescription></TemplateDescription>
 6 <TemplateTitle>Build Application Solution</TemplateTitle>
 7 <ProductVersion>3</ProductVersion>
 8 <Language>1033</Language>
 9 <TemplateID>1</TemplateID>
10 <Configuration>0</Configuration>
11 <Title>BuildApps</Title>
12 <Description></Description>
13 <CalendarType>1</CalendarType>
14 <AlternateCSS></AlternateCSS>
15 <CustomJSUrl></CustomJSUrl>
16 <AlternateHeader></AlternateHeader>
17 <Subweb>1</Subweb>
18 <Locale>1033</Locale>
19 <Collation>25</Collation>
20 <TimeZone>2</TimeZone>
21 <EnableTreeView>0</EnableTreeView>
22 <EnableQuickLaunch>1</EnableQuickLaunch>
23 </Details>
24 <WebFeatures>
25 <Feature ID="00bfea71-c796-4402-9f2f-0eb9a6e71b18" />
```

The TemplateID element (line 9) has a value of 1 and the Configuration element (line 10) has a value of 0, which means that the *SPDBuildSol* site template was based on the team site definition.

CLOSE the .cab file and SharePoint Designer.

Testing a Site Template Solution

After you have created a site template and before you allow other users to create sites from it, you should create a site based on it. Although most customizations can be saved in the site template, some cannot. For example, custom workflows that you develop by using SharePoint Designer can be saved in a site template, but they may not work in the site created from the site template. Depending on a workflow's complexity, you may need to redeploy the workflow, by opening it in SharePoint Designer and clicking Finish. If this does not work, you have the choice of creating the workflow again in the new site, or involving a developer to create a generic workflow that can be used in many sites. Similarly, if you a create Web Part connection when the Web Parts are contained in Web Part zones, you will need to re-create those Web Part connections. It is therefore important that you test your solutions to discover the customization that works successfully after packaging them in a site template and those that do not.

See Also If you are provided with a site template from elsewhere, you will need to upload the site template into the Site Template Gallery. For information about uploading and deleting site templates, refer to "Using the Book's CD" at the beginning of this book.

> **Warning** Site templates, like backup files and export files, could contain malicious code, so use site templates only from sources you trust.

You do not need to have server administrator privileges to install a site template, because the Site Template Gallery is a document library itself and not a folder on the server; therefore, if you are a site owner or administrator of the top-level site, you have sufficient rights to upload a site template into the Site Template Gallery.

In this exercise, you will create a site from a site template and test your solution.

> **USE** the site from the previous exercise.
> **OPEN** the site in the browser, if it is not already open.

1. Click **Site Actions**, and then click **Create** to display the Create page.
2. Under **Web Pages**, click **Sites and Workspaces** to display the New SharePoint Site page.
3. In the **Title** and the **URL name** text boxes, type BuildSolTest.

4. In the **Template Selection** section, on the **Custom** tab, click **Build Application Solution**.

5. Click **Create**.

   The Operation In Progress page is displayed, followed by the home page of the new site.

6. On the Quick Launch bar, under **Documents**, click **WebPages**.

   The All Documents view of the WebPages library appears, with two pages listed: SalesReport and TechNetSearch.

7. Click **SalesReport**.

   The Sales report page is displayed.

8. Under **Consignment number**, select **123**, and type 444. To the right in the same row, click **Save**.

   Note that the Customer Name for this consignment is *Adventure Works*.

9. On the Quick Launch bar, under **Documents**, click **Shared Documents**.

   The All Documents view of the Shared Documents library is displayed.

10. Click **Consignments**. If a **Microsoft Internet Explorer** dialog box opens, asking how you would like to open the file, click **OK**.

    The consignment.xml file is displayed in the browser. The first shipment element has a ConsignmentNumber element with a value of 444.

11. Open the **BuildSolTest** site in SharePoint Designer.

12. In the **Folder List** task pane, expand **Lists**, and click **Workflow History**. Then press [F12].

    The All History view of the *Workflow History* list is displayed in the browser. The list item with the most recent date and time, has the value in the Description column of *Adventure Works*, which is the name of the customer whose consignment number you modified in step 8.

Workflow History

History list for workflow.

New ▾   Actions ▾   Settings ▾   View: **All History** ▾

Workflow History Parent Instance	Workflow Association ID	Workflow Template ID	List ID	Primary Item ID	User ID	Date Occurred	Event Type	Group Type	Outcome	Duration	Description	Data
{467ba7bc-2db9-4921-b56a-cae1761206b5}	{75b25e35-d70f-4862-829e-7858dc620388}	{5f884bc9-dfe1-4d2b-bc38-39fa670298af}	{f9edcc6c-2b1a-44a1-b417-7523bac0f365}	2		11/7/2007 6:38 AM	Comment	0		0	Adventure Works	

✖ **CLOSE** all browser windows. If you are not continuing directly to the next chapter, exit SharePoint Designer.

Key Points

- You should treat a Windows SharePoint Services or SharePoint Server application solution as any other project and have a planning and requirements gathering phase, create standards, and then prototype, build, test, and deploy your solutions.

- There is no visible difference between using site templates and using site definitions.

- Site and list templates are methods of packaging solutions so that you can use them again, and are stored in the SQL Server database.

- Site definitions and Features are also methods of packaging solutions, but require the skills of a developer and access to a Web server. They are files in the 12 hive.

- Site and list templates can contain content and, by default, the limit to the size of a template file is 10 MB, which can be increased.

- Site and list templates are cabinet files, which have an extension of .stp. These files contain a number of files that describe the differences that need to be applied to a site definition or list definitions for your customizations to be achieved.

- You can use a browser or SharePoint Designer to create site templates.

Chapter at a Glance

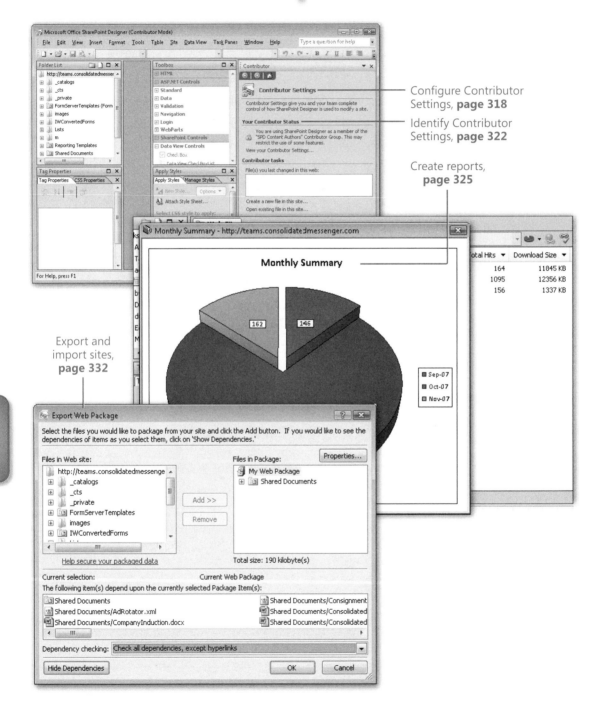

Configure Contributor Settings, **page 318**

Identify Contributor Settings, **page 322**

Create reports, **page 325**

Export and import sites, **page 332**

14 Managing SharePoint Sites

In this chapter, you will learn to:

✔ Configure Contributor Settings.
✔ Identify Contributor Settings.
✔ Create reports.
✔ Back up and restore sites.
✔ Export and import sites.
✔ Copy lists and libraries between sites.
✔ Copy documents between sites.

Microsoft SharePoint Designer provides you with more than just the ability to customize a Microsoft Windows SharePoint Services or Microsoft Office SharePoint Server 2007 site. It also helps you manage and protect your sites. SharePoint Designer includes a new component named *Contributor Settings*. With this feature, you can define Contributor groups that you will use to restrict what users can do when they use SharePoint Designer.

The reporting facilities have improved as well in SharePoint Designer 2007; for example, you can generate reports that provide change management information and help you locate errors in cascading style sheets.

In this chapter, you will learn to use Contributor Settings and to create reports. Then you will learn to copy sites, lists, and individual documents by using a variety of methods.

> **Important** No practice files are required to complete the exercises in this chapter. For more information about practice files, see "Using the Book's CD" at the beginning of this book.

> **Troubleshooting** Graphics and operating system–related instructions in this book reflect the Windows Vista user interface. If your computer is running Windows XP and you experience trouble following the instructions as written, please refer to the "Information for Readers Running Windows XP" section at the beginning of this book.

Configuring Contributor Settings

Contributor Settings is a new features included with SharePoint Designer. With Contributor Settings, you can restrict the usage of SharePoint Designer on a per-site basis and work with the permission levels you configure on your site by using a browser. The Contributor Settings for a site are dependent on Contributor groups. Windows SharePoint Services and Office SharePoint Server 2007 rely on SharePoint Designer to decide what privileges users should have.

When a site is first created, by default, three Contributor groups are available: Site Manager, Web Designer and Content Authors. Users who meet the requirements of the Site Manager and Web Designer Contributor groups have unrestricted use of SharePoint Designer on your site.

So how can you control who can do what on your site? Each Contributor group is linked to a permission level on your site. The Site Managers Contributor group is linked to the Full Control permission level, Web Designers Contributor group to the Design permission level, and Content Authors to the Contribute permission level.

Permission levels are a set of permissions that relate to a specific task. Windows SharePoint Services has five permission levels: Full Control, Design, Contribute, Read, and Limited Access. SharePoint Server creates an additional four permission levels: Manage Hierarchy, Approve, Restricted Read, and View Only. Each permission level consists of a number of permissions. *Permissions* are the smallest security access unit. Windows SharePoint Services (and, therefore, SharePoint Server) comes with more than 30 permissions, such as Add Items, Edit Items, Delete Items, View Items, Approve Items, and Create Alerts. To ease management of these permissions, they are grouped together in a manner that Microsoft thought would map to common tasks.

You can assign people to specific permission levels, but the usual practice is to put people and Active Directory directory services security groups into SharePoint Groups, which map to specific permission levels. Permission levels in turn map to SharePoint Designer Contributor groups. You then configure the SharePoint Designer Contributor groups.

You can keep track of this permission chain by using a naming convention, so that when you look at a SharePoint Designer Contributor group, you know that it affects people in specific SharePoint groups and you don't have to go through the chain every time.

Each Contributor group has a number of properties, which are divided into the seven categories listed on the next page.

- **General.** This category includes the group name and description. Use it to map the Contributor group to the appropriate permission level. You can prevent users from accessing the Code view of the document window, as well as configuring a Contributor group for unrestricted use of SharePoint Designer.

- **Folders.** Use this category to specify the location where users can edit pages, and the location where images and other files are stored.

- **Creating Pages.** Use this category to specify the creation, deletion, and renaming of pages, master pages, and Dynamic Web Templates. You can also limit users to customizing specific page types.

- **Editing.** Use this category to restrict the components a user can edit. The settings in this category affect only the WYSIWYG manipulation of components. If users still have access to Code view, they can circumvent the restriction settings on this page.

- **Formatting.** Use this category to specify the style and formatting features a user has access to.

- **Images.** Use this category to allow users to insert images and restrict the locations they can insert them in. You can also limit the size of the image, and other media files, such as videos or flash.

- **SharePoint.** Use this category to restrict users from modifying the home page; overwriting existing pages from the site definition; and creating, editing, and deleting workflows, Web Part zones, Web Parts, Data Views, and Data Forms.

One Contributor group is set as the default Contributor group. This group is used for users whose permission level does not match to any of the other Contributor groups. Because the Content Author Contributor group has the least rights when using SharePoint Designer, this group is the default group when you first install SharePoint Designer. Whatever Contributor group a user is mapped to, the permission setting within Windows SharePoint Services or SharePoint Server takes precedence. For example, if you use a browser to allow users read access to a document library, which may include pages, yet the users are assigned to the Full Control permission level elsewhere, then SharePoint Designer will not allow them to edit any files in that document library.

The Contributor Setting dialog box also allows you to define region types. Region types are associated with content regions so that you can limit the type of content users can place in those regions. Content regions are defined on master pages as content place-holder controls, which were discussed in Chapter 9, "Working with Master Pages."

In the Advanced settings of the Contributor Settings dialog box, you can disable Contributor Settings (not recommended) and you can specify one or more contact e-mail addresses, which users of SharePoint Designer can use to send queries.

> **Tip** You can prevent users from using SharePoint Designer at a global level by adding a DisableWebDesignFeatures element to a site definition. Users using SharePoint Designer cannot modify any of the sites based on that site definition. You could use this same method to prevent the users from using FrontPage 2003 on sites.

In this exercise, you will copy the default Contributor group and use it as a basis for the default Contributor group. You will then configure this new Contributor group to allow users to insert, edit, and delete of Data Views and Data Forms.

> **USE** your own SharePoint site in place of the *teams.consolidatedmessenger.com* team site.
> **OPEN** the SharePoint site in SharePoint Designer.

1. On the **Site** menu, click **Contributor Settings**.

   The Contributor Settings dialog box opens.

2. Under **Manage Contributor Groups**, click **Content Authors (Default)**, and then click **Copy**.

   Under Manage Contributor Groups, a new contributor group named Copy Of Content Authors appears.

3. Click **Copy of Content Authors**, and then click **Modify**.

   The Contributor Group Properties dialog box opens.

4. In the **Group name** text box, type SPD Content Authors.

5. In the left pane, click **SharePoint**. Then under **Web Parts and Web Part Zones**, select the **Allow insert, edit, and delete of Data Views and Data Forms** check box.

6. In the **Contributor Group Properties** dialog box, click **OK**.

SPD Content Authors appears in the Contributor Settings dialog box.

7. With **SPD Content Authors** selected, click **Set As Default**, and then click **OK**.

The Folder List task pane is redisplayed. A new folder named _contributor_settings_ appears, which contains an .htm file that defines your customized Contributor Settings. Only users with unrestricted access can see the contents of this file in Code view.

> **Note** In the Contributor Settings dialog box, you can click Reset Contributor Setting Defaults, which restores the default Contributor group settings for the site and is the same as deleting the _contributor_settings_ folder.

CLOSE SharePoint Designer.

Identifying Contributor Settings

If you do not have full access to a site using SharePoint Designer, you can use the Contributor task pane to identify the settings you have. You can also use the Contact The Site Manager button to send an e-mail message.

In this exercise, you will identify what you can do with SharePoint Designer if your credentials map to the default Contributor group.

> **Important** Complete the following exercise using the credentials of an account that has Contribute permission levels on the site you are using. By default, the Members SharePoint Group is assigned the Contribute permission level and, therefore, an account that is part of that SharePoint Group should be sufficient for the purposes of this exercise.

> **USE** the SharePoint site you modified in the previous exercise.
>
> **BE SURE TO** complete this exercise using the credentials of an account that has only Contribute permissions for the site.
>
> **OPEN** the SharePoint site in SharePoint Designer, using the login credentials of the alternative account.

1. Verify that the SharePoint Designer window has a title of **Microsoft Office SharePoint Designer (Contributor Mode)**.

> **Tip** If the SharePoint Designer window does not state that you are in Contributor mode, you may have to log off and then log on with other credentials. When you log on to a site in a browser, the credentials you use are not passed through to Windows applications, such as SharePoint Designer. If your Web site is in the browser's intranet zone, when you open SharePoint Designer, the credentials used are those that you used to log on to your computer. If the site is not in the browser's intranet zone, you will be prompted for your credentials.

2. If the **Contributor** task pane is not visible, on the **Task Panes** menu, click **Contributor**.

    The Contributor task pane displays that you are using SharePoint Designer as a member of the SPD Content Authors Contributor Group. In the SharePoint Designer status bar, a padlock icon appears to the left of the text *SPD Content Authors*.

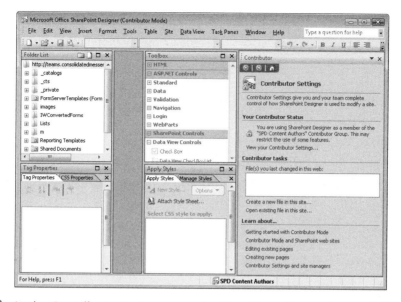

3. In the **Contributor** task pane, under **Your Contributor Status**, click **View your Contributor Settings**.

The View Your Contributor Settings dialog box opens.

4. In the left pane, click **Creating Pages**, and then click **Set page types**.

The Page Types dialog box opens. Only the Web Part Pages check box is selected. All the check boxes are unavailable, denoting that you cannot change these settings.

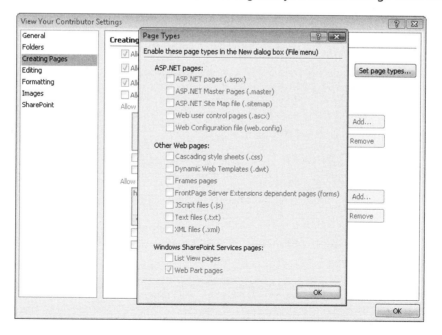

> **Tip** The New dialog box does not list Web Part pages; therefore, to create Web Part pages, you must either save an existing Web Part page in SharePoint Designer or use a browser.

5. Click **OK** to close the **Page Types** dialog box. Then click **OK** to close the **View Your Contributor Settings** dialog box.

6. In the **Folder List** task pane, double-click **default.aspx** to open the page in the document window.

7. Place the insertion point between the **Announcements** and **Links** Web Parts, and then type Consolidated Messenger.

> **Tip** If the Announcements or Links Web Parts are not on the page, click between the two Web Part zones, where they are usually placed on a newly created team site.

Save

8. On the Common toolbar, click **Save**.

The Microsoft Office SharePoint Designer dialog box opens, warning you that you are not allowed to modify this page.

9. Click **OK** to close the dialog box.

10. On the **File** menu, click **Save As** to open the **Save As** dialog box.

11. In the **Save As** dialog box, double-click **Shared Documents**, and in the **File name** text box, type SPDTestPage.aspx. Then click **Save**.

   In the Contributor task pane, the Shared Documents/SPDTestPage.aspx file appears under Contributor Tasks.

12. In the **Contributor** task pane, point to **SPDTestPage.aspx**, click the arrow that appears, and then click **Check Out**.

   The document window refreshes and in the Folder task pane, there is a check to the left of SPDTestPage.aspx.

13. Click **Announcements**. Then press ← twice. On the **Data View** menu, click **Insert Data View**.

   The Data View is place above the Announcements Web Part. The Data Source Library task pane opens, with no data sources listed, because you do not have permissions to use the contents of the Data Source Library.

14. On the Common toolbar, click **Save**.

15. Close the **Contributor** task pane.

> **CLOSE** SharePoint Designer. Log off, and then log on with a user name that has site owner permission on the SharePoint site you used earlier in this chapter.

Creating Reports

Windows SharePoint Services and SharePoint Server provide a number of reports that you can access by using a browser. Using SharePoint Designer, depending on the Contributor group you are in, you have access to additional reports. These reports are limited to the site you have open, but do go back more than 30 days, which is the limit of the reports available when using a browser. You can configure the number of months you would like to include in these reports in the Application Options dialog box, which you can access on the Tools menu. These reports are divided into five groups:

- **Summary.** These are high-level reports that provide you with an overview of the site. You can then use the links on the Summary page to produce more detailed reports.

- **Files.** These reports provide information about files, such as those recently added, changed, older, checked out, or slow to render. On the Reports View tab of the Application Options dialog box, you can configure the meaning of these terms.

- **Shared Content.** This category of reports includes files used by other files, hence the name *shared*. Files in this category include master pages, style sheets, and other files from the site definition.

- **Problems.** Use these reports to try to predict problems, such as broken links and pages that are slow to load, which does not take into account any processing time that is necessary on the Web servers.

- **Usage.** These reports provide summary and detailed usage information, which can be further dissected by day, week, or month. Most of the usage reports provide a chart mechanism. If charts do not appear, then select the Include Chart When Usage Report Is Saved check box on the Reports View tab of the Application Options dialog box.

> **Tip** Before you can view the usage report in either the browser or SharePoint Designer, Windows SharePoint Services must be configured for usage reporting. A SharePoint Central administrator configures usage reporting on the Operations page in Central Administration and if you have SharePoint Server installed, usage reporting needs to be enabled in Shared Services.

> **Tip** To view usage reports, you must have the View Usage Data permission, which is given to users who are associated with the Full Control, Manage Hierarchy, and Power User permission levels or are members of the Site Owners or Manage Hierarchy SharePoint groups. If you are not a member of these SharePoint groups or you are not associated with these permission levels, you will not be able to see Usage reports. For a discussion on how best to give users the View Usage Data permission go to *sharepoint.microsoft.com/blogs/LKuhn/Lists/Posts/Post.aspx?ID=36.*

As you review these reports, you can filter, including custom filtering, and sort them. You can also copy and paste a report in, for example, a Microsoft Office Word 2007 document or an e-mail message, or save it as an HTML file and open it in Microsoft Office Excel 2007.

In this exercise, you will review the reports available to you.

USE the site you modified earlier in this chapter.
OPEN the site in SharePoint Designer.

1. At the bottom of the **Web Site** tab in the document window, click **Reports**.

   A list of reports appears in the document window.

> **Tip** Alternatively, on the Site menu, you can point to Reports and click Site Summary to see the reports.

Name	Count	Size	Description
Usage data	1182	25,538KB	Hits and download bytes for the period from 04/09/2007 to 06/11/2C
All files	195	2,420KB	All files in the current Web site
Pictures	12	53KB	Picture files in the current Web site (GIF, JPG, BMP, etc.)
Unlinked files	14	41KB	Files in the current Web site that cannot be reached by starting from
Linked files	181	2,379KB	Files in the current Web site that can be reached by starting from yo
Slow pages	0	0KB	Pages in the current Web site exceeding an estimated download time
Older files	0	0KB	Files in the current Web site that have not been modified in over 72 (
Recently added files	37	1,777KB	Files in the current Web site that have been created in the last 30 da
Checked out files	0	0KB	Files in Web site that are currently checked out.
Hyperlinks	397		All hyperlinks in the current Web site
Unverified hyperlinks	286		Hyperlinks pointing to unconfirmed target files
Broken hyperlinks	0		Hyperlinks pointing to unavailable target files
External hyperlinks	285		Hyperlinks pointing to files outside of the current Web site
Internal hyperlinks	112		Hyperlinks pointing to other files within the current Web site
Component errors	5		Files in the current Web site with components reporting an error
Style Sheet Links	0		All Style Sheet Links in the current web site.
Dynamic Web Templates	0		All files that are associated with a Dynamic Web Template.
Master Pages	90		All files that are associated with a Master Page.
Customized pages	96	343KB	Files from the SharePoint site definition that have been customized

Web Site

Site Summary ▾

□Folders ⊞Remote Web Site ▣Reports 品Navigation & Hyperlinks

| Site Summary ▾ |

2. On the **Web Site** tab, click the **Site Summary** arrow, point to **Usage**, and then click **Monthly Summary**.

The monthly summary for this page is displayed. The visits and hits for each month are listed on a separate line, dependent on how long your site has been created.

> **Tip** If a message appears, stating that the monthly summary view cannot be displayed for this Web site, then usage reporting may not be enabled. You will need to contact your SharePoint Central administrator to configure usage reporting. Once enabled, usage statistics are analyzed on a daily basis. Therefore, you will have to wait at least one day before you will see any data in your reports.

Chart

3. In the upper-right corner of the document window, click the chart icon arrow, point to each icon in the list, and then click **3-D Pie Chart**.

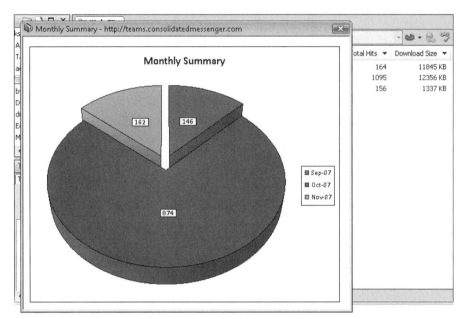

| Monthly Summary ▾ |

4. Click the **Monthly Summary** arrow, point to **Usage**, and then click **Browsers**.

The document window lists those browsers that were used when visiting the site.

| Browsers ▾ |

5. Click the **Browsers** arrow, point to **Problems**, and then click **Hyperlinks**.

The Reports View dialog box opens, asking whether you want SharePoint Designer to verify the hyperlinks in your Web site now.

6. Click **Yes**.

> **Warning** Verifying hyperlinks can take some time and can cause a considerable amount of network traffic, especially if your site contains many of them. SharePoint Designer will try to request each page that the hyperlink points to, and when a specific time elapses with no response, SharePoint Designer classifies the hyperlink as broken.

The Reports View dialog box closes. As the hyperlinks are verified, the results are displayed in the document window.

> **Tip** If there are any broken hyperlinks, you can right-click the hyperlink and click Edit Hyperlink to open the Edit Hyperlink dialog box.

| Hyperlinks ▼ |

7. Click the **Hyperlinks** arrow, point to **Shared Content**, and then click **Customized Pages**.

In the document window, all pages are listed, with the customized pages listed at the top.

Backing Up and Restoring Sites

With SharePoint Designer, you can use three different methods of packaging your sites content:

- **Backup and Restore, where you create a content migration package (.cmp).** Use this method when you need to copy or move an entire site or child site to another server or location.

- **Export and Import, using Personal Web Packages (.fwp).** Use this method to share or reuse a site, list, or library structure. It does not include list items, only the list structure. It can be used to copy files, but only as part of the library structure.

- **Export a site as a site template.** When you use this method, SharePoint Designer does not package the site for you; it opens the browser on the Save Site As Template page. More information on site templates can be found in Chapter 13, "Building a Windows SharePoint Services Application."

> **Tip** None of the above packages can be modified after they are created. If you do want to alter the contents of the package, you need to restore/import the package to a site, modify the site, and re-create the package.

The Backup and Restore method includes the most data of the three, and is, therefore, the method to use if you want to move a site or child site from one server to another. It will not include any data stored at the site collection level, such as content types, nor does it include components from the Recycle Bin. Therefore, if your site references components, such as content types, site columns, or features other than the defaults, your site may not restore successfully. Both servers should be at the same service pack levels. Even if the servers and components on both servers are the same, you could still lose some customizations or configuration settings, such as alerts and personalized content.

> **Tip** If you need to back up more than one site, your SharePoint administrator has a number of tools he or she can use.

To back up a site, you need to be a site owner for that site. You can use SharePoint Designer to back up and restore Windows SharePoint Services 2.0 sites, but they can only be restored on the same server or on another server running Windows SharePoint Services 2.0. Similarly, if you move sites between servers, verify that they have the same level of software installed, such as service packs.

With any method that moves files from one location to another, you should choose carefully what you include in the package; for example, your Data Source Library (fpdatasources), may contain *data connection* details that could include connection strings, user names, and passwords. Similarly, you should be careful about creating content by using any method, because the content will contain pages, which does contain code, and, therefore, you need to verify that the source of the packages can be trusted.

In this exercise, you will back up and restore a site.

> **USE** the site you modified in the previous exercise.
> **OPEN** the site in SharePoint Designer, if it is not already open.

1. On the **Site** menu, point to **Administration**, and then click **Backup Web Site**.

   A Backup Web Site dialog box opens, stating that this operation may take a while, and asking whether you want to back up subsites.

Backup Web Site	? X
Press OK to create a backup of the current Web site. This operation may take a while.	
☐ Include subsites in archive	
Advanced...	OK Cancel

2. Click **Advanced** to open the **Advanced** dialog box.

> **Warning** If you are completing this task on a production server or if the site you have chosen to back up is large, you should ask your SharePoint server administrator for the URL to type in this box.

3. Click **OK** to close the **Advanced** dialog box, and then click **OK** to close the **Backup Web Site** dialog box.

   The Files Save As dialog box opens.

4. Navigate to *Documents\Microsoft Press\SPD2007_SBS*, and in the **File name** text box, type SPDBackup.

> **Warning** If you are completing this task on a production server or if the site you have chosen to back up is large, you should verify that the location you specify here contains sufficient free space for the backup file.

5. Click **Save** to close the **File Save as** dialog box.

   When the Backup Web Site Progress dialog box closes, the Microsoft Office SharePoint Designer dialog box opens, stating that the Web site backup completed successfully.

6. Click **OK** to close the dialog box.

New Document

7. On the Common toolbar, click the **New Document** arrow, and then in the list, click **Web Site**.

   The New dialog box opens.

8. On the **Web Site** tab, click **General**, and then click **Empty Web Site**.

9. In the **Specify the location of the new Web site** text box, type http://<site>, where <site> is the URL of the location where you want to restore the site you just backed up. For example, <site> might be *http://teams.consolidatedmessenger.com/spdbackup*.

10. Click **OK** to close the **New** dialog box.

The new site opens in a separate SharePoint Designer program window. No content is listed in the Folder List task pane.

11. In the new SharePoint Designer program window, on the **Site** menu, point to **Administration**, and then click **Restore Web Site**.

The File Open dialog box opens.

12. Navigate to the location you used in step 4, *Documents\Microsoft Press\SPD2007_SBS*, and click **SPDBackup.cmp**. Then click **Open**.

The Restore Web Site dialog box opens.

13. Click **Advanced** to open the **Advanced** dialog box.

> **Warning** If you are completing this task on a production server or if the site you have chosen to back up is large, you should ask your SharePoint server administrator for the URL to type in this box.

14. Click **OK** to close the **Advanced** dialog box, and then click **OK** to close the **Restore Web Site** dialog box.

When the Restore Web Site Progress dialog box closes, the Microsoft Office SharePoint Designer dialog box opens, stating that the restore operation completed successfully.

15. Click **OK** to close the dialog box.

The Folder List task page displays the contents of the restored site.

CLOSE the SharePoint Designer window in which the *SPDBackup* site is open.

Exporting and Importing Sites

Using a Personal Web Package (.fwp), you can export or import a site. You can also export a list or a library or a combination of the two. In addition, you can choose which document you want to include in the package. However, the package will not include list items, version history, or permissions. You cannot package a file or a set of files without the library structure. Therefore, this method is best used when you want to duplicate the structure elsewhere. The Backup and Restore method has to create a new site each time you restore the data. With the Personal Web Package method, you can import a subset of your package.

> **Tip** Use only the Export and Import method for packaging a whole site for reuse purposes when you want to copy components selectively from it. Use Backup and Restore for regular backup purposes, if your company does not already provide those facilities.

In this exercise, you will export a site by using the Personal Web Package method, and then you will create a new site based on the exported file.

> **USE** the site you modified in the previous exercise.
> **OPEN** the site in SharePoint Designer, if it is not already open.

1. On the **File** menu, point to **Export**, and then click **Personal Web Package**.

   The Export Web Package dialog box opens.

2. In the **Export Web Package** dialog box, click **Add**.

   > **Tip** To export a complete site, select the URL of the site under Files In Web Site.

   The SharePoint Designer status bar displays messages as the files on the Web site are added to the package. When the entire site is added to the package, the total size of the package is displayed under Files In Package.

3. Click the **Properties** button above the **Files in Package** list.

   The Web Package Properties dialog box opens.

4. In the **Title** text box, type SPD Site Export, in the **Author** text box, type your name, and in the **Company** text box, type Consolidated Messenger.

> **Tip** You should always enter details on the Web Package Properties page, especially if you plan to keep the package for a while.

5. Click **OK** to close the **Export Web Package** dialog box, and then click **OK** to close the **Web Package Properties** dialog box.

   The File Save dialog box opens.

6. Navigate to *Documents\Microsoft Press\SPD2007_SBS*. In the **File name** text box, remove the spaces between **SPD**, **Site**, and **Export**, so that the file name appears as **SPDSiteExport.fwp**. Then click **Save**.

> **Warning** If you are completing this task with a large site, verify that the location you specified contains sufficient free space for the .fwp file.

7. When the **Microsoft Office SharePoint Designer** dialog box opens, stating that the Web package was saved successfully, click **OK**.

New Document

8. On the Common toolbar, in the **New Document** list, click **Web Site**.

   The New dialog box opens.

9. On the **Web Site** tab, click **General**, and then click **Empty Web Site**.

10. In the **Specify the location of the new Web site** text box, type http://<site>, where <site> is the URL of the location where you want to restore the site you just backed up. For example, <site> might be *http://teams.consolidatedmessenger.com/spdexport*.

11. Click **OK** to close the **New** dialog box.

   The new site opens in a separate SharePoint Designer program window.

12. In the new SharePoint Designer program window, on the **File** menu, point to **Import**, and then click **Personal Web Package**.

   The File Open dialog box opens.

13. Navigate to the location you used in step 6, *Documents\Microsoft Press\SPD2007_SBS*, and click **SPDSiteExport.fwp**. Then click **Open**.

   The Import Web Package dialog box opens.

14. Click **Import**.

The Microsoft Office SharePoint Designer – Security Warning dialog box opens.

15. Click **Run** to close the **Microsoft Office SharePoint Designer – Security Warning** dialog box.

> **Warning** If you do not know or trust the source of a Web package file, you should click Don't Run, because Web package files can contain code.

The Importing Package dialog box opens. During the import process, a Confirm dialog box opens, stating that _catalogs/masterpage already exists.

16. Click **Do not deploy this list** and click **OK** to close the dialog box.

    When the import process is complete, a Web Package 'SPD Site Export' Deployment Complete message appears.

17. Click **OK** to close the message box.

    The Folder List task pane and Web Site tab refresh.

18. Press F12 to view the exported site in the browser.

    The home page of the site is displayed with no home tab and no site title.

19. Click **Site Actions**, and then click **Site Settings**.

    The Site Settings page is displayed.

20. In the **Look and Feel** list, click **Title, description, and icon**.

    The Title, Description, And Icon page is displayed.

21. In the **Title** text box, type SPD Export, and click **OK**.

    The Site Settings page is displayed and the site's title appears in the top left and in the breadcrumbs.

> **Tip** To display the horizontal navigation tabs, on the Site Settings page, use the Top Link Bar option.

CLOSE the browser and the SharePoint Designer windows that have the *SPDExport* site open.

Copying Lists and Libraries Between Sites

The Personal Web Package (.fwp) method can be used to move a subset of a site. You can create a .fwp file that contains an entire site and then import only a portion, or you can choose to export only a portion. When you import a list or a library, that list or library is created in the new site. You cannot simply import, for example, only the documents into a library of your own choice.

The Import and Export method look for dependencies, which you can view. By default, your dependencies, excluding links, will be included in your package. However, this method is configurable, and you can manually choose what to include and what to exclude.

In this exercise, you will package a subset of a site and copy the contents to another site.

USE the site you modified in the previous exercise.

OPEN the site in SharePoint Designer, if it is not already open.

1. On the **File** menu, point to **Export**, and then click **Personal Web Package**.

   The Export Web Package dialog box opens.

2. Under **Files in Web site**, click **Shared Documents**, and then click **Add**.

   Shared Documents appears in the Files In Package list.

3. At the bottom of the **Export Web Package** dialog box, click **Show Dependencies**.

   Within the Export Web Package dialog box, the current selection list opens and displays those items that the Shared Document library uses.

> **Tip** The options in the Dependency Checking list are used to decide which files to add to the Web Package. Only if Do Not Check Dependencies is selected can you choose specifically the files you want to include in the package; otherwise, dependent files are also included. By default, SharePoint Designer does not check hyperlinks to find additional files to include in your Web Package; therefore, any files, for example, cascading style sheets, that that your selected files link to will not be included. To include all linked files, in the Dependency Checking list, click Check All Dependencies.

4. At the bottom of the **Export Web Package** dialog box, click **Hide Dependencies**.

5. Click **OK** to close the **Web Package Properties** dialog box.

   The File Save dialog box opens.

6. Navigate to *Documents\Microsoft Press\SPD2007_SBS*, and in the **File name** text box, type SPDLibExport.fwp. Then click **Save**.

    The Microsoft Office SharePoint Designer dialog box opens, stating that the Web package was saved successfully.

7. Click **OK** to close the dialog box.

8. On the **File** menu, point to **Import**, and then click **Personal Web Package** to open the **File Open** dialog box.

9. Navigate to the location you used in step 6, *Documents\Microsoft Press\SPD2007_ SBS*, click **SPLibExort.fwp**, and then click **Open**.

    The Import Web Package dialog box opens.

10. In the **Import Web Package** dialog box, click **Browse** to open the **Select a Folder** dialog box.

11. Under **Please select a folder below**, click **Shared Documents**, and then click **OK** to close the **Select a Folder** dialog box.

    In the Import Web Package dialog box, the Destination text box contains the URL of the Shared Document library.

12. In the **Import Web Package** dialog box, click **Unselect All**, and click the expand (+) icon for **Shared Documents**. Then select the **Shared Documents** check box, and select the check box to the left of any file.

    > **Important** You cannot import files without importing the list or library in which they are stored. When you select a file from a list or library, SharePoint Designer does not automatically select the list or library. The import process will report that the import was successful, but the file will not appear in your site. You must select the list or library to import the file.

13. Click **Import**.

    The Microsoft Office SharePoint Designer – Security Warning dialog box opens.

14. Click **Run** to close the dialog box.

    > **Warning** If you do not know or trust the source of a Web Package file, you should click Don't Run, because Web Package files can contain code.

    The Importing Package dialog box briefly appears, followed by the dialog box with the Web Package 'SPD Export' Deployment Complete message.

15. Click **OK** to close the dialog box.

The Import Web Package dialog box closes, and the Folder List task pane refreshes. A folder named *Shared Documents* appears under Shared Documents, and contains one file.

BE SURE TO keep SharePoint Designer open if continuing to the next exercise.

Copying Documents Between Sites

To copy a document from one list to another, you can use the SharePoint Designer publishing feature, also known as the *Remote Web Site command*. In no way should you consider this a backup method. It also does not support moving all types of SharePoint content. If both the source and destination have the same columns, the metadata associated with the file will be moved; otherwise, the metadata is lost. As with other methods, the permission settings and any version of the documents are not copied across sites.

In this exercise, you will copy a document from one site to another.

USE the site you modified in the previous exercise.

OPEN the site in SharePoint Designer, if it is not already open.

1. On the **File** menu, click **Publish Site**.

   The Web Site tab in the document window becomes the active tab, and the Remote Web Site is highlighted in orange at the bottom of the document window.

   The Remote Web Site Properties dialog box opens.

   > **Tip** If the Remote Web Site Properties dialog box does not open, in the document window, to the right of Folder Contents, click Remote Web Site Properties.

2. On the **Remote Web Site** tab, click **FrontPage Server Extensions or SharePoint Services**, and then click **Browse**.

   The New Publishing Location dialog box opens.

3. Navigate to **teams.consolidatedmessenger.com/spdbackup**, and then click **Open**.

   The New Publishing Location dialog box closes.

   In the Remote Web Site Properties dialog box, the Remote Web Site Location text box contains the URL of the site you want to publish content to.

4. Click **OK** to close the **Remote Web Site Properties** dialog box.

   The document window redisplays, and a SharePoint Content dialog box opens, stating that you cannot copy many types of SharePoint content.

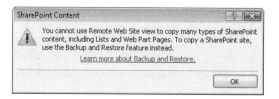

5. Click **OK** to close the **SharePoint Content** dialog box.

6. In the document window, under **Local Web site**, double-click **Shared Documents**.

   Under Local Web Site, the text *Content Of Shared Documents* appears, and the contents of the Shared Document library are listed with a question mark icon and a status of conflict, denoting that SharePoint Designer was unable to ascertain the publish status of the files.

7. Under **Remote Web site**, double-click **Shared Documents**.

   Under Remote Web Site, the text *Content Of Shared Documents* appear, and the contents of the Shared Document library are listed with question mark icons.

8. Under **Local Web site**, click a file.

   The right-pointing arrow and the two one-way arrows are highlighted in blue.

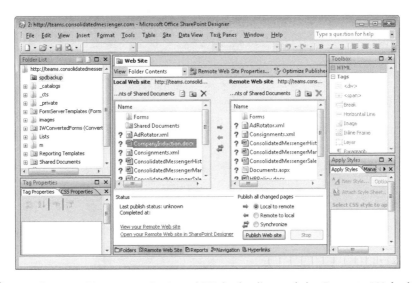

Publish Selected
Files

9. On the panel between the **Local Web site** list and the **Remote Web site** list, click the **Published Selected Files** arrow.

The Do You Want To Overwrite This File? dialog box opens.

10. Click **Yes**.

The question mark icon to the left of the file you copied on both the local and remote sites has disappeared, showing they are the same files.

> **CLOSE** the SharePoint site. If you are not continuing directly to the next chapter, exit SharePoint Designer.

Key Points

- Contributor Settings use Contributor groups to restrict the usage of SharePoint Designer on a per-site basis and work with the permission levels.

- The Site Managers Contributor group is linked to the Full Control permission level, the Web Designers Contributor group to the Design permission level, and the Content Authors (the default Contributor group) to the Contribute permission level.

- SharePoint Designer provides you with a range of reports to manage your site.

- Use Backup and Restore when you need to copy or move an entire site to another server or location.

- Use a Personal Web Package (.fwp) to export or import a site, list, or library.

- Use the SharePoint Designer publishing feature, known as the *Remote Web Site command*, to copy documents from one site to another.

Chapter at a Glance

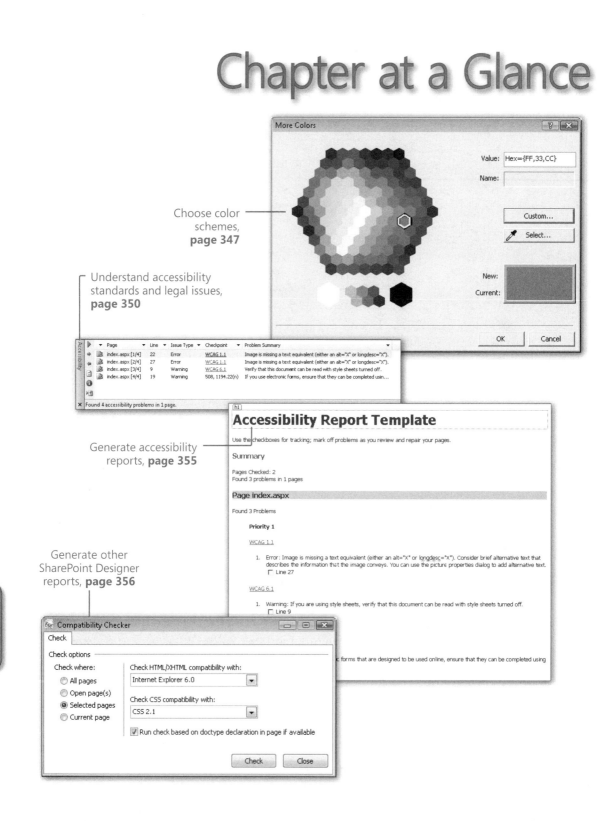

Choose color schemes, **page 347**

Understand accessibility standards and legal issues, **page 350**

Generate accessibility reports, **page 355**

Generate other SharePoint Designer reports, **page 356**

15 Understanding Usability and Accessibility

In this chapter, you will learn to:

- ✔ Understand usability issues.
- ✔ Choose color schemes.
- ✔ Understand accessibility standards and legal issues.
- ✔ Generate accessibility reports.
- ✔ Generate other SharePoint Designer reports.

Although this chapter is the last chapter of this book, do not consider its exercises and other information as the tasks you should tackle at the end of your project. You should include the methods we discuss in this chapter throughout the lifetime of any customizations or modifications you make to your site. Usability and accessibility are very important to the success of your customizations and could also save you or the company owners from being sued. Of course, in a chapter of this size, we cannot go into great depth in either of these subject areas, but we hope that it will provide you with what you need to consider. Each site is different, and you will need to research and decide on policies that suit your situation.

In this chapter, you will first explore usability issues. Next, you will learn how Microsoft Office SharePoint Designer 2007 can help you choose a color scheme when you are branding your site. You will then explore the accessibility standards and legal issues that your site may need to conform to, and how SharePoint Designer can help check your site for these guidelines and standards, as well as produce reports that you can use as checklists or as a baseline to the status of your site at a particular time.

Important Before you can use the practice files in this chapter, you need to install them from the book's companion CD to their default location. However, there is no practice starter or solution site template with this chapter.

For more information about practice files, see "Using the Book's CD" at the beginning of this book.

Troubleshooting Graphics and operating system–related instructions in this book reflect the Windows Vista user interface. If your computer is running Windows XP and you experience trouble following the instructions as written, please refer to the "Information for Readers Running Windows XP" section at the beginning of this book.

Understanding Usability Issues

As you develop your site, you need to keep in mind the people who are going to use it. People read online material differently than they do printed material; in online material, they tend to use a scanning approach. So be sure to break a story into its main points and re-structure it; write summaries, headlines and lists; and organize and label information so that it can easily be found. Get all the written elements on a Web page to work together. Consider these aspects as you develop your content pages and page layouts.

Usability is not just about the content you put on your page; it is also about where that content resides. Microsoft does not place components on a page without considerable thought and research, so ensure that you have good reasons for moving them around. For example, visitors to your site expect to see some kind of site identification in the upper-left corner of the page, a search box in the upper-right corner, and the page content in a separate area below. These are the components included on master pages. If you are new to Web usability, several books and many Internet resources are available to help you. There is even a World Usability Day (WUD) Community, visit *www.worldusabilityday.org*.

Take a practical approach to usability. For example, you can:

- Involve people who use your site. Ask them to use your site, and watch what they do. If no one uses a mobile device to visit your site, don't expend effort in making your site usable for mobile devices.
- Keep your site up to date with information that people will use, and organized in a way that they can find it.

- Ensure that you don't have broken links.
- Verify that your site renders in the browsers at the screen resolution that your users use.

> **Tip** Telerik, in an agreement between the company and Microsoft, has produced a free RadEditor, which is a cross-browser alternative to the default rich-text editor you see in Microsoft Windows SharePoint Services and Microsoft Office SharePoint Server 2007. For more information about RadEditor, see *www.telerik.com/products/aspnet/controls/editor/*.

In this exercise, you will import a page and use hyperlinks and site reports to identify any usability issues.

> **USE** the *index.aspx* page. This practice file is located in the *Documents\Microsoft Press\ SPD2007_SBS\UsabilityAccessibility* folder.
> **BE SURE TO** use *teams.consolidatedmessenger.com* or whatever site you want in the exercise.
> **OPEN** your SharePoint site in SharePoint Designer.

1. On the **File** menu, point to **Import**, and then click **Import Site Wizard**.

   The Import Web Site Wizard starts.

2. Under **How do you want to get the files**, click **File System**, and then click **Browse**.

   The Choose Import Location dialog box opens.

3. Navigate to the *Documents\Microsoft Press\SPD2007_SBS\UsabilityAccessibility* folder, and then click **Open**.

   The Choose Import Location dialog box closes. In the Import Web Site Wizard, the folder name appears in the Web Site Location text box.

4. In the **Import Web Site Wizard**, click **Next** twice, and then click **Finish** to close the Import Web Site Wizard.

5. If the **SharePoint Content** dialog box opens, click **OK**.

   On the Web Site tab, the Remote Web Site view is displayed.

6. In the document window, under **Remote Web site**, right-click **Index.aspx**, and then click **Publish Selected Files**.

   Under Local Web Site, *index.aspx* appears.

7. On the **Site** menu, click **Hyperlinks**.

   The Hyperlink view is displayed in the document window.

8. In the **Folder List** task pane, click *index.apsx*.

   A browser icon representing *index.aspx* appears in the document window, with links to a misspelled URL and JavaScript function calls.

9. In the document window, right-click the background, and then click **Hyperlinks to Pictures**.

   In the document window, an icon with the text *ConsolidatedMessenger.png* appears, with a broken line leading to *index.aspx*.

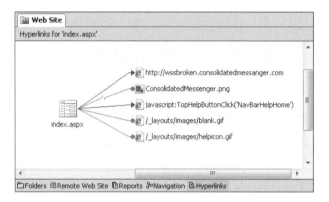

10. In the document window, right-click **http://wssbroken.consolidatedmessanger.com**, and then click **Verify Hyperlink**.

    When the Windows Vista busy-circle icon disappears, the arrow-headed line from *index.aspx* to *http://wssbroken.consolidatedmessanger.com* is broken.

11. At the bottom of the document window, click **Reports** to display the Reports view.

12. In the document window, click **Broken hyperlinks**.

13. When the **Reports View** dialog box opens, click **Yes**.

    The hyperlinks report is displayed in the document window.

14. Click the **Status** arrow, and then click **Broken**.

    In the document window, the page *index.aspx* is displayed, together with any other broken hyperlinks.

15. Right-click **ConsolidatedMessenger.png**, and then click **Edit Hyperlink**.

    The Edit Hyperlink dialog box opens.

16. In the **Replace hyperlink with** text box, type /_layouts/images/homepage.gif.

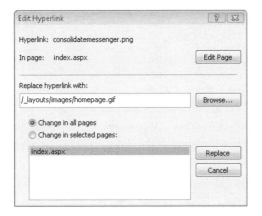

17. Click **Replace** to close the **Edit Hyperlink** dialog box.

The document window is redisplayed and no longer contains reference to ConsolidatedMessenger.png.

18. In the document window, click the **Status** arrow, and then click **(All)**.

The document window contains a list of all hyperlinks throughout the site.

19. Click the **In Page** arrow, and then click **index.aspx**.

The document window contains a list of hyperlinks on the index.aspx page.

20. In the document window, right-click **/_layouts/images/homepage.gif**, and then click **Edit Page**.

The *index.aspx* page opens in the document window.

Choosing Color Schemes

When you brand your site, you'll find that certain color schemes work better together than others. As you might take care to color-coordinate the rooms in your house, so you should take care of the colors you choose for your site.

SharePoint Designer provides you with a color wheel, similar to the one that you may have used in your home decoration exploits. Choosing colors opposite each other on the wheel, work better than those that are next to each other. This is known as the *complementary color scheme*. Similarly, picking colors from points of an equilateral triangle, triadic color scheme, are also a good choice. However, the computer color wheel is different from the home decoration color wheel. The colors you use on a site will be viewed on monitors and flat screens, and look different from colors on walls and fabrics. Web colors are defined as a hexadecimal notation that combines the Red, Green, and Blue (RGB) color values. The World Wide Web Consortium (W3C) provides 16 standard color names to refer to certain hexadecimal values.

In the past, not all browser or screen devices produced the same color when rendering these hexadecimal values or color names. Therefore, a 216 cross-browser color palette was produced, known as the *Web-safe color palette*, and the color wheel you see in SharePoint Designer is based on that color palette. When you click the color wheel in SharePoint Designer, look at the hexadecimal values it produces; you will see hexa-decimal values of only 00, 33, 66, 99, CC, and FF. In other words, you will see values of #CCFF00, #669900, and #00FFFF—not #887722, #FD3798, and #4400FF. However, tech-nology has improved; now you can choose colors that are not from the Web-safe color palette, and so SharePoint Designer provides you with an alternative visual method of choosing colors from the whole hexadecimal range.

Of course, while you design your branding, you cannot ignore the needs of people that have low vision, occurring as part of the aging process or as a result of such conditions as glaucoma, diabetes, macular degeneration, cataracts, or color blindness. Many coun-tries have laws, such as the U.K. Disability Discrimination Act (DDA) 1995, that state that businesses that provide services must make a reasonable adjustment for people with disabilities. Business are used to meeting these obligation by providing correspondence in Braille, large print or other formats, however many forget about their Web sites. In addition, although SharePoint Designer does not provide checks for this, the Internet can once again come to your aid, with such sites as Vischeck, (*www.vischeck.com/vischeck/*).

In this exercise, you will identify colors on the SharePoint Designer Web-safe palette color wheel, and check the suitability of a color scheme.

> **Important** You will need access to the Internet to complete this exercise.

> **USE** the site that you modified in the previous exercise.
> **OPEN** the site, if it is not already open, and display the *index.aspx* page in Design view.

1. On the **Task Panes** menu, click **CSS Properties**.

   The CSS Properties task pane open.

2. In the document window, click **Test for contrast and accessibility**, and in the **CSS Properties** task pane, under **CSS Properties**, click **background-color**. Then click the arrow that appears, and click **More Colors**.

The More Colors dialog box opens, displaying a Web-safe palette color wheel. The color selected for the background color is bordered in white in the wheel, and the Value text box, contains the hex values of the background color's red, green, and blue color coordinates.

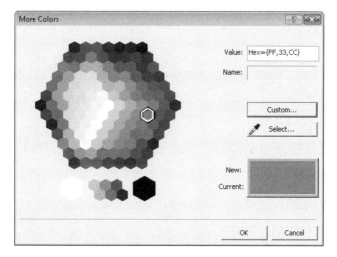

3. In the **More Colors** dialog box, click **Custom**.

The Color dialog box opens. The hue, saturation, and luminance color coordinates are displayed, together with the red, green, and blue coordinates.

4. Click **Cancel** twice to close the **Color** and **More Colors** dialog boxes.

5. Open a browser, and in the **Address** bar, type http://gmazzocato.altervista.org/colorwheel/wheel.php to open the Accessibility Color Wheel page.

6. In the **1*** text box, type #0000FF, and in the **2*** text box, type #FF33CC. Then click **Update**.

The text and background colors of Normal, Deuteranope, Protanope, and Tritanope text areas change to reflect how the color scheme looks to people who have disabilities.

> **Note** Deuteranopia is an insensitivity to green, Protanopia is an insensitivity to red, and Tritanopia is an insensivity to blue.

CLOSE the browser window.

Understanding Accessibility Standards and Legal Issues

As a Web designer, you may need to ensure that your site adheres to certain guidelines and standards. You can use SharePoint Designer to check your site against some of these standards. By considering your legal obligations at the very start of building a solution, you will save time and effort later on. Not only will this avoid any litigation, but visitors to your site will notice that it adheres to common practices and standards, and consequently, they will recognize that your site is trustworthy.

> **Tip** You can find many tools on the Internet that will help you to verify standards or guidelines that your site needs to adhere to. Such tools include *webxact.watchfire.com* and Unified Web Evaluation Methodology (UWEM). There are many other organizations, such as the Guild of Accessible Web Designers (GAWDS) and Web Accessibility in Mind (WEBAIM), as well as training courses that can help you if you are new to this area.

You should be aware of the following legal issues:

- **Accessibility.** Most of the world has accessibility guidelines, which you may legally have to meet if you publish public sites and/or internal sites for government departments and educational institutions. Such guidelines include the W3C *Web Content Accessibility Guidelines (WCAG)* 1.0 and 2.0, the U.S. government's Section 504 and 508 of the Rehabilitation Act's Voluntary Product Accessibility Template (VPAT), and the Dutch government accessibility guidelines known as *Webrichtlijnen*. Standards aside, by making your site more accessible it can be scanned by software other than screen readers, such as search engines and therefore making your site accessible is not just about people with disabilities.

- **Copyright.** Most sites include a copyright notice to prove, if necessary, when the material was produced. Sites may also contain guidelines as to the use and reproduction of material exposed on their pages.

- **Privacy.** Just as with the previous two categories, different countries have their own privacy laws, such as the Data Protection Act in the U.K., the European Commission Directive on Data Protection, and Canada's Personal Information Protection and Electronic Documents Act (PIPEDA). Many of these laws can be divided into two types of privacy policies, those concerning data that is readable by humans and those that are machine-readable; again, the W3C has produced some guidelines in this area as part of the Platform for Privacy Preferences (P3P) Project.

- **Licensing.** Both Windows SharePoint Services and SharePoint Server have licensing implications, which are different if you create intranet, extranet, and Internet sites. And even though you do not need to purchase Windows SharePoint Services, you still need to verify that you have the correct licenses in place for Microsoft SQL Server, Windows Server 2003, or Windows Server 2008—and, of course, SharePoint Designer.

- **Other legal issues.** You may need to consider other legal issues; for example, companies based in the U.K. must include certain regulatory information on their Web sites and in their e-mail footers or they will breach the Companies Act and risk a fine.

> **Warning** A visually impaired person was unable to book his tickets through the Sydney 2000 Olympic Games (SOCOG) site and successfully sued for several hundred thousand Australian dollars. During the proceedings, the site was found to be noncompliant and failed to meet the minimum accessibility requirements. There are a number of other high profile cases that you can readily find reference to on the Internet.

The list of standards, guidelines, and specifications is being added to daily, so just as with usability, you must take a practical approach to this subject. Concentrate on Web effectiveness and not on producing a site that is legally and accessibility compliant yet is unusable. Work with users who have disabilities and find out what works for them; don't go by some theoretical solution described on the Internet. If they use a screen reader, use that to check your site. Some users use options in browsers to specify a user-defined style sheet to help view pages. You may need to help them alter that style sheet to cater to your site. Some users use the browser's capability of altering text size, so in your cascading style sheets, stay away from picas, inches, and metric units of measurement, unless you are providing a print style sheet, use em, keyword, or %.

> **Tip** Cascading style sheets use units of measurement when specifying the location or size of an element or attribute. If you choose relative rather than absolute types of measurements, you will allow users to change the look and feel of the page. *Em* is one of these units of measurement that specifies the size relative to the user's font size setting on their computer. Users to your site can then choose the size of the font that they want to use to read the text on your page. Similarly, if you use keywords such as *top left* or *top center* to locate, say, an image on your page, the browser interprets the horizontal and vertical location of the image in terms of percentage of the page, again benefiting a user who uses a lower screen resolution than you may have designed the page for. Absolute units of measurement, such as centimeter, inch, pica, pixels, and point (pt), should be used only if you are creating a print style sheet.

After you decide on your implementation standards, ensure that you and your users continue to produce customizations that meet those policies. Remember that your users can make one of your pages fail accessibility or legal guidelines when they enter content on the pages. For example, adding an image to a Content Editor Web Part (CEWP) without including an alt attribute will fail the WCAG 1.0 guidelines. You should include in your solution a process that will educate your organization on the compliance issues. You should design your solution to enforce the standards you have chosen and you should conduct audits of your site that produce statistics so you can identify how close you are to meeting the standards as well as some method of assessing the users' experience of your site.

Take the worry out of making your site legal by organizing your pages so that all pages include the necessary links; for example, if you legally need to provide copyright, company, and privacy details, include these links as a footer in your master page. On publishing sites, you can use the *reusable content* functionality to add this information to page layouts.

See Also For a list of accessibility improvements in Windows SharePoint Services 3.0 compared to Windows SharePoint Services 2.0, refer to *blogs.msdn.com/sharepoint/ archive/2006/04/24/improvements-in-accessibility.aspx*. One such improvement is a "more accessible" mode, included on default.master and styled as hidden, which can be seen by screen readers.

SharePoint Designer provides you with a number of tools you can use to check your sites. Although SharePoint Designer visually interprets pages in the Designer window, many of the tools analyze the code on the page, which as you have seen, includes references to other files and to controls. Therefore, to get a true picture of the pages, you may need to view the pages in a browser, capture the code that the browser renders, and then import that code into SharePoint Designer to complete your checks.

When using either Windows SharePoint Services or SharePoint Server, many of the components rely on code that is interpreted at run time; that is, it is not precompiled into assemblies. Site definition files, cascading style sheets, and HTML\XTHML tags and XLST fall into this category. In this book, you have been customizing these components by using SharePoint Designer and a browser. However, there is a second set of components that even developers cannot fully customize, such as controls, where you can communicate with them only by using properties. Many of these controls, when processed by the Windows SharePoint Services engine, render HTML elements and reference cascading style sheet styles and JavaScript code, hence the need to check the code that is rendered to the browser and not the pages as you see them in SharePoint Designer.

Therefore, when changing some aspects to meet standards and guidelines, it may not be as easy as you had hoped, and the process will need developer skills.

Introducing the Accessibility Kit for SharePoint

Microsoft, together with HiSoftware, has released an open-source *Accessibility Kit for SharePoint (AKS)*, details of which can be found at: *aks.hisoftware.com* and *www.codeplex.com/aks/*. The initial release consists of two site definitions that replace the two publishing site definitions, with a second release targeting wikis and blogs. Other releases may implement some collaboration, list, and library accessibility–related features.

Sites based on the new site definitions have improved accessibility to the point of being fully compliant with standards such as the WCAG 1.0 Priority 1 and 2 checkpoints, known as WCAG 1.0 AA and can be used to address the exceptions that have been identified in Section 508. AKS uses a series of updates to cascading style sheets, master pages and site definitions. It uses the ASP.NET 2.0 Control Adapter Architecture to render content produced by Web Parts and controls into compliant HTML. This approach leaves untouched the default installation of Windows SharePoint Services and SharePoint Server, and therefore does not raise issues concerning Microsoft's support of your solution.

However, such sites based on AKS have a performance impact, and, therefore, you will need to analyze the effect on your existing infrastructure, after you have decided the extent to which you plan to use these site definitions.

See Also You can post questions concerning accessibility to SharePoint Products in two forums: the Microsoft MSDN SharePoint Accessibility forum at *forums.microsoft.com/ MSDN/ShowForum.aspx?ForumID=1662&SiteID=1* and the HiSofware AKS Community forum at *listserv.hisoftware.com/cgi-bin/Wa.exe?A0=AKSCOMMUNITY.*

In this exercise, you will use the Accessibility Checker.

USE the site that you modified in the previous exercise.

OPEN the site, if it is not already open, and display the *index.aspx* page.

1. On the **Tools** menu, click **Accessibility Reports** to open the **Accessibility Checker** dialog box.

2. Under **Check where**, click the **Open page(s)** option. Under **Check for**, select the **WCAG Priority 1** and **Access Board Section 508** check boxes, leaving **WCAG Priority 2** cleared. Then under **Show,** select the **Warnings** check box, leaving the **Errors** check box selected, but **Manual Checklist** cleared.

3. Click **Check**.

   The Accessibility task pane opens, displaying the results of the accessibility check.

4. In the **Accessibility** task pane, right-click the first line, and then click **Problem Details**.

   The Problem Details dialog box opens, stating that the image is missing a text equivalent, with details on how to correct this error.

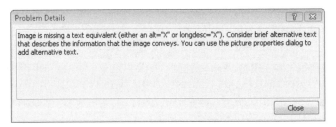

5. Click **Close** to close the **Problem Details** dialog box.

6. In the **Accessibility** task pane, double-click the first line.

   The *index.aspx* page is displayed in Code view.

`⊟ Split`

7. In the document window, click **Split** to display both the Code view and the Design view of the page.

   In Design view, the offending image is selected.

8. Right-click the offending image, and then click **Picture Properties**.

   The Picture Properties dialog box opens.

9. Under **Accessibility**, select the check box, and in the **Alternate Text** text box, type Microsoft Windows SharePoint Services logo, and then click **OK**.

   The Picture Properties dialog box closes.

10. In the **Accessibility** task pane, right-click the first line, and then click **Refresh Changed Results**.

> **Tip** You can refresh the changed results by clicking the refresh icon on the vertical pane to the left of the results.

The Accessibility task pane contains one less error.

Generating Accessibility Reports

After you have used SharePoint Designer to check your site or set of pages, you can produce an accessibility report to record the standards or guidelines adhered to at a particular point in time or to use as a checklist.

In this exercise, you will produce an accessibility report.

> **USE** the site that you modified in the previous exercise.
> **BE SURE TO** complete the previous exercise before beginning this exercise.
> **OPEN** the site, if it is not already open, and display the *index.aspx* page and the Accessibility task pane.

Generate
HTML Report

1. In the **Accessibility** task pane, click the **Generate HTML Report** button.

   The Accessibility Report.htm file opens in the document window.

[h1]
Accessibility Report Template

Use the checkboxes for tracking; mark off problems as you review and repair your pages.

Summary

Pages Checked: 2
Found 3 problems in 1 pages

Page index.aspx

Found 3 Problems

Priority 1

WCAG 1.1

1. Error: Image is missing a text equivalent (either an alt="X" or longdesc="X"). Consider brief alternative text that describes the information that the image conveys. You can use the picture properties dialog to add alternative text.
   ☐ Line 27

WCAG 6.1

1. Warning: If you are using style sheets, verify that this document can be read with style sheets turned off.
   ☐ Line 9

Section 508

508, 1194.22(n)

1. Warning: If you use electronic forms that are designed to be used online, ensure that they can be completed using assistive devices.
   ☐ Line 19

2. Close the **Accessibility** task pane, and then click **Design** so that the accessibility report is displayed the full length of the document window.

3. Close **Accessibility Report.htm**, and if prompted to save changes, click **No**.

4. Right-click the **index.aspx** tab, and then click **Save**.

Generating Other SharePoint Designer Reports

In Chapter 14, "Managing SharePoint Sites," you worked with a number of SharePoint Designer reports, which you accessed on the Reports view on the Web Site tab. These can help you maintain and predict issues you may have with your site. In addition to the Accessibility Checker, you can access other SharePoint Designer reports on the Tools menu; these reports also display their results in a task pane. In Chapter 10, "Changing the Look and Feel of Pages by Using Cascading Style Sheets," you used the CSS Reports.

You can use a third report on the Tools menu, Compatibility Reports.

By default, like any browser, SharePoint Designer uses the HTML/XHTML and cascading style sheet schemas defined in the *<!DOCTYPE>* tag on the first line of the page when deciding how to render a page. When you edit or modify a page, SharePoint Designer flags code that is invalid or incompatible, dependent on the schemas defined in the <!DOCTYPE> tag. If a page doesn't contain a <!DOCTYPE> declaration, it uses the default schemas configured in the Page Editor Options dialog box.

When you use the compatibility checker, you can specify the same or a different schema to produce the compatibility reports.

In this exercise, you will generate a compatibility report.

> **USE** the site that you modified in the previous exercise.
>
> **OPEN** the site, if it is not already open, and display the *index.aspx* page.

1. On the **Tools** menu, click **Compatibility Reports** to open the **Compatibility Checker** dialog box.

> **Tip** The SharePoint Designer status bar displays the HTML/XHTML and cascading style sheet schemas it uses to flag code as invalid or incompatible for a page.

2. Under **Check where**, click **Open page(s)**, and then click **Check**.

   The Compatibility Checker dialog box closes. The Compatibility task pane opens displaying the results of the compatibility check.

3. In the document window, click **Code** to display the *index.aspx* page in Code view. In the SharePoint Designer status bar, an incompatibility code icon appears.

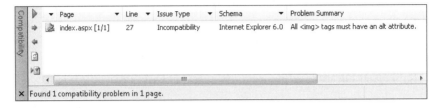

> **Tip** The incompatibility code icon appears only in Split view or Code view. If the page contains code errors, you will also see the code error icon in the SharePoint Designer window. *Quirks* in the status bar denotes that the page is using an older or none existent <!DOCTYPE>.

CLOSE the site, and exit SharePoint Designer.

Key Points

- People read online material differently than they do printed material, so be sure to keep online readers in mind when designing your site.
- SharePoint Designer can help you check your site against accessibility guidelines and compatibility standards when you choose a color scheme.
- Take a practical approach to customizing your site. Concentrate on keeping your site up to date with information that people will use, and organized in a way that they can find it.
- Define policies and tell other content authors of your site what they must do to keep the site legal and accessible.
- Use page layouts and master pages to minimize the amount of maintenance and customizations you need to complete on pages to keep your site legal.

Appendix: SharePoint Designer Workflow Conditions and Actions

Microsoft Office SharePoint Designer 2007 includes 9 workflow conditions and 23 workflow actions. Actions occur as part of a workflow step and are associated with a condition.

Conditions

A *condition* is a filter that can be used to decide which actions should be executed. The following table provides an overview of the default conditions you can use in SharePoint Designer 2007. Conditions marked with an asterisk (*) are available only for libraries.

Condition	Description
Compare [List or Library] Field	Creates a filter that allows you to select an existing column from the list or library the workflow is attached to, and specifies a value for this column. This value can also be a lookup value referring to a value from another list on the same site.
Compare Any Data Source	Creates a filter that lets you compare a specified value with another value. You can also specify lookup values referring to values from another list on the same SharePoint site.
Title Field Contains Keywords	Creates a filter that lets you specify a value for the Title column of the list or library the workflow is attached to.
Modified In A Specific Date Span	Creates a filter that lets you specify the start and end dates between which the list item must be modified. These dates can also be lookup values referring to values from another list on the same SharePoint site.
Modified By A Specific Person	Creates a filter that lets you specify the user who last modified the list item.
Created In A Specific Date Span	Creates a filter that lets you specify the start and end dates between which the list item must be created. These dates can also be lookup values referring to values from another list on the same SharePoint site.
Created By A Specific Person	Creates a filter that lets you specify the user who has created the list item.

(continued on next page)

Condition	Description
The File Size Is A Specific Type*	Creates a filter that lets you specify the file type of the list item. This value can also be a lookup value referring to values from another list on the same SharePoint site.
The File Size In A Specific Range Kilobytes*	Creates a filter that lets you specify the minimum and maximum file size of a list item. These file sizes can also be lookup values referring to values from another list on the same SharePoint site.

Actions

Although the Workflow Designer wizard of SharePoint Designer 2007 does not categorize workflow actions, in this book, we have organized them into groups of actions that complete similar tasks.

Core Actions

Core actions allow you to manipulate dates and times, build a form to collect information from users, and write information in the history list. The following table describes the default core actions.

Action	Description
Add Time To Date	Using this action, you can add or subtract minutes, hours, days, months, or years to a date. This date can also be a lookup value referring to a value from another list on the same SharePoint site. The output of this action can be saved into a new or existing workflow variable.
Assign A Form To A Group	Using this action, you can build a custom survey to collection information from one or more users. The workflow will be paused until all users have completed the survey.
Build Dynamic String	Using this action, you can create a string value containing multiple lookup values referring to values from other lists on the same SharePoint site. The string value can be saved into a new or existing workflow variable.
Do Calculation	Using this action, you can add, subtract, multiply, divide, or calculate the modulus of two numeric values. These values can also be lookup values referring to values from another list on the same SharePoint site. The output of this action can be saved into a new or existing workflow variable.

Action	Description
Log To History List	Using this action, you can write a string value to the workflow history list. This value can also be a lookup value referring to a value from another list on the same SharePoint site.
Pause For Duration	Using this action, you can specify in days, hours, and minutes the amount of time for which you want to pause the workflow. These time values can also be lookup values referring to values from another list on the same SharePoint site.
Pause Until Date	Using this action, you can pause the workflow and specify the date when workflow needs to be continued. This date can be a lookup value referring to a value from another list on the same SharePoint site.
Send An Email	Using this action, you can create an e-mail message containing string values, lookup values, formulas, and workflow variables. You can also specify the To, CC, and Subject fields of the e-mail message.
Set Content Approval Status	Using this action, you can set the current status of the list item. You can also add comments in the form of a string value or a lookup value.
Set Field In Current Item	Using this action, you can specify the value of a selected column of a list item. This value can also be a lookup value referring to a value from another list on the same SharePoint site.
Set Time Portion Of Date/Time Field	Using this action, you can set a specific time in hours and minutes and add this to a date. This date can also be a lookup value referring to a value from another list on the same SharePoint site. The output of this action can be saved into a new or existing workflow variable.
Set Workflow Variable	Using this action, you can set the value of a new or existing workflow variable. This value can also be a lookup value referring to a value from another list on the same SharePoint site.
Stop Workflow	Using this action, you can stop the workflow and write a string value to the workflow history list. This value can also be a lookup value referring to a value from another list on the same SharePoint site.
Wait For Field Change In Current Item	Using this action, you can pause the workflow until the value of a column of the list or library the workflow is attached to is equal or not equal to the specified value in this action. This specified value can also be a lookup value referring to a value from another list on the same SharePoint site.

List Actions

List actions allow you to manipulate list items, including creating, copying, and deleting list items. These actions can be applied to documents within libraries, because libraries are a form of lists. This group also includes specific document-related actions, such as undoing a check out. The following table describes the default list actions.

Action	Description
Check In Item	Using this action, you can check in the current item or select a column name and value to specify which item must be checked in. You can add a check-in comment that is either a string value or a lookup value.
Check Out Item	Using this action, you can check out the current item or select a column name and value to specify which item must be checked out.
Copy List Item	Using this action, you can copy an existing list item to another list on the SharePoint site. The list item can be the current list item or you can select a column and value to specify which list item you want to copy.
Create List Item	Using this action, you can create a new list item in a list on the SharePoint site. You can choose any list and specify the values for the required fields. The values can be lookup values referring to values from another list on the same SharePoint site. The output of this action can be saved into a new or existing workflow variable.
Delete Item	Using this action, you can delete the current item or select a column name and value to specify which item must be deleted.
Discard Check Out Item	Using this action, you can discard the check out of the current item or select a column name and value to specify for which item the check out must be discarded.
Update List Item	Using this action, you can update a list item in a list on the SharePoint site. You can choose any list you want and specify the values for the required fields. This value can also be a lookup value from another list on the SharePoint site.

Task Actions

Task actions manipulate task items. The following table describes these default actions.

Action	Description
Assign A To-Do Item	Using this action, you can assign a to-do item in the Tasks list to one or more users. The workflow will be paused until all users have completed the to-do item.
Collect Data From A User	Using this action, you can create and assign a task to one specified user. This task can contain custom form fields. The output of this action can be saved into a new or existing workflow variable.

Glossary

<!DOCTYPE> A declaration on the first line of a page that directs the browser to which rendering mode it should use to display the page.

12 hive Location on all SharePoint Web virtual servers, located in *C:\Program Files\Common Files\Microsoft Shared\Web server extensions\12*.

Accessibility Kit for SharePoint (AKS) Open-source site definitions and files from which to create sites that are accessibility-compliant.

administration page Content pages that contain *_layout* in their URLs. Such pages use the application.master page as their default master page.

Asynchronous JavaScript and XML (AJAX) A Web development language for creating interactive Web sites.

behaviors Blocks of HTML and JavaScript code that add functionality to your Web page without the need for you to write code.

breadcrumb A sequence of links that users can use to navigate or keep track of their location. See also *global navigation breadcrumb* and *content navigation breadcrumb*.

Business Data Catalog (BDC) A SharePoint Server 2007 feature that provides connectivity to backend business systems and data sources whose data is presented through the SharePoint interface.

cascading style sheet (CSS) A style sheet language interpreted by a browser that describes the presentation of a Web page.

child site A site within a site collection, where there is a hierarchy of a top-level site and one or more child sites, also called *subsites*.

class selector A style defined in a style block or in an external file, which points to a tag that uses the *class* attribute.

Closed Web Parts A Web Part that is added to a Web page, and then closed, in a browser. The Web Part is listed in the Closed Gallery, whereas in SharePoint Designer, it's shown as an opaque image.

Code view One of three views that displays markup languages such as HTML and CSS, client-side code, and user and server controls.

Collaboration Portal A site hierarchy for an intranet portal, which includes a home page, and the following Web sites: News, Site Directory, Document Center, and Search Center with Tabs. Many of these Web sites are based on the Publishing site template, which uses SharePoint Server Web Content Management functionality.

Collaborative Application Markup Language (CAML) A proprietary markup language specific to SharePoint that LVWP use to dynamically find and display SharePoint list items based on various criteria.

column An area of a SharePoint list or library that defines the kind of data to be collected for each list item or document. The values that each column contains are referred to as *metadata*.

condition See *workflow condition*.

content navigation breadcrumb A sequence of links that shows the path from the home page of a site to the current page, shown above the page title. See also *global navigation breadcrumb*. Users can use a combination of the two to navigate or keep track of their location.

content page An ASP.NET page that is combined with a Master page on the Web server to produce an HTML page that is sent to clients to be rendered in their browsers. An example of a content page is the home page of a SharePoint site, default.aspx.

content placeholder An ASP.NET control that defines regions on the master page when content from content pages can be placed. They can also define content on the master page that can be customized on content pages.

content region See *content placeholder*.

content types Content types define a reusable collection of settings that can include columns, workflows, and other attributes.

Contributor Settings Controls how SharePoint Designer is used to modify a SharePoint site.

controls Components that are commonly used on Web sites, such as displaying a calendar, changing a password, or validating entry in an input form.

CSS specificity Rules used by the browser to determine which style should be applied to an element. See also *cascading style sheet*.

custom activities Conditions or actions, created by using Visual Studio 2005, that can be deployed to Web servers and used in SharePoint Designer.

Custom List Form A SharePoint Designer menu option that allows you to add a preconfigured Data Form Web Part (DVWP) to a form page that you can customize to provide a data entry form for lists and libraries.

custom master page An alternate master page that is typically used by publishing sites. In SharePoint Server, custom master pages can be applied using the browser and inherited by all child publishing sites.

customized Web page A Web page that is stored in the SQL Server content database, previously known as an un-ghosted Web page

in Windows SharePoint Services 2.0, where you used FrontPage 2003. Using them caused significant performance implications. These implications have mostly been removed in Windows SharePoint Services 3.0 with the use of ASP.NET 2.0, master pages, and features. Web pages are customized by using SharePoint Designer.

data connection Information on how to connect to a data source, stored in the Data Source Library.

Data Form Web Part (DFWP) A Web Part that reads data from and writes data to a data source in the form of XML and applies XSLT to it. With SharePoint Designer, you can add DFWP to a Web Part Page, and it has a WYSIWYG XSLT editor so that you don't need to know XSLT to customize a DFWP.

Data View Web Part (DVWP) A Web Part created using SharePoint Designer that retrieves data in XML format from data sources such as SharePoint lists and libraries, SQL Server databases, XML files, or Web services. The data is then presented using XSLT transformations.

default master page The page applied to all pages in your site when you first create a site.

Design view One of three views that displays the Web page as it would appear in a browser and provides a WYSIWYG editing environment.

dirty page A page that you have modified in SharePoint Designer, but have not yet saved.

Dynamic Web Part A Web Part placed inside a Web Part zone. The details of these Web Parts are not saved in the same SQL Server table as the page.

Dynamic Web Template (DWT) A template that defines the layout, appearance, and colors and are attached to one or more Web pages to provide an overall design to a Web site. The Dynamic Web Template Interchange Guidelines (DWTIG) provide standards for their development.

dynamic-link library (DLL) A shared program library, also known as an *assembly*. For example, when you create a solution for SharePoint in Visual Studio .NET 2005, which includes several class or program files, and then build that solution, Visual Studio generates a file name with the extension .dll.

eXtensible Application Markup Language (XAML) A language used by the Windows Workflow Foundation (WF) to describe workflows.

eXtensible Markup Language (XML) A defined markup language for documents, which describes document content and structure rather than appearance. An XML document has to be formatted before it can be read, and the formatting is usually accomplished by using an XSL template file.

eXtensible Stylesheet Language Transformations (XSLT) A language used to create style sheets for XML, similar to cascading style sheets (CSS) that are used for HTML. Can be used to transform XML to HTML or to another type of XML.

Fabulous 40 Additional site definitions and site templates for Windows SharePoint Services 3.0 from Microsoft that can be used as a starting point to build SharePoint-based solutions. See also *www.microsoft.com/technet/ windowsserver/sharepoint/wssapps/templates/*.

Feature Allows you to activate/deactivate functionality in a site, site collection, farm, or Web application.

field controls An ASP.NET 2.0 control used on page layouts to display and modify data contained in the Pages library columns. Page layout designers use field controls to restrict the data that content creators add to publishing pages.

File Transfer Protocol (FTP) Protocol used for copying files to and from remote computer systems on a network by using TCP/IP. The mechanism cannot be used on SharePoint sites.

ghosted Web pages See *un-customized Web pages*.

global navigation breadcrumb A sequence of links displayed on all Web pages above the site name, which shows the path from the top-level site to the current site. See also *content navigation breadcrumb*. Users can use a combination of the two to navigate or keep track of their location.

Globally Unique Identifier (GUID) A unique 128-bit number that identifies a component in SharePoint, usually of the format {12345678-1234-1234-1234-123456789012}.

hidden ASP.NET controls ASP.NET controls that do not provide any visible content, often included on a page to provide data to other controls on the page that display the data. Examples of hidden ASP.NET controls are the SPWebPartManager and DataSource controls.

home page The first page to render on a Web site when you type the URL of a Web site and do not specify a Web page in the Address box of a browser. In this situation, Web servers are configured to respond with specifically named Web pages, such as index.htm, index.asp, or default.aspx. SharePoint sites, when first created, have a home page named *default.aspx*, but you can change this using SharePoint Designer.

HTTP (HTTPS) with Secure Sockets Layer (SSL) A client/server protocol that encrypts and decrypts Web pages over TCP/IP on a particular port, usually port 443.

HTTP GET A method used to pass parameter names and values to a Web server, by appending them to the URL. It is used to GET (retrieve) data.

HTTP POST A method used to pass data to a Web server by including them in the body of the request. There are usually extra headers to describe the message body. This method has many uses, such as sending parameter names and values, or submitting form data to server-side scripts.

Hypertext Transfer Protocol (HTTP) A client/server protocol used to access information on Web servers over TCP/IP on a particular port, usually port 80.

ID Selector A style defined in a style block or in an external file. Used to identify one particular element, and pointed to on a tag by using an ID attribute.

inline style A style applied as a tag attribute, named *style*.

layer An absolute positioned HTML division (div) tag. You use the <div> tag to group elements together so that, for example, you can format them with styles, create animations, or create expanding menus.

library A specialized list that contains files and metadata properties associated with those files. Windows SharePoint Services 3.0 has four types of libraries: Document, Form, Wiki Page, and Picture. SharePoint Server 2007 contains additional libraries, such as Report, Translation Management, Data Connection, and Slide. See also *lists*.

list A container that stores structured tabular data items that are related to one another with similar values, metadata, or security settings. Lists provide columns for storing metadata and user interfaces for viewing and managing the items.

List Form Web Part (LFWP) A Web Part used on form pages to provide a basic data entry form for lists and libraries.

list item An entry in a SharePoint list. Each list item can be created, reviewed, updated, and deleted individually.

list template A definition of a list that you can use as a blueprint to create a new list by using a browser. List templates are stored in the SQL Server database and include columns, list views, and general settings for a list to create new lists and optional content.

List View Web Part (LVWP) A built-in Web Part that shows the contents of a list or library.

machine state workflow An event-driven workflow that moves from state to state waiting on decisions made externally to the workflow.

master page A special ASP.NET 2.0 Web page that you can use to share code between pages. Their primary use is to provide a Web site with a consistent look and feel, and navigation for each page within a site.

metadata Data about data. For example, the metadata for a file can include the title, subject, author, and size of the file. In a document library, the metadata for a file is stored in the columns of the document library.

Microsoft .NET Framework 3.0 The managed-code model of Microsoft, which includes .NET Framework 2.0, and is included in Windows Vista and can be downloaded from the Microsoft Download Center and installed on other Microsoft operating systems.

Microsoft IntelliSense The automated completion technology used for HTML tags, cascading style sheets, variable names, functions, and methods.

Microsoft Visual Studio 2005 A tool for developers.

namespace Defines an entry point within an assembly. All controls that are similar are placed in the same namespace.

nested master pages A hierarchy of master pages, where child master pages inherit the elements of the parent master page, as well as providing elements of their own.

nodes XPath reference to XML elements, attributes, and content.

page layout A key component of SharePoint Server Web Content Management. Controls the content area of a publishing page and can contain field controls, Web Part zones, Web Parts, Data Views, and other components. Used in conjunction with either a master page or a custom master page.

parallel actions A series of predefined tasks that can start at the same time to accomplish a certain outcome.

permission level A set of permissions that relate to a specific task. Windows SharePoint Services has five permission levels: Full Control, Design, Contribute, Read, and Limited Access. SharePoint Server creates an additional four permission levels: Manage Hierarchy, Approve, Restricted Read, and View Only.

Publishing Portal A site hierarchy for an Internet site that includes a home page and subsites. Most of these Web sites are based on the Publishing Site With Workflow template that uses SharePoint Server Web Content Management functionality. Typically, this Web site has more readers than contributors.

publishing site A Web site that uses SharePoint Server Web Content Management functionality. Contributors can work on draft versions of a publishing page, which once approved, or *published*, is made visible to readers.

Publishing Site With Workflow A Web site for publishing Web pages by using the Approval workflow. When a parent site is created using this template; all subsites can be created based only on the Publishing Site With Workflow template.

quirks Pages with older transitional or no <!DOCTYPE> declarations. Browsers will display such pages by using "loose rendering" or "quirks" mode, also known as *bugwards* compatibility. This mode emulates legacy bugs and behaviors of version 4 browsers.

Really Simple Syndication (RSS) An XML standard for syndicating data. Used by Web sites and blogs to disseminate information. making updates to a Web site or blog available instantaneously. In order to receive RSS feeds, you must have an aggregator—a feed reader.

Recycle Bin It provides two-stage protection against accidental deletions. When you delete a document or other item from the Windows SharePoint Services site, it is deleted from the Web site and moved to the Web site's Recycle Bin, where it can be restored if needed. If you delete the item from the Web site's Recycle Bin, it moves to the site collection's Recycle Bin. From there, the document can be either restored to its original location or permanently deleted.

reusable content Content that needs to be repeated on multiple pages, such as copyright statements. SharePoint Server provides a feature named *Reusable Content* on publishing sites, which are centrally maintained and cannot be changed by a page content author.

ScreenTip Text that appears when you point to an icon, button or hyperlink.

sequential action A series of predefined tasks that execute in order one by one to accomplish a certain task. It is also used to depict a predictable workflow that might branch or loop or wait for user intervention. The logic is encoded as rules within the workflow.

SharePoint farm Two or more SharePoint Servers sharing a common configuration database, connected by some form of network load balance (NLC) mechanism so that users' requests are distributed among the servers.

Simple Object Access Protocol (SOAP) A protocol for transporting XML data between computer systems, normally using HTTP or HTTPS.

site collection A set of Web sites in a Web application that has the same owner and that share administrative settings. Each Web site collection contains a top-level Web site and can contain one or more subsites, also known as *child sites*. You can have multiple site collections within each Web application.

site column A reusable column that is created at the site collection or site level and can be used across multiple sites, lists, and libraries.

site definition A set of files that define the capabilities of a SharePoint site. Site definition files include .xml, .aspx, .ascx, and .master page files, as well as document template files (for example, .dot and .htm), and content files (for example, .gif and .doc). The files are located in the *Program Files\Common Files\Microsoft Shared\Web server extensions\12\TEMPLATE* subdirectories of Web front-end servers that run Windows SharePoint Services or SharePoint Server.

site master page Another name used by SharePoint Server for custom master pages for publishing sites. See also *custom master pages*.

site template A blueprint used to create a SharePoint site, which can automatically generate lists, libraries, Web Parts, and features. This term can refer to a site definition or a file that captures the configuration and customizations of a Web site at a point in time.

Split view One of three views that displays the Code and the Design view of a Web page.

Static Web Part A Web Part that is not placed inside a Web Part zone. The details of these Web Parts are saved in the same SQL Server table as the page.

style block Used to apply specific style attributes to a particular page by embedding CSS attributes into the <head> portion of the page. The attributes are surrounded with opening and closing <style> tags, such as: <style type="text/css"> p {color:red;}</style>.

subsite see *child site*.

system master page Another name used by SharePoint Server for the default master page of team sites. See also *default master pages*.

top-level site A Web site that does not have a parent Web site. The top-level site in a site collection is created from the SharePoint 3.0 Central Administration Web site.

un-customized Web pages A Web page that references files on the file system of a SharePoint front-end server. In Windows SharePoint Services 2.0, these were known as *ghosted Web pages*. From a technical perspective, the SharePoint SQL Server content database contains a row in one of its tables for each Web page on a SharePoint site. For an un-customized Web page, this row contains a pointer to the file on the file system.

un-ghosted Web pages See *customized Web pages*.

Uniform Resource Locator (URL) An alphanumeric address that is used to locate a Web site.

Universal Data Connection (UDC) An XML format that describes the connection information for data sources.

variations A publishing feature that maintains a hierarchy of Web sites where the publishing content of the source site is pushed to target sites. The target site, also known as a variation may vary from the source site in the presentation of their content, due to language, locale or device requirements.

views A Web page that displays a subset of the contents of a list or library based on specific criteria defined by the metadata. You can use views to find information easily.

Web application Previously referred to as a *virtual server*, a Web application host SharePoint site collection that users can access over HTTP or HTTPS protocol. The clients may be browsers or other servers.

Web Content Accessibility Guidelines (WCAG) The World Wide Web Consortium (W3C) guidelines, which explain how to make Web content accessible to people with disabilities.

Web Part Gallery A container for Web Parts. Web Parts are placed on pages from a Web Part Gallery.

Web Part zone A rectangular region on a Web page that facilitates working with Web Parts.

Web Parts A modular unit of information that consists of a title bar, a frame, and content. Web Parts are the basic building blocks of a Web Part Page.

Web robots Sometimes referred to as webbots, Web Wanderers, Web Crawlers, or Spiders, a Web robot is a program that automatically transverses a Web sites hypertext structure by retrieving a document, and recursively retrieving all documents that are referenced. These documents are then indexed and used by search engines.

Web-safe color palette A cross-browser color palette created to ensure that all computers display colors correctly.

Web Service Description Language (WSDL) Describes the interface to an XML Web service, which can be registered in a Universal Description Discovery and Integration (UDDI) registry.

Wiki A Web site that acts like a container for HTML content pages. One of the ten Windows SharePoint Services 3.0 built-in site definitions. Anyone can use Wiki sites to edit Web page content and link the Web pages, thus providing an effective environment for collaborative authoring.

Windows Workflow Foundation (WF) A Microsoft technology for defining, executing, and managing workflows. It was a new feature introduced by the .NET Framework 3.0.

workflow action A task that needs to be completed as part of a workflow.

workflow activity Something that needs to be done, for example, a test for a certain value in a list item's column or setting an e-mail address. Therefore, a condition and actions can be classified as activities.

workflow condition A filter that can be used to decide which actions should be executed.

Workflow History list A list that workflows use to document significant events. Based on the contents of the history list, users can create activity duration reports.

workflow rule The combination of a condition or set of conditions that trigger a number of actions.

workflow steps A workflow can contain one or more steps. A step is a self-contained set of conditions and actions that must be executed either before or after another step.

XML CDATA Text between XML CDATA tags is ignored by XML parsers. Typically used to store HTML or code in XML data.

XML data schema Defines the structure of XML data. There are languages to define the XML schema, such as Document Type Definition (DTD), XML Schema (W3C), Document Definition Markup Language (DDML) and RELAX NG.

XML Path Language (XPATH) Provides a mechanism to manipulate and navigate through XML data. XPATH models XML data as a tree of nodes. See also *nodes*.

XML Web Services Computer systems that provide services to other computer systems. The data is transferred between computer systems formatted as XML and transported using the Simple Object Access Protocol (SOAP). The computer system that requests data is named the *XML Web Service Requester* or *client*, and the computer system that provides XML data is named the *XML Web Service Provider*.

XML See *eXtensible Markup Language*.

XSLT See *eXtensible Stylesheet Language Transformations*.

Index

About the Author

Penelope Coventry is a Microsoft Most Valuable Professional (MVP) for Microsoft Office SharePoint Server 2007 and an independent consultant based in the U.K., with more than 25 years of industry experience. She currently focuses on the design, implementation, and development of SharePoint Technology–based solutions. She has worked with SharePoint since 2001 and, in recent years, has lead a team for the ATLAS Consortium on the Defence Information Infrastructure (Future) project, provided consultancy services to U.K. Microsoft Gold partners ICS Solutions and Combined Knowledge, worked for Coventry University as its Portal Strategist, and trained consultants, administrators, and end-users on Microsoft and Hewlett Packard projects. She has produced SharePoint-related courseware for Mindsharp since 2002.

Penny has co-authored a number of books, including *Microsoft Office SharePoint Server 2007 Administrator's Companion*, *Microsoft SharePoint Products and Technologies Resource Kit*, and two editions of *Microsoft Windows SharePoint Services Step by Step*. Penny is frequently seen at TechEd and IT Forum, either as a Technical Learning guide or at the SharePoint Ask-the-Experts stands.

Penny lives in Hinckley, Leicestershire, England with her husband, Peter, and dog, Poppy.

The book's Web site can be found at: *www.sharepointdesignerstepbystep.com*, where Penny will post additional information and links that she has found useful.

What do you think of this book?

We want to hear from you!

Do you have a few minutes to participate in a brief online survey?

Microsoft is interested in hearing your feedback so we can continually improve our books and learning resources for you.

To participate in our survey, please visit:

www.microsoft.com/learning/booksurvey/

...and enter this book's ISBN-10 or ISBN-13 number (located above barcode on back cover*). As a thank-you to survey participants in the United States and Canada, each month we'll randomly select five respondents to win one of five $100 gift certificates from a leading online merchant. At the conclusion of the survey, you can enter the drawing by providing your e-mail address, which will be used for prize notification only.

Thanks in advance for your input. Your opinion counts!

* Where to find the ISBN on back cover

ISBN-13: 000-0-0000-0000-0
ISBN-10: 0-0000-0000-0

Example only. Each book has unique ISBN.